Al-Qawānīn al-Fiqhiyyah

The Judgments of Fiqh Vol.1

Al-Qawānīn al-Fiqhiyyah

fī talkhīṣ madhhab al-mālikiyyah
wa-t-tanbīh 'alā madhhab ash-shāfi'iyyah wa-l-
ḥanafiyyah wa-l-ḥanbaliyyah

The Judgments of Fiqh

in Summation of the Mālikī Madhhab,
drawing attention to the Shāf'ī,
Ḥanafī and Ḥanbalī madhhabs

Vol. 1 – 'Aqīdah and 'Ibādāt

Muḥammad ibn Aḥmad ibn Muḥammad
Ibn Juzayy al-Kalbī

Translated by Asadullah Yate

Diwan Press

Al-Qawanin al-Fiqhiyyah, Vol. 1 – 'Aqidah and 'Ibadat

Published by: Diwan Press Ltd.
311 Allerton Road
Bradford
BD15 7HA
UK
Website: www.diwanpress.com
E-mail: info@diwanpress.com

Author: Ibn Juzayy al-Kalbi
Translation: Dr. Asadullah Yate
Edited by: Abdassamad Clarke

A catalogue record of this book is available from the British Library.

ISBN-13: 978-1-908892-53-9 (Casebound)
978-1-908892-54-6 (Paperback)

Dedication

to Shaykh Dr. Abdalqadir as-Sufi

This translation is based on the edition printed in Tunis by an-Nahda Nahj al-Jazeera, 1344 AH/1926 CE, the Dar al-Kitab al-'Arabi edition printed in Beirut, 1404 AH/1984 CE, the PDF version annotated by Ustadh Dr. Bin Sayyidi Muhammad Mawlay, and that edited by Majid al-Hamawi, printed by Dar Ibn Hazm.

Contents

Dedication v

Ibn Juzayy al-Kalbī xi

Translator's Preface xii

Author's Introduction 1

The Opening Discourse Concerning What is Necessarily True in Matters of *'Aqīdah* 7

PART 1 33

1 – Purification 35

2 – The *Ṣalāt* 81

3 – The *Ṣalāt* Over The Dead 172

4 – *Zakāt* 182

5 – Fasting And *I'tikāf* 209

6 – Hajj 235

7 – *Jihād* 264

8 – Oaths And Vows 290

9 – Food, Drink, Hunting And Slaughtering 315

10. *'Īd* Sacrifices, *'Aqīqah* And Circumcision 342

Detailed Table of Contents 356

Ibn Juzayy al-Kalbī

Abu-l-Qāsim Muḥammad ibn Aḥmad ibn Juzayy al-Kalbī from Granada in Andalusia was born in 693 AH into a distinguished and noble family and died *shahīd* at the great battle of Tareef in 741 AH. He was a *qāḍī*, grammarian, *faqīh*, commentator on the Qur'ān and poet. Among his teachers were Ibn az-Zubayr, Ibn Rashīd, Qāḍī Ibn Bartāl, the *khaṭīb* at-Tanjalī and Abu-l-Qāsim ibn Shāt. Among his works are *Wasīlah al-muslim fī tahdhīb Ṣaḥīḥ Muslim*, *al-Aqwāl as-sunniyyah fī kalimāt as-sunniyyah*, *Taqrīb al-wuṣūl ilā 'ilm al-uṣūl*, *an-Nūr al-mubīn fī qawā'id 'aqā'id ad-dīn*, *Taṣfiyyah al-qulūb fī wuṣūl ilā ḥaḍrah 'allām al-ghuyūb*, *al-Mukhtaṣar al-bāri' fī qirā'ah Nāfi'* and his *Tafsīr kitāb at-tas-hīl li 'ulūm at-tanzīl*.

His son, Abū Abdullah Muḥammad ibn Juzayy al-Kalbī (d. 758 AH), the scribe of the *Riḥlah* of Ibn Battuta, is sometimes confused with him.

Translator's Preface

The work presented here, *al-Qawānīn al-fiqhiyyah* 'The Judgments of Fiqh' is a concise summary of the *fiqh* of the ahl al-Madīnah – accompanied by the corresponding *aḥkām* of the other great schools of Islamic jurisprudence, some of which no longer flourish within the ummah. However it would be wrong to consider it as an apology for the fashion of *fiqh 'ala al-madhāhib al-arbi'ah* – *fiqh* according to the four madhhabs – or a democratization of legal procedure. Rather the opposite. This work is a demonstration of the superiority of the madhhab of the people of Madīnah. Just as Ibn Rushd in his *Bidāyah* did not come to the conclusion that all the madhhabs were the same, so Ibn Juzayy exclaims that those who have consciously chosen this as the school to follow are correct – as he says he is composing this work from a position of knowledge, knowledge that 'the people of our land of Andalusia and the rest of the Greater Maghrib have chosen Imam Mālik, following as an example the Abode of the Hijrah, and being fortunate in their choice because of their having been granted success by Allah, exalted is He, and confirming the words of the truthful and sincere one ﷺ that the people of the Greater Maghrib shall continue to have knowledge of the truth until the coming of the Final Hour.' In other words they are the truly successful by Allah.

It is important to note Ibn Juzayy's inclusion – in the opening pages of the *Qawānīn* – of Imam Mālik among the *salaf aṣ-ṣāliḥ*, i.e. the right-acting men and women of the earliest generations, from amongst the Companions, Tabi'īn and the *imāms* of the Muslims. Of course he was, but the term *salaf aṣ-ṣāliḥ* has been so co-opted by a certain modern, imbalanced grouping, strong on narrow 'piety and religion' but devoid of any broad understanding of Islam as *dīn*, in which life, trade, society and authority are uppermost, that one forgets that the great Imam of Madīnah was one of the *salaf.*

With some reluctance we have prepared this edition with the standard orientalist transliteration of Arabic names and terms. Words such as *ṣalāt*, *zakāt*, *mūmin*, *wuḍū'*, etc. have become part of the vocabulary of Muslims and to write them with strange additional academic markings is to persist in the nineteenth century custom of regarding Islam as strange and foreign. It is not strange, in fact it is the only real *dīn* flourishing in Europe and the Americas, the others having been diluted to the point of becoming reductive, homoeopathic additions to real life. Nevertheless as the educated reader today is probably conversant with this convention and accustomed to it, it has become standard in Muslim publishing to transliterate words thus.

Such books of *fiqh* are especially important nowadays, I mean works which contain *all* the rulings regarding the transactions of life as opposed to those which are specifically to do with *'ibādah.* It is disturbing to note how knowledge of such transactions – I refer to trade, legitimate currency, contracts etc. – has so diminished that where before one could travel to find the people of knowledge, now one usually has to look for it in books. As one 'leading' Azhari Shaykh resident in Germany advised me, when I asked him about a *mas'alah* case from the *mu'āmalāt*, 'Concentrate on *'aqīdah*, brother, we don't need to deal with such matters nowadays'. But the *mu'āmalāt* are part of our *'aqīdah* just as the reality of the Messenger ﷺ is part of *'aqīdah*, and it is this focus on *'aqīdah* devoid of the actions of life that has reduced Islam to something merely mental or at best a spiritual affair of the heart. It has become boring for the youthful generation who see clearly that it has nothing to do with action or 'real' life and has become a thing akin to Christianity or to folklore. How can we say we follow Imam Mālik – the Imām of Dār al-Hijrah, the place where the *dīn* was established, the Imām of the *'amal* of the people of Madīnah, the Imām who considered the life pattern of the people of Madīnah to be on a par with the *ḥadīth* of the Rasūl ﷺ as evidence of his *sunnah*, the Imām who recorded the madhhab of 'Umar – when the only visible thing which distinguishes us from the other three madhhabs is the *sadl* of the *ṣalāt*, i.e. the holding of one's arms at one's side during the *ṣalāt* rather than clutching them to one's breast or belly, and even this is rapidly being abandoned.

Even if one is lucky enough to find someone of knowledge who understands something of trade, contracts and the gold/silver currency of our *dīn*, it is usually a knowledge derived from research in books or the internet – and if the action, practice or thing no longer exists on the ground, then that knowledge is no longer of the quality of knowledge acquired from a face to face meeting with someone who has existential knowledge of it but rather of the rank of mere 'information'. However things have so far deteriorated that if we do not preserve this information, there can be no chance of reviving these actions.

Author's Introduction

The slave of Allah and servant of the Book and the Sunnah, Muḥammad ibn Aḥmad ibn Muḥammad ibn Juzayy al-Kalbī, may Allah turn towards him, *amīn*, says:

In the name of Allah, All-Merciful, Most Merciful

May the peace and blessings of Allah be on our Master Muḥammad and his Family and Companions

Praise belongs to Allah, the Possessor of Majesty Whose essence the intellects of the gnostics are incapable of comprehending, and of perfection the adequate praise of Whom the tongues of those who praise are incapable of expressing, and of power the dread of which causes the hearts of the fearful to tremble, and of exaltedness before Whose might the faces of the obedient and the assiduous in worship are humbled, and of knowledge which encompasses that which is above the Footstool as far as the layers of the earth, and of wisdom whose effect is manifest in everything which comes into being, is created and multiplies – what is both visible and invisible to us, and of widespread mercy whose protection has embraced all of mankind, and of abundant blessings, and of penetrating proof and of irrefutable authority for those who deny the truth and invent lies. Glory be to a Sovereign Who has not created His slaves for amusement and Who did not leave them to go on unchecked! Rather, He sent His Messengers with good news and a warning, calling people to the truth and to guidance, and calling them to forbid what is wrong and to command what is right and to be on their guard, and giving good news and a promise to those who accept the guidance and threatening those who overstep the bounds with punishment. Then He sealed the Message with our Prophet, Muḥammad ﷺ the bearer of the complete and final call to the truth and the message to all mankind and the jinn, the way of life abrogating all previous *dīn*s; the bearer of a *sharī'ah* to remain in force until the end of time and of clear Qur'anic *āyat*s, conclusive proofs and manifest evidence. He sent the Qur'ān down to him as a guidance to mankind and clear instructions to afford guidance and discrimination and rendered it a demonstrative miracle for those capable of seeing, renewing itself with the alternation of the days and nights and the succession of ages. Allah did not take him back to Himself until He had perfected the *dīn* and completed it by him, and He had elucidated the clear way, and he had established him as the Proof of Allah over all of creation and there had appeared in existence the confirmation of His words, exalted is He: '*We have only sent you as a mercy to all the worlds*' (Sūrat al-Anbiyā' 21:107). May Allah's blessings and peace be upon him, may His *barakah* and mercy be upon him, may He raise and honour him – as well as his pure family and his most honourable Companions.

This book, about the basic laws and judgments of the *sharī'ah* and detailed aspects of *fiqh*, is based on the madhhab of the Imam of Madīnah Abū 'Abdallāh Mālik ibn Anas al-Aṣbaḥī ؓ given that the people of our land of Andalusia and the rest of the Greater Maghrib have chosen him, following as an example the Abode of the Hijrah, and being fortunate in their choice because of their having been granted success by Allah, exalted is He, and confirming the words of the truthful and sincere one ﷺ 'the people of the West shall continue to have knowledge of the truth until the coming of the Final Hour'.

Then in addition to this we draw attention to many instances of agreement or difference between the aforesaid Imam and Imam Abū 'Abdallāh Aḥmad ibn Idrīs ash-Shāfi'ī, Imam Abū Ḥanīfah an-Nu'mān ibn Thābit and Imam Abū 'Abdallāh ibn Ḥanbal in order thereby to complete the benefit and render it of greater use – for those four are the models of emulation for the Muslims throughout the lands of the earth and those who are followed, well known and generally accepted. On occasion, however, I have indicated a madhhab other than theirs from amongst the Imams of the Muslims, like Sufyān ath-Thawrī, al-Ḥasan al-Baṣrī, 'Abdullāh ibn al-Mubārak, Isḥāq ibn Rahwayh, Abū Thawr, an-Nakha'ī, Dāwūd ibn 'Alī the Imam of the Ẓāhirīs whose madhhab I have transmitted on numerous occasions, al-Layth ibn Sa'd, Sa'īd ibn al-Musayyab and al-Awzā'ī as well as others, may Allah be pleased with all of them, for each of them is of the rank of a *mujtahid* regarding the *dīn* of Allah and their madhhabs are ways leading to Allah.

Know that this book is superior to other books by virtue of three qualities:

1. It combines a clear arrangement of the madhhab with mention of the differences with the other madhhabs – contrary to other books which deal with the madhhab in particular, or with the differences with other madhhabs in particular;

2. We have laid it out with clarity by dividing it up and arranging it elegantly and we have facilitated its understanding by pruning it of any superfluities or defects and clarifying the way it is expressed – so how many divisions within sections and how many detailed expositions of primary judgments have facilitated an understanding

of what was difficult and made the exceptional, anomalous judgments more accessible!

3. In it we have aimed to combine concision and explanation, despite the fact that they are rarely to be found in combination, and thus by the help of Allah it turned out to contain an ease of expression, to be subtle in its indications, complete in its meanings, but with so few words that those wishing to learn it by heart become devoted to it.

And it is Allah that we request to make this work the cause of His forgiveness of the author and a means of obtaining His good pleasure, and that it lead to the opening up of the treasures of His kindness and gracious gifts, for surely He is the Possessor of vast overflowing generosity.

AN EXPLANATION OF THE TERMINOLOGY OF THE BOOK

If we mention a judgment or ruling, in the first instance we record the madhhab of Mālik, then we follow this by the madhhabs of others, either by an explicit text or by indication and allusion, and if we refrain from speaking of the differences of judgment with respect to a matter then this generally indicates that there is no difference of judgment in this matter.

If we mention consensus and the agreed upon judgment then we refer to the consensus of the Muslim ummah. If we mention the 'majority' then we refer to the agreement of the *'ulamā'* except those whose judgments are irregular.

If we mention 'the four' then we refer to Mālik, ash-Shāfi'ī, Abū Ḥanīfah and Ibn Ḥanbal – whereby notice is given that some *'ulamā'* differ with them, and on occasion we give an explanation in this regard. If we state that 'some people (*qawm*) have said' or 'contrary to some people' then we refer to what has been said outside of the four madhhabs.

If we mention 'the three' then we refer to Mālik, ash-Shāfi'ī and Abū Ḥanīfah – whereby in this, notice is given that Aḥmad ibn Ḥanbal differs from them or that he has not transmitted a teaching in this matter.

If we mention 'the two Imams' then we refer to Mālik and ash-Shāfi'ī. If we mention the pronoun 'the two of them, or both of them', as in our saying 'according to the two' or 'contrary to the two' then we refer to ash-Shāfi'ī and Abū Ḥanīfah. If we mention the plural pronoun, such that we say 'according to them' or 'contrary to them' or the like, then we refer to ash-Shāfi'ī, Abū Ḥanīfah and Ibn Ḥanbal.

If we mention 'the madhhab' then we refer to the madhhab of Mālik whereby notice is given that others differ. If we mention the well known position *(mashhūr),* – i.e. the well-known and generally accepted judgment, then we refer to the judgment which is generally accepted in the madhhab of Mālik – whereby notice is given of a difference of judgment within the madhhab.

If we state that such-and-such has been said or there is a difference of judgment about such-and-such a matter, or there are two different judgments about such-and-such a matter then usually we refer to the madhhab of Mālik. If we say that there are two transmissions then we refer to Mālik, and we usually state the well-known judgment first of all.

An explanation of the arrangement of the book

Know that I begin the book with a concise *'aqīdah* in accordance with the Sunnah, mentioning the most important aspects first – for there is no doubt that the roots are more important than the branches, and it is only right to place what is subordinate afterwards and place the principal first.

Then I have divided the *fiqh* into two parts, the first regarding the acts of worship and the second the actions and transactions of daily life, and I have inserted ten 'books' with a hundred chapters in each section, thus the *fiqh* is contained in twenty books and two hundred chapters in all.

The first section contains the following books: the book of purification, the book of *ṣalāt*, the book of funerals, the book of *zakāt*, the book of fasting and *i'tikāf*, the book of hajj, the book of *jihād*, the book of oaths and vows, the book of food and drink, hunting and sacrifice, the book of beasts slaughtered for the *'Īd* festivals, beasts slaughtered following the birth of a child and circumcision.

The second section contains the following books: the book of marriage, the book of divorce and what is related to it, the book of sales, the book of contracts made with respect to sales, the book of judgments and testimony, the book containing chapters related to judgments, the book of compensatory payments for homicide or injury and *ḥadd* punishments, the book of gifts and similar matters, the book of setting slaves free and matters connected with it, and the book of the obligatory divisions of inheritance and testaments. Then we have sealed it with the book of miscellaneous matters containing twenty chapters. The 'books' and chapters are only contained in this number as I have inserted each matter with others like it and joined every subordinate matter with its principle, while on occasion I have gathered together in one explanation what others have explained in many different instances, out of my concern for uniting closely related and similar matters and out of my desire for brevity. Allah is the One Who helps and there is no power and no strength but by Allah the High, the Vast.

The opening discourse concerning what is necessarily true in matters of ʿAqīdah

BEING FROM AMONGST THE ROOTS OF THE VARIOUS BRANCHES OF THE *DĪN* OF ISLAM. IT COMPRISES TEN CHAPTERS, FIVE PERTAINING TO DIVINE KNOWLEDGES AND FIVE TO TRANSMITTED

1. The existence of the Creator, His majesty is majestic and His favour is cherished

Know that both the higher and lower worlds have been brought into being in time after their non-existence and both testify that they themselves are in-time creations and that their Creator is eternal from before endless time – this being apparent from the changes to the attributes of things and the succession of movements and moments of rest in physical bodies which manifest in these worlds, as well as other contingent matters which occur. Moreover for every in-time occurrence there must be that which has brought it into being and a creator which created it – given that for every action there must be an actor. Thus all existent realities in the earth and the heavens – all living creatures and non-sentient physical bodies of the mountains, oceans, rivers, trees, fruits, flowers, winds, clouds, rain, the sun and moon, the stars and the very alternation of the night and the day, indeed everything contained in it, whether large or small – are the effects of a creative act and are subtle manifestations of wisdom and arrangement. Thus in every thing there is conclusive evidence and obvious proof for the existence of the Creator, and this is Allah, the Lord of the Worlds and the Creator of all creatures, the King, the Clear Truth Who has been veiled from the sight of man by His Greatness and the sublimity of His affair but has manifested to inner sight by the might of His Authority and the clarity of His proof. How great is the proof for Allah and how many the evidences of Allah! '*Is there any doubt about Allah? The Bringer into Being of the heavens and the earth*' (Sūrah Ibrāhīm 14:10). And the *fiṭrah*, the natural pattern of human existence on which He created mankind, and what is necessarily found in the self of the neediness of slavehood and recognition of Lordship is enough for you: '*If you asked them, "Who created the heavens and the earth?" they would certainly say, "Allah!"*' (Sūrah Luqmān 31:25).

2. The Attributes of ALLAH, exalted is He and mighty is His affair and His authority is overwhelming!

It is customary for those who study *kalām*, the rational study of '*aqīdah,* to affirm seven attributes, namely: life, power, will, knowledge, hearing, seeing and speech.

'Life'

Allah is the Eternal First from before endless time before the existence of created times and eras. There was nothing other-than-Him with Him, and He is now as He was. He is the Living, the Everlasting, the Last Who does not die, whereas '*Everyone on it will pass away*' (Sūrah ar-Raḥmān 55:26).

'Power'

He has power over all things, nothing frustrates His power and ability, nothing is difficult for Him and: *'He has the Dominion of all things in His Hand'* (Sūrah Yāsīn 36:83). Do you not see the result of His Power in the origination of the existent realities and how He keeps a firm hold on the earth and heavens, and in the execution of His command regarding the way the created realities behave – such that every day He causes some to die some to live, He creates and he causes to pass away, He impoverishes some and enriches others, He guides and He leads astray, He gives sovereignty to whomever He wills and He takes sovereignty from whomever He wills, He gives and He withholds, He brings low and He raises, He makes some happy and others miserable and He spares some and tests others? *'His command when He desires a thing is just to say to it, "Be!" and it is'* (Sūrah Yāsīn 36:82).

'Will'

He, glory be to Him, is the One Who wills all beings, the One who directs the occurrences in creation, Who determines the time, degree, nature and extent of all decrees, Who does what He wishes – so anything of benefit or harm, anything sweet or bitter, unbelief and belief, obedience and disobedience, increase and decrease, and profit and loss is by His will from before endless time, by His judgment and power and by His desire based on wisdom. There is no averting His command and no deferring His judgment, there is no remonstrating with Him regarding His action – *'He will not be questioned about what He does, but they will be questioned'* (Sūrah al-Anbiyā' 21:23). Every blessing from Him is an overflow of His generosity, and every affliction from Him is justice; His dominion and His wisdom require that – for the owner does what he wants in his property and the king decides as he wishes for his subjects. Moreover the man of wisdom knows better what his wisdom requires – '*and Allah knows but you do not know*' (Sūrah al-Baqarah 2:216). He has determined the creatures' amount of provision, their life-spans, their actions and whether they are to be unhappy or happy, unfortunate or fortunate – '*everything is in a clear Book*' (Sūrah Hud 11:6). He has created some people for the Garden and has made the way to ease easy for them, such that it is the actions of the people of the Garden which they perform; and He has created some people for the Fire and made their way to difficulty easy such that it is the actions of the people of the Fire which they perform – '*Your Lord does not wrong His slaves*' (Sūrah Fuṣṣilat 41:46).

'KNOWLEDGE'

He, blessed and exalted is His name, knows all that is to be known, encompasses what is in the depths of the earth right up to what is beyond the heavens, encompasses everything in His knowledge, has accounted for everything by number, knows what was and what will be and what will not be – such that if it were to be, He knows how it would be. He is present by His knowledge in every place and He is the One watching over every person – '*He knows what you keep secret and what you make public and He knows what you earn*' (Sūrah al-An'ām 6:3). He is equally aware of the manifest and the hidden and He has knowledge of the most concealed secrets and what is in the most hidden recesses of the minds and hearts of mankind, so much so that He knows even what occurs to the awareness of the fish in the depths of the oceans – '*Allah knows what the heart contains*' (Sūrah al-Anfāl 8:43).

As for 'hearing and sight'

He, exalted is He, hears and sees; nothing which may be heard escapes His hearing however muffled, and nothing which is visible escapes His sight however fine and subtle it may be – '*He knows your secrets and what is even more concealed*' (Sūrah Ṭā–Hā 20:7) – even a black ant crawling on a hard rock in a dark night – '*from Allah nothing is hidden, either on Earth or in Heaven*' (Sūrah Āli 'Imrān 3:5), and what better way to follow this up than with the proof of: '*It is He who forms you in the womb however He wills*' (Sūrah Āli 'Imrān 3:6).

'Speech'

He, majestic and mighty is He, speaks, commanding and forbidding, in an eternal manner, from before endless time, but not with letters nor with voice, a speech which does not admit of non-existence, nor anything that may be understood in the same sense such as silence, division into parts, coming before or coming after chronologically, such that it does not resemble the speech of created beings, just as His essence does not resemble the essences of created beings. Nor can His words be exhausted just as His knowledge of things cannot be enumerated or His determining of things encompassed – '*Say: "If all the sea were ink to write down the Words of my Lord, it would run out long before the Words of my Lord ran out," even if We were to bring the same amount of ink again*' (Sūrah al-Kahf 18:109).

The proof for the truth of these attributes has three aspects:

1. That they are attributes of perfection

So describing Allah with them is necessarily true. Moreover their opposites are attributes of imperfection and so it is necessarily true that He is free of them – '*Allah's is the Highest Likeness*' (Sūrah an-Naḥl 16:60).

2. That the traces of His wisdom demonstrate them

The thoroughness and precision of the creation is proof of the life, power, knowledge of the Creator, as well as all His other attributes.

3. That which has been transmitted of explicit texts in the Qur'ān and sound narrations.

3. The beautiful names of Allah, exalted is He

The Messenger of Allah ﷺ said: 'Allah has ninety nine names, whoever understands them shall enter the Garden' (al-Bukhārī and Muslim), and a specific number has been transmitted in the *ḥadīth* related by at-Tirmidhī in the chain of narration of Abū Hurayrah ﷺ. People have differed regarding those specific names as to whether they may be attributed to the Prophet ﷺ as with the root of the *ḥadīth* or whether they are a saying of Abū Hurayrah – given that Allah, exalted is He, has other names besides those specific ones, some mentioned in the Qur'ān and the *ḥadīth*, while others are names derived from His actions.

Know that the names and attributes of Allah as a whole may be classified in three divisions: that which refers to the essence; to the attributes of the essence; and to the attributes of action. They may be classified in detail in ten ways according to their meanings:

1. A name that indicates the essence

Namely our saying 'Allah', and it is has also been said that it is the greatest of Allah's names;

2. Names that indicate oneness

Such as His name 'al-Wāḥid – the One', 'aṣ-Ṣamad – the everlasting Sustainer' and 'al-Witr – the Single';

3. Names that indicate life

Such as 'al-Ḥayy – the Living', 'al-Awwal – the First' and 'al-Ākhir – the Last';

4. Names that indicate the bringing into being of created realities

Namely the most particular names of Lordship, like 'al-Khāliq – the Creator', 'al-Bāri' – the Maker' 'al-Fāṭir – the One Who brings forth';

5. Names that indicate power

Like 'al-Qadīr – the Powerful', 'al-Muntaqim – the Avenger' and 'al-Qahhār – the One Who has absolute mastery';

6. Names that indicate will

Like 'al-Murīd – the One who wills', 'al-Faʿʿāl limā yurīd – the Doer of what He wills', 'al-Qābiḍ – the One Who restricts' and 'al-Bāsiṭ – the One Who expands';

7. Names that indicate perception

Like 'al-ʿAlīm – the all-Knowing', 'as-Samīʿ – the All-Hearing', 'al-Baṣīr – the One Who sees';

8. Names that indicate greatness and majesty

Like 'al-Aẓīm – the Magnificent', 'al-Kabīr – the Most Great', 'al-ʿAlī – the All-High';

9. Names that indicate dominion and mastery/ownership

Like 'al-Malik – the King', 'al-Mālik – the Master/the Owner' and 'al-Ghanī – the Rich Beyond Need;

10. Names that indicate mercy

Like 'ar-Raḥmān – the All-Merciful', 'ar-Raḥīm – the Most Merciful', 'al-Ghaffār – the Endlessly Forgiving', 'at-Tawwāb – the Ever-Returning' and 'al-Wahhāb – the Ever-Giving'.

4. The Tawḥīd of Allah, exalted is He

Tawḥīd is the gist of our saying *lā ilāha illa-llāh* – 'there is no god, only Allah', meaning that you should have *īmān* – have trust – that He is One God, Unique, that He is the Everlasting Sustainer of all, that He has not taken a wife, nor has He a son and that He has associated no one as a partner in His rule, that He has no partner in His Lordship, has no equal and has no adversary, no rival, no challenger or helper in His kingdom.

The clear proof of this oneness is what may be understood by the intellect from four *āyat*s:

1. His saying, exalted is He: '*If there had been any gods besides Allah in Heaven or Earth, they would both be ruined*' (Sūrah al-Anbiyā' 21:22). And it is from this that the *mutakallimūn* have taken the proof based on mutual exclusion – although the Qur'ān is more eloquent and clearer;

2. His saying, exalted is He: '*If there had, as you say, been other gods together with Him, they would have sought a way to the Master of the 'Arsh*' (Sūrah al-Isrā' 17:42) – so the absence of any contention is proof of the absence of any contender;

3. His saying, exalted is He: '*Allah has no son and there is no other god accompanying Him, for then each god would have gone off with what he created and one of them would have been exalted above the other*' (Sūrah al-Mūminūn 23:91) – so the fact that the nature of existence is all interconnected is a proof that its Owner is one;

4. That which may be understood by the intellect from His saying,

exalted is He: '*but they have adopted gods apart from Him which do not create anything but are themselves created*' (Sūrah al-Furqān 25:3) – for among the attributes of God is the fact that He is a creator, but there is no creator other than Allah and so there is no god except Allah and all that is other-than-Him is created and a created reality is not a partner with the One Who has created it: '*Is He who creates like him who does not create? So will you not pay heed?*' (Sūrah an-Naḥl 16:17).

Supplement: the various groups holding to contradictory interpretations of tawḥīd

They are the Christians, Magians, Sabeans, star worshippers or astrologers and advocates of the elements and humours.

The Christians

Their *kufr*, their denial of *tawḥīd*, is by their false utterances and their deviant teachings regarding 'Īsā and his mother, may Allah grant peace to both of them. The most conclusive rejection of them is contained in five *āyat*s:

1. His saying: '*Both of them ate food*' (Sūrah al-Mā'idah 5:75) – for this is a contingent, in-time attribute and an attribute of slavehood, not one of lordship;

2. His saying: '*The likeness of 'Īsā in Allah's sight is the same as Ādam*' (Sūrah Āli 'Imrān 3:59) – that is, He Who is capable of creating a person without a mother or father is also capable of creating another person with a mother but not a father;

3. His saying: '*They say, "Allah has a son." Glory be to Him! He is the Rich Beyond Need*' (Sūrah Yūnus 10:68) – for the One Who has absolute richness beyond need has no need of a wife, son or any other person;

4. His saying: '*It is not fitting for the All-Merciful to have a son. There is no one in the heavens and earth who will not come to the All-Merciful as a slave*'

(Sūrah Maryam 19:92-93) – for lordship and slavehood cannot be combined;

5. The saying of 'Īsā ﷺ: '*I am the slave of Allah*' (Sūrah Maryam 19:30) and his saying: '*Tribe of Israel! worship Allah, my Lord and your Lord*' (Sūrah al-Mā'idah 5:72) – so his acknowledging himself as being in the state of slavehood is a clear rebuttal of the lie of those who describe him with the attributes of lordship.

Magians

The adherents of Mazdaism, their *kufr*, their covering up of the truth of *tawḥīd*, is on account of their worship of light. The rebuttal of their claim is His saying: '*and He appointed darkness and light*' (Sūrah al-An'ām 6:1) – for that which is a contingent in-time creation is not a god.

Sabeans

Their *kufr*, their covering up of the truth of *tawḥīd*, is on account of their worship of angels and ascribing them to Allah, and the rebuttal of their claim is His saying: '*No, they are honoured slaves!*' (Sūrah al-Anbiyā' 21:26).

ASTROLOGERS

They assert that the stars have an influence in existence – and the rebuttal of their claim is His saying: '*the sun and moon and stars are subservient to His command*' (Sūrah al-A'rāf 7:54) – and that which is subservient is owned and compelled – and His saying: '*Do not prostrate to the sun nor to the moon. Prostrate to Allah who created them*' (Sūrah 41:37) – so how is something created supposed to be a partner to its Creator?

Advocates of the elements and humours (tabā'i'iyyun)

They ascribe actions to nature – and the rebuttal of their claim is

His saying: '*fruits of varying colours*' (Sūrah Fāṭir 35:27) and His saying: '*all watered with the same water. And We make some things better to eat than others*' (Sūrah ar-Ra'd 13:4) – for the divergence of shapes, colours, smells and flavours, and the fact that some are useful and some harmful is proof of a Maker Who is free to choose as He wishes.

A Sufi indication

Tawḥīd is of two kinds, general and particular. The general refers to the absence of any manifest association of Him with other gods, and this is the station of *īmān*, i.e. trust, obtained by all the *mūminūn*. The particular is the absence of any hidden association of Him with other gods, and this is the station of *iḥsān* and this is particular to the *awliyā'* who are gnostics of Allah, may Allah be pleased with all of them.

5. Tanzīh – freeing Allah, exalted is He, of any defect

This is the meaning of our saying, '*Subḥāna llāh* – glory be to Allah!' – that is, you have *īmān* that there is nothing like Him, that He is not like anything, that He is not similar to anything and that nothing is similar to Him – exalted is He above having any similarity, likeness or any match or equal or companion-associate! – and that He is not in need of anything but that everything is in need of Him and that it does not befit Him to have any defect or imperfection; rather His absolute purity renders him free of any defect and He is exempt from any imperfection; and that He is not subject to drowsiness or sleep; and nothing hurts Him, and He is not afflicted by incapacity, tiredness or weariness; and neither the obedience of the slaves brings benefit to Him nor is He harmed by the wrong actions of the slaves; and He does not die, does not cease to be, does not go astray, does not forget, and there is nothing in His kingdom but that which He wishes should be – so that which He wishes to be, is and what He does not wish to be is not; and he does not treat anyone unjustly; and there is never any decrease in His stores and nothing that is with Him ever perishes.

NOTE

There are statements in the Qur'ān and the *ḥadīth* which might cause one to imagine a likeness between Allah and man, like His saying, exalted is He, that: '*the All-Merciful is established firmly upon the* 'Arsh' (Sūrah Ṭā-Hā 20:5) and: '*both His hands are open wide*' (Sūrah al-Mā'idah 5:64) and like the *ḥadīth* reporting the coming down of Allah every night to the lower heaven – and other reports of this nature. There are many of them and people have split into three groups in their regard:

1. THE EARLIEST RIGHT-ACTING GENERATIONS

The Companions and the *Tābi'ūn* i.e. the generation after the Companions, and the *imāms* of the muslims have *īmān* in these statements but do not investigate their meanings any further, nor do they interpret them, [i.e. in order to reconcile them with fundamentals of *'aqīdah*]; rather they reject those who speak in this regard – '*Those firmly rooted in knowledge say, "We have īmān in it. All of it is from our Lord"*' (Sūrah Āli 'Imrān 3:7) – and this is the way of submission and acceptance which leads to safety and which is the way adopted by Mālik, ash-Shāfi'ī and most of the transmitters of *ḥadīth*.

2. THOSE WHO UNDERSTAND SUCH STATEMENTS ACCORDING TO THEIR LITERAL MEANING

So they are obliged to attribute corporeality to Allah, and this is ascribed to the followers of Ibn Ḥanbal and some of the transmitters of *ḥadīth*.

3. Those who interpret these statements

And they infer from their literal meanings an interpretation required by rational proofs, and they include most of the scholars of *kalām*, and Allah knows best.

6. Īmān in the Angels of Allah, His Books and His Messengers

Know that the angels are worshipper-slaves to Allah who are honoured in His eyes. They worship Him, they glorify Him, they obey Him, do not disobey Him, do not venture to say anything before He does and they act in accordance with His command. Among them are those who bear the *'Arsh*, those who inhabit the heavens, those who watch over the sons of Adam, those responsible for the rain, plants, the sperm of man, the womb, and seeking out the gatherings of *dhikr*. No one knows their number but Allah.

Allah has sent Prophets and Messengers who have brought good news and a warning, some of whom Allah has named in the Qur'ān while others He has not. The first of them was Ādam, the father of humankind, and the last of them was our master Muḥammad ﷺ the unlettered Prophet, the seal of the Prophets to whom Allah sent down Jibrīl, the trustworthy, with the Clear Qur'ān, just as He sent the Torah down to Mūsā, the Injīl to 'Īsā, the Zabūr to Dāwūd and other books to other Prophets, may the blessings of Allah be upon them all. Thus Allah, exalted is He, said: '*Say, "We have īmān in Allah and what has been sent down to us and what was sent down to Ibrāhīm and Ismā'īl and Isḥāq and Ya'qūb and the Tribes, and what Mūsā and 'Īsā were given, and what all the Prophets were given by their Lord. We do not differentiate between any of them. We are Muslims submitted to Him*"' (Sūrah al-Baqarah 2:136).

Allah has made it incumbent upon all nations to enter into the *dīn* of

Islam: '*If anyone desires anything other than Islam as a dīn, it will not be accepted from him, and in the* ākhirah *he will be among the losers*' (Sūrah Āli 'Imrān 3:85). Allah gave each Prophet certain signs similar to those on the basis of which humankind came to have *īmān*. Since the message of our Prophet Muḥammad ﷺ is more general and his *sharī'ah* abrogates what came before, this requires that his proofs be more obvious, his *āyat*s more brilliant and the evidences for his truthfulness greater and more conclusive in establishing the argument and in explaining the way forward on this path. Thus Allah helped him with various kinds of brilliant *āyat*s and manifest signs in which there is a teaching for those of core understanding. As for his states, his sayings and his actions, they contain the most wondrous of wonders. Our *'ulamā'* ﵏ have enumerated a thousand miracles with respect to him – which are comprised in five categories:

1. The magnificent Qur'ān which both people and jinn are unable to imitate '*even if they backed each other up*' and which contains divine knowledges, Lordly wisdoms and secrets which had been hidden from the intellects of creatures – all of which indicate conclusively that it is a revelation sent from the All-Merciful, the Most Merciful;

2. The extraordinary miracles manifested at his hands ﷺ which were very numerous;

3. Prior tidings about him and the good news of his coming;

4. The miraculous marks of honour (*karamāt*) which appeared at the hands of the rest of his ummah – for they are evidence of the soundness of their *dīn* and the genuine nature of their following him ﷺ. Just look at the dominance of his *dīn* in the east and the west, its protection from any alteration or change for more than seven hundred years, and it will become obvious to you that this is on account of a heavenly command and concern emanating from a divine Lord;

5. The qualities of vast character and of a nobly generous nature given to him by Allah and which Allah only gathers together in the case of His most beloved slaves, of those most honoured in His eyes – and His saying is enough for you in this respect: *'Indeed you are truly vast in character'* (Sūrah al-Qalam 68:4).

Know too that his miracles ﷺ may be classified in three ways with respect to their transmission:

1. Those miracles whose soundness we may be absolutely sure of and so we may use as proof

This is even if the transmission in question is a single one, being an isolated report, like the Magnificent Qur'ān, or like the splitting of the moon – on account of its mention in the Qur'ān, or like the gushing of water from between his fingers ﷺ and a little food becoming abundant, on account of the famousness of this incident and its being widely reported and the reliability of its narrators and the fact that it occurred in the presence of a large gathering of people;

2. Those transmissions about which we are absolutely sure on account of their multiple occurrences

This is even if we do not consider as absolutely sure those reports among them narrated by single narrators – like the transmissions regarding matters of the unseen and Allah's answering *duʿā*s, for there are many of these transmitted from him ﷺ such that they have become a group in themselves about which people are absolutely sure;

3. Those narrated on this matter by single persons

But which, if compared with other narrations, are then considered to afford absolute certainty as to the occurrence of miracles.

7. Īmān in the Abode of the Ākhirah

It comprises twelve matters

1. Īmān in the barzakh, i.e. the interspace after death, and in the punishment in the grave

Which is meted out to those whom Allah wishes, this being referred to in His saying in the Qur'ān: *'before them there is an interspace until the Day they are raised up'* (Sūrah al-Mūminūn 23:100), and His saying: *'a most evil torment engulfed Pharaoh's people – the Fire, morning and night, to which they are exposed; and on the Day the Hour takes place: "Admit Pharaoh's people to the harshest punishment!"'* (Sūrah al-Ghāfir 40:46) – for this is proof of the punishment before the Day of Raising Up; and there are sound reports too from the corpus of the traditions.

2. The questioning of the two angels

And this has been mentioned in the sound *ḥadīth*s and is indicated in His saying: *'Allah makes those who have īmān firm with the Firm Word in the life of the* dunyā *and the* ākhirah' (Sūrah Ibrāhīm 14:27).

3. The raising up of creation from their graves

And the gathering of them for the reckoning, reward and punishment. The proof that this is conceivable is the power of Allah to do this, may His power and majesty be honoured, for it is He: '*Who brings creation out of nothing, then reproduces it? That is easy for Allah*' (Sūrah ar-Rūm 30:27), '*Your creation and rising is only like that of a single self*' (Sūrah Luqmān 31:28); and the proof that it shall occur is its occurrence in the various *sharī'ah*s, that the Messengers and the Books speak about it, and in particular our *sharī'ah*, which has expressed itself in terms of warnings and the giving of good news so that the argument for or against human beings may be established. Moreover, divine wisdom requires that the person who does good be rewarded for his good actions and the person who commits wrong be punished for his wrong actions: '*so that Allah may repay every self for what it earned*' (Sūrah Ibrāhīm 14:51) – and this manifests in the Abode of the *ākhirah* not in the *dunyā*; and if there were no requital in the *ākhirah* then the *mūmin* and the *kāfir*, the obedient person and the disobedient one would all be equal: '*Would We make the Muslims the same as the evildoers?*' (Sūrah al-Qalam 68:35)

4. The reckoning up of actions

This has been mentioned in the Book and the Sunnah.

5. The settlement of accounts between the slaves

And this has also been mentioned in the Book and Sunnah.

6. The weighing of one's actions in the scales

And this has also been mentioned in the Book and Sunnah.

7. The giving of the record (of one's actions) either in the person's right or left hand

And this has also been mentioned in the Book and Sunnah.

8. People's passing over the Ṣirāṭ

That is the bridge extending over Jahannam; and the speed with which people will pass over it will vary in accordance with their actions; and some will fall headlong into the Fire of Jahannam. The proof for all this is His saying in the Qur'ān: '*and guide them to the Path of the Blazing Fire!*', (Sūrah aṣ-Ṣaffāt 37:23) and there are also sound *ḥadīth*s in the Sunnah.

9. The Pool of the Prophet ﷺ

From it his ummah will drink, and no one who drinks from it will ever be thirsty but those who substituted or changed matters in the *dīn* will be driven away from it. The proof of this is His saying from the Qur'ān: '*Truly We have given you the Great Abundance*' (Sūrah al-Kawthar 108:1) and the interpretation of '*the Great Abundance*' as the Pool has been narrated in sound *ḥadīth*, and there are many sound *ḥadīth*s in the Sunnah in this respect.

10. The intercession of the Prophet ﷺ for his ummah

And proof of this is His saying in the Qur'ān: '*It may well be that your Lord will raise you to a Praiseworthy Station*', (Sūrah al-Isra 17:79) and there are also sound *ḥadīth*s in the Sunnah. Intercession takes place in five instances:

1. People are granted ease in the place of standing, and the separation of the people of the Garden from those of the Fire occurs more quickly for his ummah – and this is peculiar to our Prophet ﷺ;
2. The saving of those for whom the Fire is fitting;
3. The taking the wrongdoers out of the Fire;
4. The bringing about of a quick entry into the Garden;
5. People will be raised in stations in the Garden.

11. The entry of people into the Fire

Of them there are two kinds:

1. All of the *kuffār*, and they shall be tortured in different ways, some more intensely than others, and they shall remain there for ever: '*It will not be eased for them. They will be crushed there by despair*' (Sūrah az-Zukhruf 43:75);
2. Those of the disobedient from among the *mūminūn* whom Allah wishes should enter – but then they will leave the Fire by the mercy of Allah, exalted is He, and the intercession of the Prophets and angels, the *shahīd*s, the right acting slaves and the rest of the *mūminūn*.

A precise determination

Those of the *mūminūn* will enter the Fire who have the following six characteristics:

1. They are people of wrong actions, but excluding the *muttaqūn*, the people of *tawqā*, who guard themselves from *kufr* but not every wrong action;

2. Those who die without making *tawbah*, i.e. without turning for forgiveness to Allah, from their wrong actions – for the person who turns from his wrong actions is like the person who has no wrong actions;

3. That their wrong actions are major wrong actions, for the minor ones are forgiven if the major ones are avoided;

4. Those whose good actions do not outweigh their wrongdoing, for if they do outweigh them, even if by an atom's weight, then they will be saved from the Fire;

5. That they are not from among those who will be saved by virtue of a previous action such as the people of Badr and of the *bay'at ar-Riḍwān*, i.e. the oath of allegiance taken at Ḥudaybiyah;

6. That they are not from amongst those for whom someone has interceded;

7. That they are not from amongst those forgiven by Allah.

12. Entering the Garden

Only the *mūminūn* will enter, and they will delight in various kinds of blessings, will look upon the noble face of Allah – the proof of this being His saying, exalted is He: '*Faces that Day will be radiant, gazing at their Lord*' (Sūrah al-Qiyāmah 75:22-23) as well as sound *ḥadīth*; and they will abide there forever, may Allah make us from among them by His overflowing generosity and mercy!

8. Imamate,

This comprises two matters

1. Affirmation of the imamate of the four Khalīfahs ﷺ

The proof of the imamate of each of them has three aspects:

1. Each of them fulfilled completely the conditions of imamate;

2. The Muslims of their time reached consensus on pledging the oath of allegiance to them and obeying them – and this consensus is itself a proof;

3. The fact that before becoming *Khalīfah*s, each of them lived as Companions to the Messenger ﷺ. Each emigrated from Makkah to Madīnah, each possessed outstanding characteristics, each enjoyed the commendation of Allah, and his ﷺ bearing witness that they would be accorded the Garden.

Moreover, the Messenger also indicated the *Khilāfah* of Abū Bakr and 'Umar and commanded that they be followed, and he put Abū Bakr forward on the occasion of the Farewell Hajj and had him lead the people in *ṣalāt* when he himself became ill prior to his death – this being proof that he appointed him as *Khalīfah*; then Abū Bakr appointed 'Umar as *Khalīfah*; then 'Umar instructed that the matter of succession be decided by *shūrā*, i.e. consultation, among six men and they agreed to the appointment of 'Uthmān – until he was killed unjustly, this having been testified to previously by the Prophet ﷺ who also gave him a promise of the Garden on account of this killing. Then the person with the most rightful claim after him was 'Alī on account of his noble rank and his aspects of excellence.

As for the dispute which arose between 'Alī and Mu'āwiyah and those Companions who were with each of them, the best thing is to refrain from mentioning it, but if the matter is mentioned, then these

Companions should be mentioned in the best manner and one should seek the best explanation for them, for the matter was one of *ijtihād*, i.e. it was open to legal interpretation.

As for ʿAlī and those with him, they were in the right as they made *ijtihād* and came to the correct decision and are correspondingly rewarded for this; as for Muʿāwiyah and those who were with him, however, they made *ijtihād* but came to the wrong decision and are correspondingly forgiven for this. They should both be honoured – as well as all the other Companions with them, and they should be loved on account of what has been mentioned in praise of them in the Qur'ān and their companionship of the Messenger ﷺ. He said ﷺ '[Fear] Allah! [Fear] Allah! with respect to my Companions! Do not make them the target of your attacks after me! Whoever loves them, loves them on account of his love for me; whoever hates them, hates them on account of his hatred for me. He who hurts them, has hurt me, and he who hurts me, has hurt Allah.'

2. The conditions of imamate

They are eight in number: that the person be Muslim, have reached puberty, be sane, male, be just, have knowledge, be sufficiently qualified and that he be related to the Quraysh, although there is a difference of opinion about this latter. However, if people unite under a person who does not fulfil the conditions, then his imamate is permitted lest *fitnah*, i.e. chaos and civil strife, break out.

Moreover it is not permitted to disobey those in authority even if they act unjustly – until they openly manifest *kufr*, and it is obligatory to obey them in both matters which are pleasing and abhorrent to one – unless they command to disobedience, for no obedience is due to any creature when it means disobedience to the Creator.

9. Iman and Islam

AND THIS COMPRISES TWO MATTERS

1. What they mean

Islam

It means absolute submission, linguistically speaking, while its meaning in the *sharī'ah* means submission to Allah and His Messenger ﷺ by expressing this on the tongue and acting in accordance with it with the limbs of the body;

Iman

Linguistically speaking, it means absolute affirmation, while in the *sharī'ah* it means the affirmation of Allah, His angels, His Books, His Messengers and the Last Day. Thus Islam and *īmān*, according to this definition, are different – and this corresponds to His saying: '*The desert Arabs say, "We have īmān." Say: "You do not have īmān. Say rather, 'We have become Muslim'"*' (Sūrah al-Ḥujurāt 49:14). However they are used as synonyms, as for example in His saying: '*We brought out all the mūminūn who were there but found in it only one house of Muslims*' (Sūrah adh-Dhāriyāt 51:35-36). They are also used in an overlapping sense with respect to their general and particular meanings: thus Islam is more general if it refers to submission on the tongue, in the heart and with respect to the limbs, because *īmān* is particular to the heart; but *īmān* is more general if we say that it refers to the declaration on the tongue, sincerity of intent in the heart and the action of the limbs – and this is the view of many of those from the earliest generations.

2. The legal rulings covering both

There are four possible forms:

1. That Islam and īmān are combined

This is such that the slave has *īmān* in his heart and is submitted with respect to his limbs – in which case he is deemed sincere in the eyes of Allah;

2. The opposite of this such that both attributes are absent

In this case he is a *kāfir*, eternally in the Fire;

3. Submission with respect to the limbs but not having īmān in his heart

Such a person is eternally in the Fire and such a person at the time of Prophethood was called *munāfiq*, i.e. a hypocrite, while afterwards he was called a *zindīq*, i.e. someone who manifests Islam and is secretly a *kāfir*;

4. The opposite of this, that is having īmān in the heart but without expression on the tongue or in action

If this is on account of being coerced or lack of time, like someone for example who becomes Muslim, then dies immediately after this before he has had the opportunity to declare it on the tongue or make any actions, then he is excused and deemed sincere in the eyes of Allah, while if this is not the case, then there is a difference of opinion on the matter.

10. Holding fast to the Sunnah

and this comprises two matters

1. Refraining from innovation

The Messenger of Allah ﷺ said, 'I have left you with two matters. You shall never go astray as long as you hold fast to them: the Book of Allah and my Sunnah'. And he said ﷺ 'My Companions are like stars, whoever of them you follow you will be guided'. He also urged people to follow the *Khalīfahs* who took the right way. Thus all good lies in holding to the Book and the Sunnah and following the right-acting men and women from the earliest generations and avoiding all invention and innovation.

Those of earlier generations used to denigrate innovation in the most absolute manner while the later generations said that innovation may be classified in five ways. That which is:

Obligatory, like recording knowledge;

Recommended, like the *ṣalāt* of *tarāwīḥ* in Ramadan;

Ḥarām, like taxes and other imposed payments apart than *zakāt*, such as customs duties, tolls, market dues and sales taxes;

Makrūh, i.e. disliked, such as specifying certain days for certain acts of worship;

Mubāḥ, i.e. permitted, such as new customs in food and dress invented by people – and 'Ā'ishah said ﷺ that at the time of the Prophet ﷺ there were no sieves.

2. Rational examination and theoretical speculation as opposed to imitation and following others (taqlīd)

Firm trust and conviction as to the truth of the *dīn* may be obtained either by means of the first or the second. As for imitation and following, there is a difference of opinion amongst the *'ulamā'*. According to the teaching of the *mutakallimūn* it is not permitted and it does not suffice. However most of the scholars of *ḥadīth* say that it is permitted and that it is perfectly acceptable in the eyes of Allah – and this is correct because the Messenger of Allah ﷺ was content for people to obtain *īmān* by whatever means, be it through rational examination or through imitation, and if he had imposed rational demonstration or speculative examination upon them he would have made it difficult for many people to enter the *dīn*, such as the desert Arabs and others. Rational demonstration and speculative reasoning are for those of superior intellect and strong minds – and the *'ulamā'* differ with respect to their degree of understanding, and this is from the overflowing generosity of Allah, and He gives this understanding to whom He wills.

Moreover the best reasoning, demonstration and proof is that made according to the way of those of right action from amongst the earliest generations – from amongst the Companions, the *Tābi'ūn* and the *imāms* of the Muslims, namely the proofs afforded by the Book of Allah, reflection upon its *āyat*s, contemplation of the marvellous created realities of Allah and the wonders of His handiwork as well as by following the sayings of Muṣṭafā, the Chosen One ﷺ, and the beauty of his *sīrah*, i.e. his life and behaviour and his radiant characteristics, by having a sincere love for him and the pure people of his household and his wives, the mothers of the *mūminūn*, and his devoted, most noble Companions and those who follow them in the best possible manner until the Day of Judgment, and may Allah be pleased with them all.

Part 1

THE ‘IBĀDĀT – LAWS OF FIQH REGARDING THE ACTS OF WORSHIP

AND THIS COMPRISES TEN BOOKS

1 – Purification

Comprising an introduction and ten chapters

Introduction

Comprising two matters

1. Kinds of purification

Purification in the terminology of the law is both spiritual and physical. As for the spiritual it is the purification of the limbs and the heart from the impurity of wrong actions; as for the physical they are the legal aspects of *fiqh* by means of which one wants to perform the *ṣalāt*, and they consist of two kinds: purification from a state of impurity and purification from some physical impurity adhering to the body.

The purification from a state of impurity is of three kinds: major, namely *ghusl* (consisting of a ritual washing of the whole body); minor, namely *wuḍū'* (consisting of a ritual washing of the face and the limbs); and that which may substitute for these two when they cannot be performed, namely *tayammum* (consisting of rubbing over the face and the forearms having struck with the hands on clean earth).

Purification from physical impurity is of three kinds: washing, wiping and sprinkling with water.

2. Conditions for the obligation of purification

Purification is obligatory for the person for whom the *ṣalāt* is obligatory, and this is according to ten conditions:

1. That the person is Muslim, although it is also said that it is conditional on the invitation to Islam having been made to a person. Thus according to the former, it is not obligatory for the *kāfir* while according to the second it is – this difference of opinion being based on the difference of opinion regarding the necessity of having first explained the detailed, applied aspects of the *ṣalāt* to the *kāfir*. However, the *ṣalāt* is not valid from the *kāfir* according to consensus and if a person who has reneged on Islam becomes a Muslim once again, he does not have to make up the *ṣalāt*s he missed during his rejection of Islam, contrary to ash-Shāfi'ī;

2. That the person be of sane mind. It is not obligatory for a mad person, or a person who faints and has lost consciousness, unless he returns to his senses and the prescribed time for a particular *ṣalāt* has not elapsed, contrary to the drunk person, for the obligation of the *ṣalāt* is not removed for him;

3. That the person has reached the age of puberty, the signs of which are five in number: the emission of sperm during sleep, the growth of pubic hair and under the arms, menstruation and pregnancy or a person having reached the age of maturity, namely fifteen years old or according to others seventeen. Thus it is not obligatory for a child although he is instructed to do it at the age of seven and beaten at the age of ten if he does not do it. If a child performs the *ṣalāt* then comes of age during the time remaining prescribed for a particular *ṣalāt* or reaches puberty during the *ṣalāt* itself then it is incumbent on him to repeat it, contrary to ash-Shāfi'ī;

4. That the menstrual blood or that after childbirth ceases to flow;

5. That the time prescribed for a particular *ṣalāt* begins;
6. That one is not asleep;
7. That one has not forgotten;
8. That one is not being compelled to perform it. Furthermore, the person who was asleep, the one who forgets and the person compelled to perform the *ṣalāt* all must make up what they missed according to the consensus;
9. The existence of water or clean earth, dust or sand. There is a difference of opinion if they are not to be found, the difference being whether one should perform the *ṣalāt* or not and whether one has to make it up or not;
10. The capacity to perform the *ṣalāt,* i.e. as much or as far as possible.

1. Wuḍū'

Comprising four sections

1. Kinds of wuḍū'

There are five in all: the obligatory, recommended, *sunnah*, permitted and forbidden.

One may only perform the ṣalāt with the obligatory wuḍū'

i.e. the *wuḍū'* performed for the obligatory and the voluntary *ṣalāt*, for the prostration while reciting those *āyat*s of the Qur'ān necessitating this, according to the consensus; and for the *janāzah* i.e. *ṣalāt* for a funeral, according to the majority; and for touching the *muṣ-ḥaf*, i.e. the written or printed Qur'ān, contrary to the Ẓāhirīs; and for the *ṭawāf*, i.e. going around the Ka'bah, contrary to Abū Ḥanīfah. Thus anyone who makes *wuḍū'* for any one of these is permitted to perform all of them.

Sunnah wuḍū'

This may be done by the person who is in a state of *janābah*, i.e. who is in a state of ritual impurity because of a seminal emission or intercourse, when he wants to go to sleep before purifying himself, but this kind of *wuḍū'* is judged to be obligatory by Ibn Ḥabīb and the Ẓāhirīs.

Recommended

This is the *wuḍū'* one may make for every *ṣalāt*, according to the majority, contrary to those who have deemed that it is obligatory; and the *wuḍū'* that may be made for every *ṣalāt* in the case of the *mustaḥāḍah*, i.e. woman whose menstruation extends beyond the normal time, or the person suffering from incontinence, contrary to the three *imams* who judge it to be obligatory; and the *wuḍū'* which may be made prior to performing the *qurubāt*, i.e. anything which brings one closer to Allah, like the recitation of Qur'ān, *dhikr*, i.e. remembrance of Allah, *du'ā* i.e. supplications, acquiring knowledge and when faced with something one fears, such as embarking on a journey by sea, entering into the presence of the Sultan or others one finds intimidating.

Permitted wuḍū'

It is that which is done to clean oneself or to cool down.

Forbidden

It is to renew one's *wuḍū'* before any act of worship has been performed.

2. The farḍ, i.e. obligatory aspects of wuḍū'

They are six in number: the intention, washing the face, washing the hands, wiping over the head, washing the feet and performing each of these straight after each other.

THE INTENTION

This refers to the aim of the person performing the *wuḍū'* and it is obligatory for every *qurbah*, i.e. act bringing one closer to Allah, and has four characteristics:

The intention is for an action, not for leaving something out, other than fasting;

It pertains to the rights of Allah, exalted is He, and excludes repayment of debts and the like;

It is something undertaken by the person himself and excludes the act of performing the *ghusl* on the dead person or someone who performs *wuḍū'* on someone else;

And it should be for a rational meaning – and for this reason it is not obligatory when removing physical impurity, according to the consensus, whereas it is obligatory in the case of *tayammum,* according to the four, and it is obligatory in the case of *wuḍū'* and *ghusl,* according to the two Imāms, contrary to Abū Ḥanīfah.

TWO SECONDARY POINTS

1. The person who purifies himself makes the intention to carry out the *farḍ* obligation or to remove the state of ritual impurity or to make licit those acts of worship for which purification is obligatory, irrespective of whether this is a general intention or one for a specific act of worship.

2. The timing of the intention is at the beginning of the purification, while it has also been said that it is at the beginning of the first of the *farḍ* elements of the act of purification in question – in agreement with ash-Shāfi'ī, while it has also been said that it should be remembered

from the first element of the purification to the first *farḍ* element. If one delays its timing or makes it some considerable time before, then it is invalid; if, however, it is made just a short time before, then there are two judgments in this regard.

THE FACE

Lengthways it extends to the usual place on the head where the hair first grows to the end of the chin, so it does not include any baldness of the foremost part of the head or baldness of the temples. As for the breadth, the area extends from ear to ear, in agreement with ash-Shāfi'ī, while it has also been said from one cheek to the other, and it has also been said that the first applies when the cheek is devoid of any facial hair and the second applies when the beard extends to it. Qāḍī 'Abd al-Wahhāb is alone in saying that the area between the temples and the ears is a *sunnah*. It is obligatory to rub water thoroughly in between the hair on the face when it is thin while there is a difference of opinion in the case of thick hair. It is also obligatory to wipe over the beard, while there are two judgments as to whether one should rub the beard thoroughly with water.

THE HANDS AND FOREARMS

The washing is from the ends of the fingers to the elbows, and it is obligatory to wash the whole of the elbows and ankles, including the joints, according to the well-known judgment, in accordance with both of them. As for thoroughly rubbing water in between the fingers and toes, there are two judgments in this regard, namely obligation and recommendation. As for removing a ring, there are three judgments, the third being that one removes it when it is tight-fitting but not if it is loose – this being the judgment of Ibn Ḥanbal.

The head

It is obligatory to wipe over the whole of it once from the place where the hair begins to grow on the forehead to where growth ends on the nape of the neck, contrary to Ibn Maslamah who says that two thirds is enough, and to Abi-l-Faraj who says a third, and to Abū Ḥanīfah who says a quarter, and to ash-Shāfiʿī who says a single hair. Moreover it is not permitted to wipe over any head covering, contrary to Ibn Ḥanbal, and there is no extra merit in repeating the wiping, contrary to ash-Shāfiʿī. The preferred way of wiping is that one begins at the front of the head and wipes over to the end of the hair then returns to where one began – the return being a *sunnah*. It is obligatory to wipe over long hair, according to the well-known judgment.

The feet

The obligation is to wash them up to the ankles, according to the well-known judgment, although aṭ-Ṭabarī says [feet] are to be wiped over. The ankles refer to the two points on either side of the shin, there being two ankles to each foot, although it has also been said that it refers to the two points at which one's shoelaces are tied up, there being just one ankle in this case for each foot.

Performing each aspect of the washing and wiping immediately after each other

This is obligatory as long as one remembers this and one is physically able, according to the well-known judgment. Thus on the basis of this one makes a distinction between the person who forgets or is incapable, who carries on from whatever he has forgotten or was unable to do, and the person who deliberately misses out something, in which case he must start again from the beginning. However it has also been said that it is a *sunnah*, while ash-Shāfi'ī and Abū Ḥanīfah have omitted this.

3. The Sunnah aspects

They are six in number: washing one's hands before putting them into the receptacle containing the water, rinsing one's mouth, sniffing up water into the nose and then blowing it out, wiping over the ears and doing all these in this order.

Washing one's hands before putting them in the receptacle

This is a *sunnah* according to the three for anyone making the *wuḍū'* or *ghusl* whose hands are free from any impurity, while the Ẓāhirīs have made it an obligation when getting up after sleep, and Ibn Ḥanbal restricts it specifically to sleep at night. As to whether washing them is done as worship or in order to clean them, there are two judgments in this respect – two secondary judgments being based on these two, namely, are they to be washed as part of the *wuḍū'* as a whole, or separately, and does one repeat their washing if one becomes ritually impure during one's purification or not, each of these aspects having two judgments.

Rinsing of the nose

This is a *sunnah* for the *wuḍū'* according to the four.

Snuffing up of water and expelling it from the nose

They are both *sunnah*s for the *wuḍū'*, according to the three, while Ibn Ḥanbal deemed them obligatory.

As for the manner in which one should rinse the mouth, you should shake the water vigorously in your mouth and then expel it. While the manner in which one should rinse one's nose is that one should draw up water into both nostrils – and it is recommended to do this with the utmost meticulousness, unless one is fasting. As for the *sunnah* of expelling water from the nose, one should place one's thumb and forefinger on one's nose and then expel the water with the air from the nose. It is permitted to rinse the mouth and draw up water into the nose with one handful of water or with two or more.

The ears

Wiping over them is a *sunnah,* according to the four, but one group have said that they should be washed together with the face, while wiping over them is a *sunnah* according to the two Imams, and Abū Ḥanīfah has deemed it obligatory; and one renews the water used when wiping them, contrary to Abū Ḥanīfah.

The order

It is a *sunnah* according to the well-known judgment, in agreement with Abū Ḥanīfah, although it has also been said that it is obligatory, in agreement with ash-Shāfi'ī.

4. Excellent and disliked aspects of wuḍū'

Aspects of excellence

They are six in number:

1. Use of the *miswāk* toothbrush before it, and the Ẓāhirīs have deemed it obligatory. The fresh, green stick is the best, except in the case of the fasting person. If there is no *miswāk* stick available then one should rub over one's teeth with one's fingerl;

2. Saying *bismillāh* 'in the name of Allah' at the beginning of it, although it has also been said that it is not to be said. It has been deemed obligatory by one group, contrary to the four;

3. Repeating the washing twice or thrice, and three times is the best;

4. Beginning with the right before the left;
5. Beginning the wiping at the front of the head;
6. Remembering Allah during the *wuḍū'*, and saying:

أَشْهَدُ أَنْ لَا إِلَهَ إِلَّا اللهُ وَحْدَهُ لَا شَرِيكَ لَهُ، وَأَشْهَدُ أَنَّ مُحَمَّدًا عَبْدُهُ وَرَسُولُهُ صَلَّى اللهُ عَلَيْهِ وَسَلَّمَ، اَللَّهُمَّ اجْعَلْنِي مِنَ التَّوَّابِينَ وَاجْعَلْنِي مِنَ الْمُتَطَهِّرِينَ

Ash-hadu al-lā ilāha illa-llāhu waḥdahu lā sharīka lah, wa ashhadu anna Muḥammadan ʿabduhu wa rasūluh, ṣalla-llāhu ʿalayhi wa sallam. Allahumma-jʿalnī mina-t-tawwābīna wa-jʿalnī mina-l-mutaṭahhirīn

I bear witness that there is no god but Allah, alone without partner, and I bear witness that Muḥammad is His slave and His Messenger, may Allah bless him and grant him peace. O Allah make me one of those who turn constantly to You in *tawbah* and make me one of those who purify themselves.

Ash-Shāfiʿī has added the wiping of the neck. As for placing the receptacle on the right, this a person may do.

The disliked aspects

They are six in number. First, making the *wuḍū'* in the toilet, talking other than *dhikr*, i.e. remembrance of Allah, exalted is He, using a lot of water, restricting the washings to a single washing for each limb except in the case of someone who knows how to do the *wuḍū'* properly, washing more than three times, performing *wuḍū'* from receptacles of gold or silver, although it has also been said that this is prohibited.

Wiping oneself with a towel is permitted, although ash-Shāfiʿī recommends it not be done.

Remark

When washing one's face, forearms/hands and feet one must bring the water to them and rub the water on them with one's hand – it is not permitted to let the water drop from one's hand before touching the limb in question with the water for then it would be a wiping; nor is it permitted that one allow the limbs to come into contact with water without rubbing it in; nor that one rub the limbs when there is no longer any water on them. One must also make sure to seek out any places where the skin is not immediately exposed to the washing, like the creases on one's forehead, the soft parts of the nose, those parts of the eyelids which are sunken, the places where the skin is split on hands and feet, and beneath the toes and the ends of the nails.

Secondary point

As for whoever forgets any *farḍ* element of the *wuḍū'*, if he remembers when his limbs have dried after making the *wuḍū'*, then he does that particular thing which he has omitted; if he remembers before the limbs dry, then he must begin the *wuḍū'* anew. At-Talaytali has said that he should repeat what he has forgotten and any other elements of the *wuḍū'* following it – and not begin it anew, and this is correct, and Allah knows best; and likewise if he omitted it deliberately; but if he has already performed the *ṣalāt* then he must repeat it both in the case where he deliberated missed something out or forgot to do it.

As for anyone who omits a *sunnah* out of forgetfulness, then his *ṣalāt* is valid – and he does whatever he has forgotten for any *wuḍū'* after this; if he deliberately omits a *sunnah* then he is like the person who has forgotten, although it has also been said that this invalidates his *ṣalāt* on account of his lack of respect

If, however, he omits an aspect of excellence, then there is no harm in this.

2. Things which invalidate wuḍū'

Comprising two sections

1. Things which invalidate wuḍū' in the madhhab

They are three in number: the physical changes which break ritual purity, the cause of these physical changes, and renunciation of Islam. As for the physical changes, they refer to what is expelled from either the penis or the anus, they being five in number: urine, excrement, breaking wind noisily or breaking wind silently, the thick white fluid excreted after urination (*wady*) and the thin white pre-seminal fluid excreted after experiencing sexual pleasure (*madh-y*).

Three secondary matters

1. If what is expelled from either the penis or the anus occurs when the person is in good health

This invalidates *wuḍū'* according to the consensus. If what is expelled comes out of the body from a place other than the penis or anus, then there are two judgments in this respect. If something unusual is expelled like [kidney or gall bladder] stones or worms from either of them then this does not invalidate *wuḍū'*, contrary to Ibn Abi-l-Ḥakam and them [i.e. ash-Shāfi'ī, Abū Ḥanīfah and Ibn Ḥanbal].

2. If urine or madh-y are excreted due to persistent incontinence

This does not break *wuḍū'*, contrary to the two. If the person in question is able to stop the incontinence with medicine or by means of sexual intercourse then there are two judgments as to whether it is broken. If the person subject to incontinence excretes the thin white pre-seminal fluid usually excreted after experiencing sexual pleasure (*madh-y*) or urinates in a normal way, then he must make *wuḍū'* – and he recognises this by the fact that the normal excretion of *madh-y* is accompanied by sexual arousal, and ordinarily urine accumulates [in the bladder] but may be retained.

3. Whoever is sure that he is in a state of ritual purity then has doubts as to whether something has occurred to change this

He must make *wuḍū'*, contrary to them. If he is sure that something has occurred to change his state of purity and has doubts as to his state of purity, then he must also make *wuḍū'*.

The causes of the physical changes which break someone's wuḍū'

They include intoxication, madness and fainting, which break *wuḍū'*, according to the consensus irrespective of whether these [states] are severe or mild, and sleep – the effect on a person's state depending on which of the two kinds of sleep he has had.

The first is determined by examining the position of the person sleeping: if it is not conducive to inducing any excretion, as in the case of someone sitting, then the *wuḍū'* is not broken, contrary to the person who is lying down – in agreement with the two.

The second is determined by examining the kind of sleep a person has had, this being of four types: a long, deep sleep breaks *wuḍū'* while the opposite does not; as for a long, light sleep and its opposite, there are two judgments.

Other causes include the touching of women. If this is accompanied by sexual pleasure the *wuḍū'* is broken, if not then it does not, irrespective if the touching is done over clothing or not, irrespective of whether the person touched is one's wife or some other woman. Any sexual pleasure experienced counts alike for the person who touches and the person touched. According to ash-Shāfi'ī, *wuḍū'* is broken in all cases while according to Abū Ḥanīfah it is not broken in all cases. If he intends to find sexual pleasure but does not obtain it, there are two judgements non-acceptance. Obtaining sexual pleasure is not stipulated in kissing [directly on the mouth], according to the well-known judgment (*mashhūr*), [which breaks *wuḍū'*].

Wuḍū' is not broken by touching a boy's penis or that of an animal, contrary to ash-Shāfi'ī.

Another cause is a woman's touching her vagina, there being three narrated judgments in this respect: it is said that it breaks *wuḍū'* in agreement with ash-Shāfi'ī, that it does not, in agreement with Abū Ḥanīfah, and that it depends on whether she experiences pleasure or not.

As for touching one's anus, this does not break *wuḍū'*, contrary to Ḥumdays and ash-Shāfi'ī.

As for having an erection without any emission of the thin white pre-seminal fluid excreted after experiencing sexual pleasure (*madh-y*), there are two judgments.

As for reneging on one's Islam, it breaks *wuḍū'*, according to the well-known judgment (*mashhūr*), although it has also been said that it does not, in agreement with ash-Shāfi'ī.

2. The causes – recognised outside of the madhhab – which break one's wuḍū'

Vomiting breaks it, as does belching, bleeding from the nose, cupping with scarification and, according to Abū Ḥanīfah and Ibn Ḥanbal, the exuding of pus, and guffawing during the *ṣalāt*, according to Abū Ḥanīfah, and eating raw or cooked camel meat, according to Ibn Ḥanbal, and eating anything touched by fire, according to some from the earliest generations – although there was then a consensus that this had been abrogated, and carrying a corpse, according to Ibn Ḥanbal, and slaughtering animals, according to Ḥasan al-Baṣrī – although this narration from him is not sound, touching one's testicles, according to 'Urwah ibn az-Zubayr, and touching one's armpits, according to Ibn 'Umar, although this narration from him is not sound.

3. Ghusl i.e. the ritual washing of the whole body

IT HAS THREE SECTIONS

1. Types of ghusl

They are either obligatory, *sunnah* or recommended.

Obligatory

This is done because of the state of *janābah*, i.e. the ritual state of impurity caused by emission of sperm or intercourse, because of menstrual bleeding, bleeding after childbirth and a person becoming Muslim.

Sunnah

This refers to the *ghusl* made for the *jumu'ah ṣalāt* – and the Ẓāhirīs regard it as obligatory, that made for the two *'Īd ṣalāt*s, entering into the state of *iḥrām* for the hajj, entry into Makkah, washing the dead person, although it has also been said that it is obligatory.

Recommended

This is that made for the *ṭawāf*, i.e. circling the Ka'bah, and the *sa'y*, i.e. walking and trotting seven times between aṣ-Ṣafā and al-Marwah, standing at 'Arafah and al-Muzdalifah, making *ghusl* for any extended bleeding from the womb after the normal menstrual cycle, and that made after washing a corpse.

2. The five farḍ aspects of the ghusl

The intention, contrary to Abū Ḥanīfah, covering the whole body with water, according to the consensus, rubbing in of water, according to the madhhab and contrary to them, performing the various stages of the *wuḍū'* immediately after each other – as long as one remembers and is able to do this, contrary to the two, and combing the fingers through the beard to ensure the water reaches the skin, in agreement with ash-Shāfi'ī, although it has also been said that it is a *sunnah.*

3. The sunnahs

They are five in number: the washing of one's hands before bringing them into contact with the water contained in the receptacle used for the *ghusl*, vigorously rinsing the mouth, snuffing up water into the nostrils – and Abū Ḥanīfah deeming it obligatory for the *ghusl*, wiping inside the nostrils, combing the fingers through one's hair to make sure the water reaches the scalp, although it has been said that this is an aspect of excellence, and ash-Shāfi'ī deemed it obligatory.

4. The aspects of excellence

They are five in number: saying *bismillāh,* i.e. in the name of Allah, scooping up water three times to the head, making *wuḍū'* beforehand, beginning at the top and to the right of the body.

5. The makrūh, i.e. disliked aspects

They are also five in number: pouring a lot of water over one's body, not washing in the preferred order and manner mentioned previously [i.e. at the top and to the right], repeating the washing of the body when it has already been done thoroughly all over, washing in the privy, and talking, other than *dhikr,* i.e. remembrance of Allah.

6. The form of the ghusl

One begins by washing one's hands, then one removes any impurity from his hands, then washes one's private parts to remove any impurities from the state of *janābah*, i.e. sperm and vaginal fluid, lest one touch these after making *wuḍū'*, then one makes *wuḍū'* as if one were making *wuḍū'* prior to the *ṣalāt* – and it is permitted to leave the washing of the feet to the end of one's *ghusl*, then one rubs in water with one's hands to the roots of one's hair, then one pours three scoops of water over one's head – and in the case of a woman she washes roughly her hair in tresses but does not have to undo the braids, contrary to ash-Shāfi'ī – and then one washes the rest of one's body.

Five subsidiary matters

1. One must check that one has reached the hidden areas of the body such as underneath one's beard, the armpits, the groin, the inner side of the knees, the navel and other such areas.

2. Whoever breaks his *wuḍū'* while still making *ghusl* repeats his *wuḍū'* – and there is a difference of opinion as to whether one should make a particular intention for it.

3. It suffices in the case of a woman who is both in menstruation and in a state of *janābah* that she make a single *ghusl* for both the menstruation and the *janābah*; and the intention made for the *ghusl* does for the *wuḍū'* as the latter is included in the former, but not vice versa.

4. If one makes *ghusl* for *janābah* and the *jumu'ah* then this may have various ways of performance, the best being that one makes the intention for the *ghusl* of the *janābah* then one follows it with that of the *jumu'ah* – in order that both be acceptable, according to the agreed judgment.

5. The *dhimmī* woman, i.e. a Christian or Jewess living under the authority of the Muslims, who is married or possessed by a master must make the *ghusl* to fulfil the husband's due – even if she does not make the intention; and according to Ibn al-Qāsim the husband or the master should coerce her into making the *ghusl* after her menstruation, but not on account of her state of *janābah*, while Ashhab has said that she is not to be coerced.

4. Those matters which make the ghusl obligatory

These comprise the *janābah*, entry into Islam, termination of menstruation and the flow of blood after birth – and these will be dealt with in the corresponding chapters.

Janābah

It is of three kinds: emission of sperm while awake, the disappearance of the glans of the penis during intercourse, and emission of sperm while asleep.

The emission of sperm

This refers to the thick, white liquid which gushes out and which smells of palm-tree pollen or dough – if it is emitted accompanied by the customary feeling of pleasure as a result of intercourse or any other sexual activity then, according to the consensus, it is obligatory to make a *ghusl*; if it is emitted without this pleasurable feeling or with some feeling of pleasure other than the customary, such as when scratching one's body, washing with hot water or through pain, like receiving a blow, then it is not obligatory to make a *ghusl*, although it has also been said that it is obligatory, in agreement with ash-Shāfi'ī; and if the customary pleasure is present but is not simultaneous with emission, as for example when one has intercourse or sets about it and no emission takes place but then one has an emission after the pleasure has disappeared, then there are three judgments: the *ghusl* is obligatory, in agreement with ash-Shāfiʿī, the negation of obligation, and a judgment based on the distinction between the person who has intercourse and makes a *ghusl* before the emission of sperm – in which case he does not repeat the *ghusl* – and the person who has not made the *ghusl* – in which case he then makes the *ghusl*; in the case where one decides that it is not an obligation to make the *ghusl*, then there are two judgments as to the obligation or recommendation to make *wuḍū'*.

The disappearance of the glans – or an amount corresponding to its length – into the front or back passage of an animal or human being

This renders the *ghusl* obligatory, irrespective of whether sperm is emitted or not, according to the consensus – after a difference of opinion amongst the earliest generations, based on the *ḥadīth* 'the water [of the *ghusl*] becomes necessary from the water [i.e the sperm emitted]' which was then abrogated.

Additional remarks

Know that just as the 'disappearance of the glans' or an amount corresponding to it makes *ghusl* obligatory, it also makes the *ḥadd* punishment for adultery obligatory, it assures a married couple the state of *ihsān*; it renders both obligatory and voluntary fasting invalid – and makes the payment of *kaffārah*, i.e. the reparation which 'covers up' the wrong action, obligatory in Ramadan, making it obligatory only on the man who coerces his wife to intercourse; it also renders invalid the consecutive nature of the fasting of the two months stipulated in reparation for the breaking of the fast in Ramadan; it renders the hajj invalid if it happens before the standing at 'Arafah, and renders the *'umrah* obligatory, i.e. the lesser pilgrimage, and slaughter of a *hady*, i.e. a sacrificial animal, if it happens after *jamrah al-'aqabah*, i.e. the place of the final stoning, and before the [*ṭawāf*] *al-ifāḍah*, and it renders the slaughter of a *hady* obligatory if after the [*ṭawāf*] *al-ifāḍah* and before the *jamrah al-'aqabah* for the person who delays the stoning; and it also invalidates the *i'tikāf*, and invalidates *'umrah*; and it makes it obligatory for the man who has coerced his wife into having intercourse to enable her to perform another hajj; it fulfils the oath of a man who has sworn to have intercourse; and it necessarily results in the breaking of the oath of the person who has sworn not to have intercourse; it necessitates payment by the father of the price of his grandson's female slave if he has intercourse with her; it necessitates payment by whoever usurps the ownership of a slave girl; it necessitates payment by one of two partners if he has intercourse with a slave girl who is jointly owned by them; it breaks the inviolability of the marriage bond of the husband whose whereabouts were unknown and with whose wife another party has intercourse; it also prevents the first husband returning to his wife who wants to return not knowing [that she has had intercourse in a second marriage] – and by it is validated the marriage of the second husband if two male guardians who did not know about each other married her off in two separate marriages; by means of it also is validated the purchase of the second purchaser if the master of the slave girl or his representative sells her to two men and neither of the two is aware of the other's purchase; it renders marriage to a step-daughter prohibited; and it necessarily invalidates the marriage of the daughter if he marries the mother and penetration takes place; and it renders marriage to a second sister prohibited if he owns the first; and it renders marriage to a paternal aunt prohibited if he owns the daughter of her brother; and it renders marriage to a maternal aunt prohibited if he owns the daughter of her sister; and it renders prohibited the marriage to a wife who is in her *ʿiddah* [from another marriage]; and it makes payment of the full dowry (*ṣadāq*) obligatory; and it makes payment of the dowry obligatory in the case of the man who usurps possession of a woman or in the case of a fornicator; it also validates a marriage contracted with an incorrect dowry; and it obliges the father to consult the daughter if he marries her off after it occurs; and it renders the *ʿiddah* obligatory; and it renders the waiting period (*istibrāʾ*) of the slave girl obligatory; and it renders the waiting period (*istibrāʾ*) obligatory in the case of fornication; and it renders obligatory the husband's return to his divorced wife; and it renders the wife who has been divorced three times licit for the husband who divorced her; it also necessitates that the wife have the right to choose [a divorce] if her husband had granted her that he would not take a concubine along with her; and it rescinds the right to her choosing [divorce] in the case of a slave girl set free while married to a slave; and it renders obligatory payment of the expiation (*kaffārah*) for *ẓihār*; and it renders commencement (*ibtidāʾ*) of the *kaffārah* obligatory if he has intercourse after he had commenced it; and it rescinds the *īlāʾ* oath of the one who pronounces it; it obligates the rescinding of the *liʿān*; and it renders the *ḥadd* punishment obligatory for the husband's sworn allegation if he has intercourse with her after the claim of her adultery; it removes the obligation of upkeep on behalf of the father whose daughter had been divorced; and it validates the incorrect sale of a slave girl; and it rescinds the right of option in the case of a sale of a slave girl; and it rescinds the right to claim for defect in the case of a slave girl; it rescinds the father's right to take back the gift of a slave girl if the son has intercourse with her; and it renders the payment of the price of a slave girl obligatory if she was gifted with the intention of receiving some recompense. The aforementioned judgments are fifty in number.

Summary

The rulings governing sexual intercourse may be subdivided in four ways:

The first division is concerned with intercourse which is *ḥalāl* within marriage – not with ambiguous or *ḥarām* matters – like *iḥlāl*[1] or making *muḥṣan*;

And a division concerned with the *ḥalāl* and the ambiguous – but not with the *ḥarām* – like genealogy and relations, the *'iddah* waiting period, the full dowry, the prohibition of marrying those related by marriage and the like;

And a division concerned with the absolutely *ḥarām* like the instances governed by the *ḥudūd* punishments and other offences;

And a division concerned with *ḥalāl*, *ḥarām* and ambiguous cases, like the obligation to make the *ghusl* and invalidation of the acts of worship – among them fasting, hajj, *i'tikāf* and the like.

Iḥtilām i.e. the emission of semen during sleep

This obligates the making of *ghusl* whether it be on the part of a man or a woman, according to the consensus;

It does not however render it obligatory if someone has a dream of a sexual nature without emission, according to the consensus;

If one wakes up and finds a damp area on one's self or clothing and does not know if it is semen or the thin white pre-seminal fluid excreted after experiencing sexual pleasure (*madh-y*) – and has no

1 Making a thrice divorced woman *ḥalāl* for her original husband.

recollection of having had a dream of a sexual nature – then there are two judgments as to the obligation to make a *ghusl*;

If someone sees semen on his clothing but is unsure as to when the emission occurred then, if it is still damp, he repeats the *ṣalāt* made after his most recent sleep, but if dry, then he repeats all the *ṣalāt* that he has made from the first time he wore those clothes, although it has also been said that he repeats the *ṣalāt* made after his most recent sleep.

NOTE

Janābah prevents every kind of *ṣalāt*, according to the consensus, as well as the prostration made after reading the specific *āyat*s of prostration from the Qur'ān, according to the consensus, touching the *muṣ-ḥaf*, according to the four but contrary to the Ẓāhirīs, also prevents *ṭawāf* and *i'tikāf*, according to the consensus, recitation of the Qur'ān by heart, according to the four but contrary to one group, although Mālik has permitted recitation of short *āyat*s in order to seek refuge from Shayṭān, contrary to ash-Shāfi'ī; it also prevents one from entering a mosque, while ash-Shāfi'ī has permitted this, as well as passing through it, while Ibn Ḥanbal has permitted the person in *janābah* to sit in it.

As for the *kāfir* who enters Islam, he is obliged to make a *ghusl*, in agreement with Ibn Ḥanbal, although it is also said that it is recommended, in agreement with ash-Shāfi'ī; and there is a difference of opinion as to whether he has to make a *ghusl* if he is convinced of the truth of Islam in his heart – before actually manifesting it in his actions, and whether he should make *tayammum* if he does not find water.

5. Water

This is divided into three sections

1. The five ways in which water is classified

1. Water of absolute purity

That remains in its original state, it being both pure in itself and capable of purifying other than it, according to the consensus, irrespective of whether it is sweet or salty, from the sea, the sky or the earth;

Included in this is water which has changed after standing for a long time or because of what has come into contact with it or what has been generated by it like water moss or what cannot normally be separated from it or that which is immediately adjacent to it;

It is not changed by dust or earth which is thrown into it, according to the well-known judgment (*mashhūr*);

As for whether it changes by the addition of salt, there are three judgments, in the third there being a distinction made between natural mineral salt and that made by man;

As for the change which occurs because leaves fall into it, there are three judgments, there being a distinction made in the third between the time when many leaves fall into it and it would be difficult to clear the water of them and the time when few leaves fall in it.

2. Water with which something pure has come into contact

If no change occurs with respect to its colour, taste or smell then it is as water of absolute purity;

If one of its three attributes changes, then it is pure, according to the two Imams, but is not capable of purifying other than itself, while according to Abū Ḥanīfah it is both pure in itself and capable of purifying other than itself, as long as it has not been boiled and as long as this change in one attribute does not dominate the whole of the amount or body of water.

3. If it comes into contact with something ritually impure

If it causes a change in the water, then it is neither pure in itself or capable of purifying other than it, according to the consensus;

If the change caused by the ritual impurity disappears then there are two judgments;

If the change does not disappear, then if there is a large amount of water it is deemed to be pure water in its original state – and there is no defining limit as to what constitutes a large amount within the madhhab, whereas ash-Shāfiʿī defines it as being two earthenware bottles of the type that come from Hajar in Bahrain, this being equal to about fifty water skins, while Abū Ḥanīfah defined it as being a body of water which if disturbed on one side would not be disturbed on the other. If the amount is small and it does not change then it is ritually impure, in agreement with ash-Shāfiʿī and Abū Ḥanīfah, although it is also said that it is *makrūh*, and it is also said that it is of dubious quality in which case one combines use of it with *tayammum*.

4. Water already used in making wuḍū' or ghusl

Then it is pure in itself and capable of purifying other than itself if its use has not changed the water, although its use is *makrūh* when other water is available, while it has also been said that it is pure in itself but not capable of purifying other than itself, in agreement with ash-Shāfiʿī, and it has been said that it is of dubious quality and one should make *wuḍū'* with it together with *tayammum*, while Abū Ḥanīfah has said that it is ritually impure.

The surplus water left over after use by someone in *janābah* or a menstruating woman is pure in itself and capable of purifying other than itself and it is permitted for a man to purify himself with the surplus water of a woman, contrary to Abū Ḥanīfah, and vice versa is permitted, contrary to one group.

5. WATER IN WHICH DATES OR OTHER FRUIT HAVE FERMENTED

It is ritually impure if it intoxicates; if it does not intoxicate but has changed, then it is pure in itself but not capable of purifying other than itself, although it is reported of Abū Ḥanīfah that he permitted *wuḍū'* with *nabīdh* but that he later rescinded this.

2. WHAT IS LEFT OVER [OF DRINK]

IT CONTAINS FIVE MATTERS

1. THE LEFTOVERS OF A MAN

If he is a Muslim and he does not drink wine then his leftovers are both pure in themselves and capable of purifying other than themselves, according to the consensus;

If he is *kāfir* or drinks wine and there is some ritual impurity in his mouth then it is like water which has come into contact with ritual impurity, but if there is no ritual impurity in his mouth, then it is both pure in itself and capable of purifying other than itself according to the majority, although one group has said that the leftovers of a *kāfir* are ritually impure, and likewise anything which his hand has come into contact with.

2. THE LEFTOVERS OF A DOG

One washes the receptacle with water seven times to clean after its licking according to the four, while ash-Shāfi'ī has added to this the cleaning of it by sprinkling dust or earth over it; and there are two judgments as to the obligation or recommendation of this washing. As to whether that which the dog has lapped is to be emptied out or not, there are two judgments; and there are also two judgments as to whether one washes food clean that it has licked seven times; and there are two judgments as to whether the washing should be repeated in the case of a number of dogs or in the case where one dog has repeatedly licked something; and there are two judgments as to whether something licked by a dog whose possession is legitimate is to be washed seven times.

3. The leftovers of a pig

They are pure, contrary to ash-Shāfiʿī, and there are two judgments as to whether the receptacle used by it is to be washed seven times.

4. The leftovers of animals that consume what is ritually impure, like cats and mice or rats

If something ritually impure is seen in their mouths, then it is as if it has come into contact with something ritually impure, but if one can ascertain that their mouths are clean then it is pure;

If it is not known, then one may overlook what one finds difficult to be on one's guard about; and there are two judgments as to whether what one is on one's guard about should be deemed ritually impure.

5. The leftovers of wild beasts and predatory animals

They are pure according to the two Imams, while Abū Ḥanīfah has said the ruling for such leftovers follows that of the meat of such animals.

3. Receptacles

Comprising four matters

1. Receptacles made of leather the animal of which has been slaughtered and whose meat is permitted to eat

It is permitted to use them according to the consensus, while there is a difference of opinion about leather of an animal which has been slaughtered but whose meat is *ḥarām* to eat, like that of predatory animals.

As for the leather of pig, it is ritually impure in all circumstances.

As for the leather of carrion, if it has not been tanned then it is ritually impure and if it has been tanned, then the well-known judgment (*mashhūr*) is that it is impure, in agreement with Ibn Ḥanbal, although it is permitted within the madhhab to use it for dry things and, with respect to liquids, for water alone, but it is not permitted to sell it, to make *ṣalāt* on it or in it, although it has also been said that it is pure, in agreement with ash-Shāfiʿī.

2. Receptacles made of fired clay or earthenware, iron, lead, brass, copper, wood, and pure bone

It is permitted to use them, according to the consensus. There are two judgments as to the purification of earthenware after having been immersed in something ritually impure like wine.

3. Receptacles of gold and silver

Their use is *ḥarām* for both males and females, while there is a difference of opinion as to whether it is permitted to have them but not to use them; or whether one may attach precious stones other than gold or silver to them like ruby and pearls; or if they are covered with lead or the like; and with respect to permitted vessels, if they are embellished with gold or silver or they are used to repair a crack.

4. In the case where vessels have been mixed up

And they resemble each other and one does not know which of the two is pure, and one does not have any other vessels, then it is said that one does *tayammum* and does not use them, in agreement with Ibn Ḥanbal; although it has also been said that one should examine one of them carefully and do *wuḍū'* with it, in agreement with the two; and it has also been said that one does *wuḍū'* with one and performs the *ṣalāt*, then makes *wuḍū'* with the other and performs the *ṣalāt*; and Muḥammad ibn Maslamah said that one should wash his limbs with the second before he makes *wuḍū'* with it.

6. Najāsāt – ritually impure things

Comprising three sections

1. Discriminating between najāsāt

There are four kinds of ritually impure things: inanimate things, animals, animal excretions and excrement, and parts of animals.

Inanimate things

These are ritually pure except for things which intoxicate.

Animals

If they are alive, then they are ritually pure in all circumstances although it has also been said that dogs, pigs and those who associate other gods with Allah are ritually impure;

If dead, then they must necessarily have died of natural causes or been slaughtered;

If they were slaughtered, then the animal slaughtered is ritually pure if its meat is permitted to eat, according to the consensus, while there is a difference of opinion regarding animals which are slaughtered and whose meat it is not permitted to eat;

If they died of natural causes and are of the sea then they are ritually pure, contrary to Abū Ḥanīfah, while if land-based and not warm-blooded then they are pure, contrary to ash-Shāfiʿī;

If land animals and warm-blooded then they are ritually impure, according to the agreed judgment.

The various parts of animals

If they are cut from them while they are alive, then they are ritually impure, according to the consensus, except for hair, wool and fur.

If cut from them after they have died, then in the case where we rule that it is pure, then all parts of the animal are pure, while if we rule that it is ritually impure then its meat is *najas.*

As for bone and that which is understood in the same way such as horns, teeth and cloven hooves, these are *najas* when from a dead animal, contrary to Abū Ḥanīfah.

As for wool, fur and hair from an animal that has not been slaughtered ritually they are pure, contrary to ash-Shāfiʿī, and mention has already been made of hides.

As for the excretions of animals, if they have no particular location, like tears, sweat and saliva, then they are pure in the case of all animals, although there is a difference of opinion in the case of the saliva of dogs and the sweat of someone who consumes ritually impure things such as the person who drinks wine, or the person who comes into contact with dung.

If these excretions have a particular location, then in the case of the urine and excrement of man it is *najas,* according to the consensus, although there is a difference of opinion regarding the urine of a child who has not yet begun to eat solid food.

And the urine of other animals is classified within the madhhab according to their meat, such that:

The urine of animals whose meat is *ḥarām* is *najas*;

While that of animals whose meat is *ḥalāl* is pure;

And that of animals whose meat is *makrūh* is *makrūh*.

Ash-Shāfi'ī has said that the urine and excrement of all animals is *najas*.

As for blood, if a large amount from a land animal then it is *najas*, while a little may be overlooked, the amount in this case being limited to the size of a Baghlī Dirham coin.

Ibn Wahb has said a little menstrual blood may be overlooked while a lot is *najas*.

There are two judgments regarding the ritual impurity of fish blood and the blood of flies, while musk is pure according to the consensus.

As for pus and vomit, it is said that one may overlook a little, as in the case of blood, although it has also been said that it is treated like urine.

As for milk, that of women and of animals whose meat is eaten is pure while that of pigs is *najas* according to the consensus;

As for the milk of other animals whose meat is *ḥarām*, there are two judgments;

As for the milk of animals which have consumed *najāsah* there are two judgments.

As for the thin white pre-seminal fluid excreted after experiencing sexual pleasure (*madh-y*) and the thick white fluid excreted after urination (*wady*) they are both *najas* according to the agreed judgment.

As for human sperm it is *najas*, contrary to ash-Shāfi'ī and Ibn Ḥanbal.

Summary

There are twelve najāsāt unanimously agreed upon within the madhhabs

Urine of an adult human being, their excrement, the thin white pre-seminal fluid excreted after experiencing sexual pleasure (*madh-y*), the thick white fluid excreted after urination (*wady*), the flesh of animals that are not ritually slaughtered, pig and the bones of both of the latter, the skin of pigs in all cases, the skin of a dead animal if not ritually slaughtered, whatever has been cut from an animal while alive other than its hair and anything like hair, the milk of pigs and intoxicants.

What is agreed upon within the madhhab are: the urine of animals whose meat it is *ḥarām* to eat and their excrement, sperm and a lot of blood and a large amount of vomit.

There are also eighteen matters about which there is a difference of opinion within the madhhab

The urine of a child which does not yet eat solid food, the urine of animals whose meat is *makrūh* to eat, the skin of a dead animal if it has been tanned, the skin of a slaughtered animal whose meat is *ḥarām*, and its meat and its bones, and the ashes of a dead animal, the tusks of an elephant, the blood of fish, the blood of a fly, a small amount of menstrual blood, a small amount of pus, the saliva of a dog, the milk of animals other than pig whose meat is not eaten, the milk of animals which have consumed something ritually impure, the sweat of someone who has consumed something impure, the hair of a pig, and wine if changed to vinegar.

2. Judgments pertaining to najāsāt

They are ten in number

1. The removal of najāsah is obligatory

If one is aware of it and if one is able to remove it, according to the well-known judgment. If one then performs the *ṣalāt* with *najāsah* on one, one must repeat it if one is aware of it and capable, but one does not if one is not aware and not capable, although it has also been said that it is obligatory in all circumstances, in agreement with the two – such that if one makes the *ṣalāt* with it on one, one must repeat it in all cases, although it has also been said that it is a *sunnah* and that it is recommended to repeat it within the prescribed time.

2. There is a licence to make the ṣalāt with najāsah on one

If it is not possible to avoid it or if it is difficult, as in the case of a wound or running sore, or a woman who is suckling, or someone who is incontinent.

As for whether it is permitted for them to be *imāms* of the *ṣalāt*, there are two judgments, like the *ghāzī* warrior who has to hold on to his horse.

3. It is obligatory to remove any najāsah

From the body of the person making *ṣalāt*, from the place of *ṣalāt*, from the clothing in which he is making the *ṣalāt*, from anything he is carrying or to which he is connected.

4. The removal of najāsah is effected in three ways

By washing, wiping, sprinkling/moistening. A sprinkling or moistening of clothing is made if one has doubts as to whether there is any *najāsah* on it, while there is a difference of opinion as to sprinkling one's body or the place of *ṣalāt* with water if one has doubts as to whether there is any *najāsah*; and there is a difference of opinion as to whether this sprinkling needs an intention. Wiping is done over that which might be damaged through washing, like a sword, sandals or *khuffs*. Washing is done for anything other than this.

5. It is not enough when washing off najāsah just to wipe over with water

Rather one must remove the actual *najāsah* itself and its traces such that the water used in the washing then comes away unchanged after separating from this *najāsah*; if after separating from it it is changed, then the water itself is *najas* as well as the place of *najāsah*.

6. If the place of the najāsah on clothing or the body may be identified

Then this alone is to be washed; if it cannot be identified, then the whole item of clothing or the whole body are to be washed.

7. It is not permitted to remove the najāsah with any liquid other than water

Although Abū Ḥanīfah permits it with all liquids, for example vinegar or rose water.

8. If a woman walks over some dry najāsah wearing a long dress

The latter is purified by the earth she walks over after this; there is a difference of opinion if it is wet. It is similar if someone walks over *najāsah* when his foot is wet and then walks over dry earth. And one may overlook any mud one walks in as long as most of it is not *najāsah* or the actual location or source of the *najāsah* is where one is walking.

9. If an unclean animal falls into a well and the water changes

Then all of the water must be drawn out of it; if it does not change then it is recommended to draw out of it an amount equal to the size of the animal and the water.

10. If najāsah falls into a liquid other than water

Then it becomes *najas* irrespective of whether it changes or not; and if a mouse or rat falls into liquid fat and dies in it then the whole of it is thrown away; if it is solid then the mouse and what surrounds it are thrown away, unless, Ṣaḥnūn has said, it remained a long time in it [in which case the whole of it is thrown away].

3. Nosebleeds

Anyone who has a nosebleed and knows that the bleeding will not stop, should make the *ṣalāt* while in this state; if he hopes it will stop, and it began before the *ṣalāt*, then he should wait until it stops; if it does not stop before the final moment of the prescribed time, then he must make the *ṣalāt*; if it starts to bleed during the *ṣalāt*, then he should squeeze his nose with his fingers and carry on; if drops of blood fall or blood flows then he should leave the *ṣalāt* to wash his nose, and it is permitted for him to interrupt the *ṣalāt* by saying *as-salāmu 'alaykum* or saying something, then washing and beginning the *ṣalāt* again, and carrying on the *ṣalāt* where he left off after washing away the blood, although Ibn al-Qāsim prefers that he interrupts the *ṣalāt*, while carrying on from where he left off is the preference of Mālik; and it is not permitted, outside of the madhhab, to carry on from where one left off. It is only permitted within the madhhab according to five conditions: that is that he does not talk, that he does not walk on *najāsah*, that the blood does not fall on his body or clothing, that he washes off the blood in the closest place available and that he has already completed a *rak'ah* with its two prostrations – although there is a difference of opinion in this matter; and carrying on from where one left off is permitted in the madhhab for the *imām* and those following him, while there is a difference of opinion with respect to someone who is alone; and if someone comes after the *ṣalāt* has begun and has a nosebleed and wants to carry on from where he has left off, there is a difference of opinion whether he should begin by carrying on from where he left off or making up what he has missed.

7. INSTINJĀ' AND ASSOCIATED MATTERS

COMPRISING TWO SECTIONS

1. THE COURTESIES OF GOING TO THE LAVATORY

One should go away from people and keep oneself hidden from view, and avoid places where one would call down on oneself the general curses of people, that is roads and streets, the places where people sit, the shady areas in front of walls and trees and the banks of rivers; one should not urinate in burrows, standing water, or in a place exposed to the wind; one should remember Allah when entering it, saying:

أَعُوذُ بِاللهِ مِنَ الْخُبُثِ وَالْخَبَائِثِ

A'ūdhu billāhi mina-l-khubuthi wa-l-khabā'ith

'O Allah, I seek Your protection from male and female devils'
and when coming out:

الْحَمْدُ لِلهِ الَّذِي أَذْهَبَ عَنِّي الْأَذَى وَعَافَانِي

Al-ḥamdu lillāhi-lladhī adhhaba ʿanni-l-adhā wa ʿāfānī
'Praise be to Allah, Who has removed from me impurity and given me good health', or one says:

غُفْرَانَكَ

Ghufrānak
'I seek your forgiveness';

One should not face the *qiblah* nor turn one's back to it unless one is between buildings, in agreement with ash-Shāfiʿī, while Ibn Ḥanbal has prohibited this in all cases; one should not speak; one should count that which removes the impurity; one should not stand to go to the lavatory unless the ground is soft, for example sand.

2. Making instinjā' with water and istijmār with stones

Comprising five matters

1. The best

The best is to combine *istijmār* and *instinjā'*, and to make *istijmār* first; then, to make only *instinjā'*; then to make only *istijmār* – and this is permitted both when water is not available and when it is, although Ibn Ḥabīb has said it is only permitted when water is not available. It is not permitted to make *istijmār* to clean oneself of sperm or of the thin white pre-seminal fluid excreted after experiencing sexual pleasure (*madh-y*), nor if the urine or faeces have spread well beyond the two orifices or even near them.

2. The way istinjā' is done

One pours water into one's left hand before touching the impurity, then one washes one's genitals – if it is just of urine then it is enough that one just washes the orifice of the penis, while if it is of the thin white pre-seminal fluid excreted after experiencing sexual pleasure (*madh-y*) then one must wash the whole of the penis, although it has also been said that one should wash in the same way as if there is urine; then one washes one's back passage pouring water in a continuous manner while rubbing with the left hand, and one allows oneself to relax a little, and one should rub vigorously to clean properly, and one should not make *istinjā'* with the right hand or touch one's penis with it.

3. It is permitted to make istijmār with stones

And with anything like them i.e. anything solid which is pure and cleaning, which is not edible, nor prohibited because *ḥarām*, nor involving wastefulness, nor something over which another has a rightful claim, nor dung, or bones, nor charcoal as this has been prohibited, although if one makes *istijmār* with what is not permitted then it discharges the duty, contrary to Ibn 'Abd al-Ḥakam, while the Ẓāhirīs have said that it is only permitted with stones.

4. It is obligatory with respect to istijmār that cleaning is effected

Even if this is by means of a single stone, while three are preferable, although it has also been said that this number is obligatory; if then the cleaning is not effected with one, then one must use more stones using an odd number of them.

5. One must make istibrā' before instinjā'

That is: to ensure that the two orifices are free of urine and faeces, and there is no limit to the degree to which this is done, rather one should follow what people customarily do, although ash-Shāfi'ī has said that one should 'milk' the penis three times to ensure the urine is expelled.

8. Tayammum

Comprising four sections

1. The conditions for its permissibility

In general they are two in number: the absence of water or one's having an excuse for not being able to use it. As for a more detailed description, it refers to the absence of water while travelling, and illness, according to the consensus, and in the case where one is resident – i.e. not travelling – contrary to Abū Ḥanīfah, and when one finds insufficient water, contrary to ash-Shāfi'ī, and the absence of any implement to reach the water like a bucket or well-rope, and when one fears one would go thirsty or others would go thirsty, in the case of both humans and animals, and when one fears thieves or predatory animals if one were to go out to get water, or when water is expensive and buying it would be prejudicial to him, or he fears the prescribed time would pass if he were to go to get water or wait for it or use it, contrary to ash-Shāfi'ī, or he fears death from the cold or that he might fall ill or that [his illness] would be aggravated or that he would he take longer to get better, or that he is ill and cannot find anyone to give him water, or wounds or ulcers cover most of his body in the case of the person in the state of *janābah* or the parts of the body washed for the *wuḍū'* in the case of someone in a state of minor ritual impurity as a result of urinating or discharging faeces (*muḥdith*).

2. The farḍ aspects of tayammum

That it be done after the prescribed time for the *ṣalāt* in question has begun; that one has looked for water, contrary to Abū Ḥanīfah with respect to both of the previous aspects; intention, according to the four; wiping over the face and the hands or arms, according to the consensus; that the two wipings be done immediately after each other, contrary to the two; and it is done using earth, and it is permitted to make *tayammum* with what is on the surface of the earth – in its various forms, like stones, pebbles, sand and gypsum, contrary to ash-Shāfi'ī.

Its sunnah aspects are

Wiping the face before one's hands or arms; striking the earth with one's palms again before wiping over the arms or hands; wiping up to one's elbows, although it has also been said that this is obligatory in agreement with ash-Shāfi'ī and others.

Its aspects of excellence are

That one begin with one's right hand; and that one say *bismillāh* when commencing; the manner in which one wipes one's forearms, i.e. that one wipe over one's right forearm with one's left hand from the back of the hand to the elbow, then from the inner part of the elbow to the wrist, then one wipes over one's left forearm with one's right hand in the same way, although it is acceptable whatever way it is done, if done properly.

3. Tayammum stands in place of

Tayammum stands in place of *wuḍū'*; and in place of *ghusl* done to free oneself of the state of *janābah*, or from menstruation, and bleeding after giving birth, although it is not permitted for the husband of the menstruating woman to have intercourse with her until she makes a *ghusl* with water, according to the well-known judgment (*mashhūr*).

Tayammum is broken by those things which break *wuḍū'* and *ghusl*, and it is also broken by water being found before the *ṣalāt*, according to the agreed judgment, but it does not after the *ṣalāt* has been commenced, contrary to Abū Ḥanīfah and Ibn Ḥanbal, nor after completing it – so one does not repeat it according to the consensus.

4. Tayammum renders permissible that which is rendered permissible by purification using water

One does not however make two prescribed *ṣalāt*s with one *tayammum*, contrary to Abū Ḥanīfah. One may combine a *nāfilah ṣalāt* with an obligatory one if the latter is made first, although ash-Shāfiʿī has said that one may make *nāfilah* before and after the prescribed ones.

9. Wiping over khuffs and splints/ligatures/bandages

As for the two *khuff*s, according to the four *imām*s it is permitted to wipe over them on a journey and while resident if six conditions are fulfilled:

That the *khuff* is made of leather, excluding thereby socks; that they cover up to the ankles; that they be in sound condition or have only a minor tear or a small hole – a major tear being something which renders walking impossible, while according to Abū Ḥanīfah it is a tear three fingers wide; and that they be single, and there are two judgments regarding wiping over a *khuff* on top of another *khuff*; and that one has put them on having full ritual purity from having used water; that it is licit to wear them, excluding thereby those that are *ḥarām* for one to wear, or in the case of someone having misappropriated them.

It is obligatory to wipe over the uppers of the *khuff*, while it is recommended to wipe over their soles, although it has also been said that it is obligatory.

And one may continue to wipe over them without time limit as long as one does not take them off or do something which necessitates making *ghusl*. If one does take them off, then the wiping over is no longer valid and one must wash one's feet, and if a *ghusl* is obligatory then one does not make the wiping as wiping is done in the case of *wuḍū'*. Ash-Shāfi'ī and Abū Ḥanīfah have said that the traveller may wipe for three days and nights, and the resident for a day and a night.

Splints

They are those which are strapped over wounds, ulcers and vein openings for blood-letting – it is permitted to wipe over them and over ligatures and bandages which are fastened over them irrespective of whether these cover the limbs washed in *wuḍū'* or *ghusl*, or if they cover the specific area in question or reach beyond it; this is not conditional upon them having been attached while one is in a state of ritual purification; and one does not repeat the *ṣalāt* if one becomes well again; and if one removes the splint to treat the area and then replaces it, one repeats the wiping; and if one becomes well again and one removes it, then one washes the area immediately; and if the splint falls off while one is making the *ṣalāt*, one breaks off the *ṣalāt* as the purity of the area affected is broken by its being uncovered.

10. Menstruation, bleeding after childbirth, the period of purity and the istiḥāḍah

As for menstruation, this refers to the bleeding from the vagina of a woman who is normally able to become pregnant, but which is not from childbirth and not a prolongation of the normal period of menstruation, and it comprises two matters:

1. Its measure

There is no minimum limit with respect to the acts of worship, contrary to *'iddah* and *istibrā'*, rather any strong bleeding is menstruation, although ash-Shāfi'ī has said its minimum is a day and a night and Abū Ḥanīfah has said three days.

As for the maximum, this varies according to the differences in women, and they are of four categories: the beginner, the woman accustomed to specific periods of menstruation, the pregnant woman and the woman who has irregular periods.

As for the beginner, she reckons in accordance with others of her age, and if bleeding continues beyond this, then she makes a *ghusl* and is deemed to be in the state of *istiḥāḍah*, although it has also been said that she should use precaution by waiting three days after this before doing the *ghusl* and making *ṣalāt*, and it has also been said that she should complete fifteen days.

As for the woman accustomed to specific periods of menstruation, she counts the days she customarily experiences as her period and if bleeding extends beyond that, she does a *ghusl* and is considered to be in *istiḥāḍah*. And it has been said that she should use precaution by waiting three days after this before doing the *ghusl* and making *ṣalāt*, and it has also been said that she should complete fifteen days.

As for the pregnant woman, if she sees blood then this is menstruation, according to the two Imāms, contrary to Abū Ḥanīfah; and if her usual period does not alter then she is as a woman who is not pregnant; if her usual period does alter, then there are three judgments with respect to her, as in the case of the woman accustomed to specific periods of menstruation; and Ibn al-Qāsim has said that she should pause and wait for fifteen days after three months, twenty days after six months and thirty days at the end of the pregnancy, and the like of that, while it has also been said that she should wait and double the number of days of her usual period.

As for the woman who has irregular periods, that is she sees blood for one or more days and then is clean of blood for a day or more, such that she never has a full time in which she is free of blood: then according to the two Imāms she should join the days of bleeding together and keep a count of them until the maximum number of days for menstruation is reached for her, and she should ignore the days between them in which she was clean of blood, and not count them, and so if she has completed the maximum number of days for menstruation she is then deemed to be in the state of *istiḥāḍah*; and if a time when she is clean of blood corresponding to the minimum period of purity intervenes between the days of bleeding, then she makes a new start of another period of menstruation; and during the whole period in which she joins together the days of bleeding and ignores the clean days in her calculation, each day she does not see any blood she makes a *ghusl* anticipating that it will be a period of full purity, and every day she sees bloods she avoids that which the menstruating woman would avoid.

2. Menstruation and bleeding after childbirth

They prevent a woman from doing twelve things. She is prevented from seven of them by the state of *janābah*, namely all of the *ṣalāt*s, the prostration made for recitation, touching a copy of the Qur'ān, entering the mosque, *ṭawāf*, *i'tikāf*, and recitation of the Qur'ān, although it is also said that it is permitted her to recite from heart.

And then there are five more things: fasting, but she must make it up whereas she does not have to make up missed *ṣalāt*s according to the consensus; divorce; intercourse in the vagina before bleeding has stopped, according to the consensus; and intercourse apart from in the vagina before bleeding has stopped, contrary to Aṣbagh and the Ẓāhirīs – it is only permitted to take pleasure in her upper body, according to the four, after she has tightened a wrap around her waist – and it is not permissible to have intercourse with her after bleeding has stopped before she has made a *ghusl*, contrary to Abū Ḥanīfah.

If intercourse is had during menstruation he must seek forgiveness from Allah but does not have to pay *kaffārah*, although Ibn Ḥanbal has said that he pays *ṣadaqah* of one dinar or half a dinar.

The body of the menstruating woman, her perspiration and any food and drink left over by her are pure, and likewise the person in a state of *janābah*.

As for bleeding from the vagina on account of childbirth there is no minimum to this, although Abū Ḥanīfah has said twenty-five days, and the maximum is sixty days, in agreement with ash-Shāfi'ī, while Abū Ḥanīfah has said forty; if the bleeding after childbirth stops, then the bleeding returns after a full period of purity then this is menstruation, but if it returns before the period of purity is completed then it is bleeding from childbirth, and if it continues for longer than the period then it is *istiḥāḍah*.

Purity refers to the time for which a woman becomes free of the blood of menstruation or childbirth, and there is no maximum time according to the consensus, while the minimum is fifteen days, in agreement with the two, although it has also been said that it is ten, eight, five and it has also been said that she should reckon in accordance with what is customary with her.

Purity is recognized in two ways: dryness after bleeding and the thin, white fluid which appears at the end of the menstruation. If the woman with menstruation or bleeding after childbirth sees these signs of her purity then she makes *ghusl* immediately and is permitted everything which is not permitted for a woman menstruating or with bleeding after childbirth.

As for the blood of *istiḥāḍah*, which is bleeding from the vagina because of ill health, the woman with *istiḥāḍah* does not become subject to rules governing the menstruating woman unless three conditions are fulfilled:

1. That the number of days which elapse when she is in a state of *istiḥāḍah* equals the minimum reckoned in the case of purity;

2. That the blood of her *istiḥāḍah* changes in quality to that of menstruation, the blood of menstruation being black and thick while that of *istiḥāḍah* is red and thin, and the yellow and turbid is also menstruation;

3. That she is capable of discriminating between menstruation and *istiḥāḍah*. *Istiḥāḍah* does not prevent her from doing anything which menstruation would stop her from doing. And it is recommended for the woman with *istiḥāḍah* to make *wuḍū'* for every *ṣalāt*, while ash-Shāfi'ī has made it obligatory; and there is a difference of opinion as to whether she make a *ghusl* if the blood of *istiḥāḍah* stops.

2 – The Ṣalāt

Comprising thirty chapters

1. There are five kinds of ṣalāt

Those which are *farḍ ʿayn*, *farḍ kifāyah*, *sunnah*, *faḍīlah*, and *nāfilah*.

The farḍ ʿayn ṣalāts

They are five in number, according to the consensus, namely the *ṣubḥ ṣalāt* which is that of dawn, *ẓuhr* (midday), *ʿaṣr* (afternoon), *maghrib* (following sunset) and *ʿishāʾ* (night), this being the *ṣalāt* which it has been prohibited to call *ʿatamah*. The 'middle *ṣalāt*' refers to the *ṣubḥ ṣalāt* according to Mālik and the people of Madīnah, while it refers to the *ʿaṣr ṣalāt* according to ʿAlī ibn Abī Ṭālib ﵁ and to *ẓuhr* according to Zayd ibn Thābit.

The farḍ kifāyah

This refers to the *ṣalāt* over the deceased person according to the well-known judgment, although it has also been said that it is a *sunnah*.

The Sunnah

This applies to ten *ṣalāt*: the *witr* and it is the most particularly stressed of the *sunnah*s, and Abū Ḥanīfah considers it obligatory; the two *rakʿah*s of the dawn prior to *ṣubḥ*; the *ʿĪd al-fiṭr ṣalāt*; the *ʿĪd al-Aḍḥā*; the *ṣalāt*s of the eclipse of the sun and the eclipse of the moon; the *ṣalāt al-istisqā*; the prostrations for reciting certain *āyat*s; the two *rak'ah*s for the *ṭawāf*; the two *rak'ah*s for entering *iḥrām* on hajj – although it has also been said that the two *rak'ah*s of *fajr* before *ṣubḥ*, those for the eclipses and the prostrations for recitation are among the acts of excellence.

The acts of excellence (faḍā'il)

They are ten in number: two *rak'ah*s after *wuḍū'*; two *rak'ah*s to greet the mosque, and the Ẓāhirīs deemed them obligatory; the Ḍuḥā *ṣalāt*, and there is a difference of opinion ranging from twelve to two *rak'ah*s; standing in the night; standing in Ramadan, this being a *sunnah* of particular importance; 'the bringing to life' of the time between *maghrib* and *'ishā'*; four *rak'ah*s before *ẓuhr*; two *rak'ah*s after it, although four have also been said; two *rak'ah*s before *'aṣr*, although four have also been said; two *rak'ah*s after *maghrib*, although six have also been said; and it has also been said that these are all *sunnah*s.

The nāfilah

They are divided into two: those for which there is no particular occasion, and this refers to voluntary ones made at permissible times; while there are others for particular reasons, they being ten in number: *ṣalāt* prior to starting out on a journey; when returning from it; for entering one's house and leaving it; the two *rak'ah*s of *ṣalāt al-istikhārah* recorded by al-Bukhārī; the two *rak'ah*s of the *ṣalāt* of need recorded by at-Tirmidhī from 'Abdallāh ibn Abī Awfā but he regarded its chain of narration as weak; the four *rak'ah ṣalāt at-tasbīḥ* recorded by at-Tirmidhī and Abū Dāwūd from Abū Rāfi' – al-Qabbāb mentioned from [Qāḍī] Ibn al-'Arabī that this *ḥadīth* of Abū Rāfi' has no basis among either the sound *ḥadīth* or those which are good (*ḥasan*); two *rak'ah*s between the *adhān* and the *iqāmah*; four *rak'ahs* after the sun has passed its zenith; two *rak'ahs* upon turning to Allah in *tawbah*; and some have added two *rak'ahs* when making supplication; and two *rak'ahs* for someone about to be put to death, following the example of Khubayb.

Section

Someone who abandons doing the *ṣalāt* and claims that it is not obligatory is a *kāfir* according to the consensus; if he confirms that it is obligatory but refuses to do it, then he is put to death in accordance with the *ḥadd* punishment not as a *kāfir*, in agreement with ash-Shāfi'ī, while Ibn Ḥabīb and Ibn Ḥanbal have said that he is put to death as a *kāfir*, and Abū Ḥanīfah has said that he is lashed and imprisoned until he dies or returns to the *ṣalāt*.

2. The times of the ṣalāt

Comprising three sections

1. The optimal (ikhtiyārī) time

Ẓuhr

The beginning of its time is when the sun has passed its zenith, according to the agreed judgment, the zenith being the moment when the sun is at its highest, its having passed this point being known by the shadows beginning to lengthen after their having reached a minimum; and the end of its time is when the shadow of every object becomes as long as this object after including the amount of shadow resulting from the sun passing its zenith, and Abū Ḥanīfah has said it is when the shadow of every object becomes twice as long as the object.

ʿAṣr

The beginning of its time is the end of the time of *ẓuhr*, this being common to both, the commonality being in the end of the first length of shadow of the object while it has also been said that it is in the beginning of the second length of shadow, and it has also been said that there is no commonality between the two, in agreement with ash-Shāfiʿī, while Abū Ḥanīfah has said that the beginning of the time is after the shadow has become two lengths; as for the end of the time it is when the shadow of every object becomes twice the length of the object, in agreement with ash-Shāfiʿī, although it has also been said it is the time of the yellowing of the sun in agreement with Ibn Ḥanbal, whereas the Ẓāhirīs have said it extends up to the setting of the sun.

Maghrib

The beginning of its time is the setting of the sun according to the consensus, and the time span is short, not extended, in agreement with ash-Shāfiʿī, although it has also been said it extends until the twilight has disappeared in agreement with Abū Ḥanīfah and Ibn Ḥanbal.

ʿIshā'

The beginning of its time is the disappearance of the redness of twilight according to the two Imāms, but the disappearance of the whiteness of twilight according to Abū Ḥanīfah; the end of its time is a third of the night, in agreement with the two, but Ibn Ḥabīb and the Ẓāhirīs have said half of the night.

Ṣubḥ

The beginning of its time is the breaking of true dawn according to the consensus; the end is sunrise, in agreement with them, while Ibn al-Qāsim has said it is the clear yellowing before sunrise.

Secondary matter

The most excellent according to ash-Shāfiʿī is to perform the *ṣalāt*s at the beginning of the time except *ẓuhr* when the heat is intense; and the most excellent according to Abū Ḥanīfah is to delay them to the end of the time except *maghrib*. As for the ruling within the madhhab, the most excellent according to the well-known judgment is to delay *ẓuhr* until the shadow of a quarter of the length of an object has been reached, to delay *ʿishāʾ* in mosques, and to do *ṣubḥ*, *ʿaṣr* and *maghrib* at the beginning of the time.

2. The ḍarūrī times

They extend beyond the *ihtiyārī* times, according to the three but contrary to the Ẓāhirīs, and this refers to the time which is shared in common between *ẓuhr* and *ʿaṣr* and the time shared in common between *maghrib* and *ʿishāʾ*, while *ṣubḥ* does not have a *ḍarūrī* time according to the well-known judgment.

The *ḍarūrī* times are particularly for those people who have a valid excuse such as menstruation, bleeding after childbirth, a fit of insanity, fainting, *kufr*, still being a youth prior to puberty, and forgetfulness.

As for forgetfulness, it has a ruling particular to it, while all the other excuses have two modes: the circumstances in which [the excuse] ceases to exist and the circumstances of the [excuse's] onset.

If [the excuse] ceases to exist and not enough time remains to make at least one *rakʿah*, then both *ṣalāt*s are cancelled, while if enough time remains for a *rakʿah* or more – or for the whole of one *ṣalāt*, whether it is the full *ṣalāt* of the person who is resident or the shortened *ṣalāt* for the traveller – then the second of the two is obligatory and the first is cancelled; if there remains enough time for more than this, enough for one *rak'ah* of the other *ṣalāt*, whether it is the full *ṣalāt* of the person who is resident or the shortened *ṣalāt* for the traveller, then both *ṣalāt*s are obligatory.

As an elucidation, if the woman menstruating becomes clean of bleeding, the mad person comes to his senses, the young person reaches puberty, or a *kāfir* becomes Muslim, and there remains enough time before *maghrib* to make five *rak'ah*s in the case of the resident or three in the case of the traveller, then they must make *ẓuhr* and *'aṣr*; if however less than this remains – up to the point where there is only enough time for one *rak'ah* for example, then only *'aṣr* is obligatory; and if there is not enough time to make even a single *rak'ah* then the two *ṣalāt*s are cancelled.

With respect to *maghrib* and *'ishā'*, if there remains enough time after there is no longer any valid excuse before the break of dawn for five *rak'ah*s then the two *ṣalāt*s are obligatory, while if there is only enough for three, then *maghrib* is cancelled, and if there is enough for four then it is said that *maghrib* is cancelled as he is able to fulfil the amount required for *'ishā'* in particular, although it has also been said that the two *ṣalāt*s are obligatory as he makes the *maghrib* in full and is able to catch one *rak'ah* of *'ishā'*.

As for the onset of the reason for these valid excuses, this is conceivable with respect to a fit of insanity, fainting, menstruation and bleeding after childbirth, but is not conceivable with respect to *kufr* and youth prior to puberty. If one of these happens during the time common to both *ṣalāt*s, then both *ṣalāt*s are cancelled, while if it happens during the time particular to one of the two, then the one particular to the time is cancelled and he makes the other up. This is such that the first time immediately after the sun has passed its zenith is particular to *ẓuhr* – comprising four *rak'ah*s with regard to the resident and two *rak'ah*s for the traveller, then the two *ṣalāt*s have a common time up to the point where *'aṣr* has its particular time for four *rak'ah*s before *maghrib* with respect to the resident and two *rak'ah*s for the traveller, contrary to ash-Shāfi'ī who says that the common *ḍarūrī* time extends from when the sun has passed its zenith to sunset.

So if a woman begins menstruation within the common time, then *ẓuhr* and *'aṣr* are cancelled, and if she begins in the time which is particular to *'aṣr*, and she has not yet performed *ẓuhr* or *'aṣr*, then only making up *'aṣr* is cancelled for her; and if she begins menstruation in the time particular to *ẓuhr*, then it is cancelled, and if the menstruation continues to the common time then *'aṣr* is cancelled – but if it stops before it, then it is obligatory; and the same applies for all the other valid excuses in *ẓuhr* and *'aṣr*, and *maghrib* and *'ishā'*.

As for forgetfulness, it is included in this section if one has forgotten one of the two common *ṣalāt*s while resident – and then travels and remembers it, or vice versa: as for whether one does it in full or shortens it, then the ruling is that if he remembers the *ṣalāt* before the *ḍarūrī* time for it has finished, then he makes it according to the time in which he remembers it whether resident or travelling, such that he shortens it if he remembers it while travelling and does it in full if he remembers it while resident; and if he does not remember it until the *ḍarūrī* time for it has expired, then he does it according to what of its time remains with respect to the person resident or travelling, as for example if one forgets *ẓuhr* and *'aṣr* while resident, then one travels and one remembers them while travelling with enough time before sunset for three *rak'ah*s then one performs them in the shortened form, but if one has enough time to catch two or one *rak'ah*s then one makes *ẓuhr* in full and shortens *'aṣr*, and if one remembers them after *maghrib*, then one makes them both in full.

So if one forgets them both while travelling, then remembers them when resident with enough time before sunset for five *rak'ah*s, then one makes them both in full, but with time for any number less than this – up to one *rak'ah* – one shortens *ẓuhr* and makes *'aṣr* in full; if one remembers after sunset, then one shortens them both;

If one forgets *maghrib* and *'ishā'* while resident then remembers them while travelling with enough time for four *rak'ah*s before dawn then one shortens *'ishā'*, but there is a difference of opinion regarding when there is time for any number less than this – up to one *rak'ah* – as to whether one shortens them or makes them in full. And if one remembers them after the dawn, then one makes them in full,

If one forgets them while travelling, then remembers them while resident with enough time for four *rak'ah*s before dawn, then one makes *'ishā'* in full, and there is a difference of opinion regarding when there is time for any number less than this – up to one *rak'ah* – as to whether one does it in full or shortens it; and if one remembers after the dawn then one shortens it.

Three secondary matters

1. Only if one catches one *rak'ah* together with its two prostrations, has one caught the *ṣalāt*, while Ashhab said if one catches the bowing in particular, and ash-Shāfi'ī and Abū Ḥanīfah said if one catches the *takbīratu-l-iḥrām*.

2. What counts with respect to catching the *ṣalāt*, in the case of those who had an excuse, is that their excuse is no longer valid and they have made the purification, and Ibn al-Qāsim has said that in the case of a *kāfir* the purification does not count.

3. The *ṣalāt* is not to be delayed until the *ḍarūrī* time and whoever does delay it and is not one of those who has a valid excuse, then he is at fault, and there is a difference of opinion as to whether he is carrying out the *ṣalāt* properly or making it up.

3. The times when ṣalāt is prohibited

These are ten in number: when the sun is rising; when setting; after the *ṣubḥ ṣalāt* up to the sunrise; after *'aṣr* until *maghrib* – but, the *ṣubḥ ṣalāt* of the day or its *'aṣr* are permitted within these four times for anyone who has missed doing them, according to the consensus, and it is permitted to make up missed *farḍ ṣalāt*s at these times and at other times, contrary to Abū Ḥanīfah. *Ṣalāt*s other than these are not allowed, except that in the madhhab the *janāzah ṣalāt* is permitted after the *ṣubḥ ṣalāt* as long as the dawn has not become fully bright [before sunrise] and after *'aṣr* as long as the sun has not become yellow, and likewise the prostration of the recitation of the Qur'ān as narrated in the *Mudawwanah*, in agreement with ash-Shāfi'ī but contrary to what is in the *Muwaṭṭa'* and in agreement with Ibn Ḥanbal. Ash-Shāfi'ī added that it is permissible to perform *nawāfil* which are for specific occasions, like greeting the mosque, the two *rak'ah*s for *ṭawāf* and entering *iḥrām*.

Also among the times [when *ṣalāt* is prohibited] is the time after dawn and before the *ṣubḥ ṣalāt*, although it is permissible to make up missed *ṣalāt*s, the two *rak'ah*s of *fajr* and the *witr* and that one make up one's reading of the *ḥizb* of the night if one has missed it and there is a difference of opinion as to the *ṣalāt* of greeting the mosque during this time.

Also among the times [when *ṣalāt* is prohibited] is when the sun is passing its zenith, although it is not a time when it is prohibited according to the well-known (*mashhūr*) judgment [of Mālikīs], although it is a time of prohibition according to ash-Shāfi'ī, except on the day of the *jumu'ah*.

Also among the times [when it is prohibited] is after sunset and before *maghrib* according to the well-known judgment.

And among these times is the making of *nāfilah ṣalāt* on the day of *jumu'ah* when the *imām* is on the minbar delivering the *khuṭbah* and before it, and on account of the *ṣaḥīḥ ḥadīth* ash-Shāfi'ī and others permitted the greeting of the mosque for the person who enters at this time.

And among them the making of *nāfilah ṣalāt* after the *jumu'ah* in the mosque, which is not permissible within the madhhab, contrary to Abū Ḥanīfah and others.

And among them is the *ṣalāt* after and before the *'Īd ṣalāt*, it not being permissible in the *muṣallā* but permissible in the mosque, although according to ash-Shāfi'ī it is permissible in both, and according to Ibn Ḥanbal it is not permitted before but is permitted after, and Allah knows best what is correct.

3. The adhān and the iqāmah

Comprising five sections

1. The ruling on the adhān

It is a *sunnah mu'akkadah*, in agreement with ash-Shāfi'ī and Abū Ḥanīfah, although it has also been said that it is a *farḍ kifāyah*, and it has also been said that there are five kinds of *adhān*: the obligatory, being that of the *jumu'ah*; the recommended, being that of the other *farḍ ṣalāt*s in the mosque; the *ḥarām* being that made by a woman, although ash-Shāfi'ī has permitted women to make the *adhān*; the *makrūh*, being that of the *nāfilah ṣalāt*s and the *ṣalāt*s which have been missed, although Ibn Ḥanbal and Abū Ḥanīfah have permitted it for missed *ṣalāts*; and the *adhān* which is licit, being that made by the person alone, although it has also been said that it is recommended.

2. The way the adhān is called

There are four madhhabs in this regard:

1. The adhān of Madīnah

This comprises saying *Allāhu akbar* twice and the *tarjīʿ* of the two *shahādahs*.

2. The adhān of Makkah of ash-Shāfiʿī

This comprises *tarjīʿ* of the *Allāhu akbars* and the two *shahādahs*.

3. The adhān of Kufa of Abū Ḥanīfah

This comprises saying *Allāhu akbar* four times and the two *shahādahs* twice.

And the three are in agreement as to saying the two *ḥayya ʿalas* twice and the saying *Allāhu akbar* twice after them, and the saying the *tahlīl* once after this.

4. The adhān of Basra of al-Ḥasan al-Baṣrī

This comprises saying *Allāhu akbar* four times, the *ḥayya ʿalas* twice and the two *shahādahs* twice.

According to the madhhab there are seventeen phrases in the *adhān*, to which the *tathwīb* before the *ṣubḥ ṣalāt* after the two *ḥayya ʿalas* is added, that is saying ‘الصَّلاَةُ خَيْرٌ مِنَ النَّوْمِ – *aṣ-ṣalātu khayrun mina n-nawm* – *ṣalāt* is better than sleep’ twice, and once according to Ibn Wahb, although it is omitted according to Abū Ḥanīfah.

Secondary note

Tarjīʿ is repeating the two *shahādah*s twice, louder than the first two times.

3. The qualities and courtesies required of the mu'adhdhin

His obligatory attributes are six in number: islam; being of sound mind; male; having reached the age of puberty – although there is a difference of opinion on this within the madhhab; of equitable and proper character; having a knowledge of the times of the *ṣalāt*s; and it is recommended that he be of fine and strong voice.

Its courtesies are ten: that he make the *adhān* while in *wuḍū'*; standing; in an elevated place; facing the *qiblah*, and it is permitted for him to turn to another direction during the saying of *ḥayya 'ala-ṣ-ṣalāh* and *ḥayya 'ala-l-falāḥ*; that he not speak during the *adhān*, neither by saying the *as-salāmu 'alaykum* to someone or returning the *salām* of someone, or any other utterance; nor that he recite it backwards or interrupt its delivery, rather he should pronounce it in a continuous fashion, pronouncing it according to *tartīl* – in a distinct and accurate manner; he should pause after his pronouncing the various phrases, contrary to the *iqāmah*; he should avoid trilling, quavering or chanting, and excessive elongation of the long vowels; and it is permitted for him to put his fingers in his ears, and Abū Ḥanīfah and Ibn Ḥanbal deemed this to be recommended; and [it is permitted] that someone other than the person who calls the *adhān* makes the *iqāmah*; and [it is permitted] that more than one person make the *adhān* except that of *maghrib* [i.e. multiple *adhān*s – but from different *mu'adhdhins*]; and that one does not call it before its time other than for the *ṣubḥ ṣalāt* – which one may call to before the dawn, contrary to Abū Ḥanīfah.

4. What the person who hears the adhān says

He is instructed to say the same as what is called but instead of the two *ḥayya 'ala ṣ-ṣalāh*s, *ḥayya 'ala-l-falāḥ*s he should say *lā ḥawla wa lā quwwata illā billāh*, although it has also been said that he should restrict such repetition to the saying of the two *shahādah*s, and it has also been said that he should say the *shahādah* once only. If he hears the *adhān* while performing his *ṣalāt*, then it is said that he should repeat it during his *nāfilah* but not his *farḍ ṣalāt*, although it has also been said that he does not repeat it in either, and it has also been said that he does repeat it, but that he does not say more than the two *shahādah*s and that if he does say more than these two, then there are two judgments as to whether his *ṣalāt* is invalidated. And the person who hears the *adhān* should send blessings on the Prophet ﷺ and ask for rank and favour from Allah for him, then make a *du'ā* for whatever he wishes.

5. The iqāmah

It is a *mu'akkad sunnah* for the *farḍ ṣalāt*s within their time, for those which are out of their time, for the person alone, for the *jamā'ah* and both for men and women, although it has also been said that a woman does not have to make the *iqāmah*.

The form of it is that each phrase is said once except for the *takbīr* which is said twice, and the number of phrases within the madhhab amounts to ten, while the madhhab of ash-Shāfi'ī and Ibn Ḥanbal is to say the *takbīr*s and the saying *qad qāmati ṣ-ṣalāt* twice, while that of Abū Ḥanīfah is to repeat each phrase twice.

4. Mosques and places for ṣalāt

Comprising two sections

1. Mosques

Comprising three matters

1. Mosques are the best places on earth

The best mosques are the mosque of Madīnah, the *Ḥaram* mosque of Makkah and the al-Aqṣā mosque, and the best of these three is that of Madīnah according to Mālik, while according to ash-Shāfi'ī and Abū Ḥanīfah it is that of Makkah; likewise Mālik gives preference to [the city of] Madīnah over Makkah, contrary to the two of them, whereas Ibn Rushd agrees with them both.

2. One should say the following when entering a mosque:

اَللَّهُمَّ افْتَحْ لِي أَبْوَابَ رَحْمَتِكَ

Allāhumma-ftaḥ lī abwāba raḥmatik

'O Allah open the doors of Your mercy for me' and when leaving:

اَللَّهُمَّ إِنِّيَ أَسْأَلُكَ مِنْ فَضْلِكَ

Allāhumma innī as'aluka min faḍlik

'O Allah I ask of You from Your overflowing bounty' – these being said after calling for blessings on the Prophet ﷺ. However, it has also been reported that one should say when entering:

أَعُوذُ بِاللهِ الْعَظِيمِ وَبِوَجْهِهِ الْكَرِيمِ وَسُلْطَانِهِ الْقَدِيمِ مِنَ الشَّيْطَانِ الرَّجِيمِ

A'ūdhu billāhi-l-'aẓīmi wa biwajhihi-l-karīmi wa sulṭānihi-l-qadīmi mina-sh-shayṭāni-r-rajīm

'I seek refuge by Allah the Magnificent and by His noble

face and by His from before-endless-time dominion from the accursed Shayṭān'.

3. The things which do not belong in the mosque

That is buying and selling and all other activities involving earnings; announcing a stray animal; raising one's voice, even for the Qur'ān or matters of knowledge; spitting, which must be made good by removing it; reciting poetry, except that permitted in the *sharī'ah*; and Ṣaḥnūn considered it *makrūh* to make *wuḍū'* in it; one may be indulgent regarding the traveller and resident person sleeping during the day in it; and strangers staying overnight in it, and it is not fitting that it be used as a place of dwelling – except for the person devoted entirely to worship.

Concession is granted to eat a little food in it; children are barred from it as well as mad persons and anyone who eats garlic and onions.

Women have a concession to perform the *ṣalāt* in it if there is no danger of immorality, although it is *makrūh* for a young woman to go out to it.

One should not pass through it using it merely as a pathway; nor should one draw one's sword in it – rather one should do in it that for which it has been built.

It is not permitted for the *mushrik* to enter the mosque, although ash-Shāfi'ī permitted it except in the Ḥarām Mosque, while Abū Ḥanīfah has permitted it in all mosques.

2. Places where the ṣalāt may be performed

It is permitted in any clean, pure place.

It is prohibited in seven places: rubbish tips on account of the filth; abbatoirs on account of the blood; cemeteries – this having been said by some with general import, while others said that it is particular to the cemeteries of the *mushrik*s; roads and pathways as they would not be secure from the vagaries of passers-by and traffic or from impurities; *ḥammām*s and bath houses, although it is permitted if there is a clean, pure place in them; where the camels lie around their watering trough – but no reason is known for that according to the most valid judgment; on top of the Ka'bah, although it has been said that if there is some part of the building in front of the person then it is permitted; and within the madhhab it is prohibited to perform *farḍ* *ṣalāt*s inside the Ka'bah, contrary to the two; and it is *makrūh* within the madhhab to make the *ṣalāt* on anything other than the earth and what grows from it.

5. The conditions and essential elements of the ṣalāt

They comprise the *farḍ*, *sunnah* and *nāfilah* aspects, those aspects which annul it and those which are *makrūh*, they being twenty in all for each aspect.

FARḌ ASPECTS

Ten preconditions

Being ritually purified of anything which breaks one's state of purity; clean from any *najas* – physical impurities; knowing that the time for the particular *ṣalāt* has begun; covering the area of one's private parts; facing the *qiblah*; making the intention; performing the various elements in their correct order; performing them immediately after each other; desisting from saying anything other than what pertains to the *ṣalāt* or what is uttered to put something right; desisting from excessive movements – other than those pertaining to the *ṣalāt*.

Among the farḍ aspects there are ten essential elements

The *takbīratu-l-iḥrām* – the initial *takbīr* marking a person's entry into the ritual state of the *ṣalāt*; standing for this *takbīr*; recitation of the Umm al-Qur'ān – the Fātiḥah *sūrah*; continuing standing for this; bowing; straightening up after it; prostrating; the separation between the two prostrations; the saying *'as-salāmu 'alaykum'* at the end; sitting for this; and to these have been added that one be still and composed and to be inwardly humble.

The sunnahs

They are the *adhān*; the *iqāmah*; the *ṣalāt* with the *jamā'ah*; the recitation of a *sūrah* together with the Umm al-Qur'ān; continuing standing for this; reciting the Umm al-Qur'ān before the other *sūrah*; reciting aloud in the places where one should recite aloud; being silent in the places where one should be silent; saying *sami'a-llāhu liman ḥamidah* and *rabbanā laka-l-ḥamd*; the *Allāhu akbar*s other than the *takbīratu-l-iḥrām*; reciting *tartīl* – in an unhasty, clear and accurate manner; prostrating while the seven parts of the body – the face, palms, knees and toes – are touching the floor; saying the first *tashahhud*; sitting for it; saying the second *tashahhud*; sitting for it; calling for blessings on the Prophet ﷺ; taking each position correctly and making a moment's relaxation of the joints between them; saying the final *'as-salāmu 'alaykum'* to the right. However it has also been said of many of the above that they are aspects of excellence.

The prostration of negligence

It is done for [missing any one of] eight things: a *sūrah*; reciting aloud; reciting silently; the *takbīr*; missing out the *sami'a-llāhu liman ḥamidah*; the two *tashahhud*s; missing out the sitting for these two.

The aspects of excellence

These refer to: making the *ṣalāt* at the beginning of the time; wearing a loose outer garment; placing a *sutrah* – something set up to screen the person performing the *ṣalāt* [from persons passing in front of him]; raising one's hands while making the *takbīratu-l-iḥrām*; keeping the feet apart while standing; placing the right hand over the left; saying the *amīn*; reciting the measure of a complete *sūrah* be it of long, medium or short length; reciting the *qunūt* during the *ṣubḥ ṣalāt*; placing the hands on the knees during the bowing; glorifying Allah in the bowing and prostration; making *du'ā* during the prostration and the final sitting; keeping the legs apart during bowing and prostration; placing the palms of the hand flat on the ground in prostration; sitting in the particular way; shortening the middle sitting; not saying the *Allāhu akbar* when rising to stand for the third *rak'ah* until one is standing straight; returning the *salām* of the person to one's left; making prostration when an *āyat* of prostration is recited; the *imām* standing up from his place immediately after he has said the final *as-salāmu 'alaykum*.

However many of these are considered to belong to the Sunnah. Some have said that the actions of the *ṣalāt* are all *farḍ* except for three: raising the hands, the middle sitting, and turning to the right for the final *salām*, and that none of the spoken elements of the *ṣalāt* are *farḍ* except for three: the *takbīratu-l-iḥrām*, the recitation of Umm al-Qur'ān, and the *as-salāmu 'alaykum*.

The things which invalidate

They are: omission of the intention or breaking it off; omission of one of its essential elements, such as recitation, bowing or any other *farḍ* element – or the measure of them that one is capable of doing although having an excuse for not doing it fully, on account of some difficulty or impediment – irrespective of whether one omits it deliberately, out of ignorance or from heedlessness – these invalidate the *ṣalāt*, except not turning to the *qiblah*, not removing *najāsah* or not covering one's private parts, for if one omitted these out of forgetfulness then it may be overlooked and one repeats it [if one discovers it] within the time; likewise when ignorant of the *qiblah* and likewise if the middle sitting has been omitted, which is one of the *sunnahs*, or one omitted three *takbīrs* or *sami'a-llāhu liman ḥamidah*, anything like these similarly invalidate the *ṣalāt* if not made good by the prostrations for negligence; it is similar in the case of having deliberately or accidentally made additional movements or having forgetfully done a great deal of that; likewise it is invalidated in the case of reneging on one's *dīn*, guffawing in whatever manner or speaking, except to correct something said or done by the *imām*; likewise if one eats or drinks or does a lot of anything which does not belong to the *ṣalāt*, or when the urge to restrain oneself from passing wind, or urinating or restrain the bowels or stomach rumbling is so intense as to dominate one's thoughts; and likewise excessive anxiety and worry which cause one to be diverted from the *ṣalāt* so much that one is no longer aware what part of the *ṣalāt* one is performing; and leaning against a wall or on a stick without an excuse while standing during the *ṣalāt* such that if the thing he is leaning against were to be taken away he would fall; and his *ṣalāt* is also invalidated if he remembers another *farḍ ṣalāt* during it that should have been done in its order before; *ṣalāt* in the Ka'bah or on its roof is also invalidated; likewise if someone who has done *tayammum* remembers where water is to be found during his *ṣalāt*; and if the intention of the person behind the *imām* differs from that of the *imām*; likewise if the *ṣalāt* of the *imām* is invalidated except from forgetfulness; by his losing his ritual purity, by the presence of *najāsah*, by the *imām*'s establishing a *ṣalāt* when he owes another *ṣalāt*; likewise according to some of them, the deliberate omission of one of the aforementioned *sunnah*s invalidates the *ṣalāt*.

THE THINGS THAT ARE MAKRŪH

Then the *ṣalāt* of a man who is restraining 'the two places of filth', i.e. the urge to urinate or defecate; being distracted or listening to the whisperings of the self regarding matters of this world; interlacing one's fingers and cracking them and playing with them or one's beard or ring; or smoothing out the pebbles; or *iq'ā'* which is squatting on both heels when sitting or when getting up from the prostration, rather he should support himself with both hands when getting up; also *makrūh* is *ṣafd,* which is placing one's feet tightly next to each other when standing as if they were fettered; as is *ṣafn,* which is standing with one foot slightly raised as an animal might do when standing; or *ṣalb,* which is placing one's hand on one's hips and stretching them out when getting up like someone being crucified; or *ikhtiṣār,* which is placing one hand on one's hip when getting up; or performing the *ṣalāt* while veiling one's face; or gathering up one's hair or clothes to stop them falling during the *ṣalāt*; or someone carrying something in his mouth, or carrying something on another part of his body if this preoccupies him; or one performs the *ṣalāt* when angry, hungry or when food is ready or in narrow *khuff*s or the like such that this diverts him from understanding the *ṣalāt*; or he performs the *ṣalāt* on a pathway or road where people pass by in front of him; or one kills a flea or lice; or he makes a *du'ā* while bowing, or before the recitation while standing; or he recites Qur'ān when bowing or prostrating; or he recites the *tashahhud* aloud; or raises his head or lowers it during his bowing; or looks up to the sky during his *ṣalāt;* or prostrates on a rug or velvet-like carpet, or on something which does not grow from the earth or on something which is wasteful to use in this way or something luxurious; or in clothing which does not cover his shoulders; likewise anything which is contrary to aspects of excellence or recommended things; and anything which distracts him from being present with his heart during the *ṣalāt* or which diverts his thoughts from it.

Summary

The aspects of the *ṣalāt* may be divided in ten ways with respect to that about which there is agreement and that about which there is disagreement:

1. That about which there is agreement as to its obligation. This is the purification from anything which breaks one's ritual purity, facing the *qiblah*, carrying out the various elements of the *ṣalāt* in their proper order, bowing, prostration and rising from it.

2. That about which there is a difference of opinion as to its obligation. This is the *takbīratu-l-iḥrām*, the recitation of the Umm al-Qur'ān, the saying of the *bismillāh*, the *as-salāmu 'alaykum* and the rising from the bowing.

3. That about which there is a difference of opinion as to whether it is *farḍ* or *sunnah,* namely the removal of *najāsah*, the covering of one's private parts, the two *shahādah*s, the sitting for them both, the *takbīr*s other than the *takbīratu-l-iḥrām*, making sure one is standing straight after rising from the *rukū'* or prostration.

4. That about which there is a difference of opinion as to whether it is *farḍ* or *mustaḥabb,* namely pausing to relax one's limbs before going on to the next action within the *ṣalāt*, the saying *subhāna-llāh* during bowing and prostration and seeking refuge from the four during the sitting.

5. That about which there is a difference of opinion as to whether it is *farḍ*, *sunnah* or *mustaḥabb*, namely the raising of one's hands.

6. That about which there is agreement that it is Sunnah, namely reciting a *sūrah* in the first two *rak'ah*s.

7. That about which there is agreement that it is *mustaḥabb*, namely reciting the *sūrat*s in their order and reciting the longest first and splaying out one's elbows.

8. That about which there is a difference of opinion as to whether it is *sunnah* or *mustaḥabb*, namely the *qunūt* supplication, the saying of *rabbanā wa laka-l-ḥamd* and the saying of *amīn* by those who follow the *imām*.

9. That about which there is a difference of opinion as to whether it is *mustaḥabb* or not, namely turning one's face towards the *qiblah*, seeking refuge from *shayṭān*, looking at the place of prostration, performing the *ṣalāt* at the beginning of its time, the saying Amin by the *imām*, moving the index finger during the *tashahhud*, making the middle sitting shorter, placing one's hands on one's knees during the bowing, placing one's hands on the ground before one's knees when prostrating and sitting after the second prostration.

10. That about which there is a difference of opinion as to whether it is *mustaḥabb* or *makrūh*, namely squatting on both heels; and placing one's right hand on one's left while standing – and the explanation of this shall follow in its place, and Allah knows best.

6. Clothing to be worn for the Ṣalāt

And an examination of what is to be covered and the covering

What is covered

This is the area of the *'awrah* – the private parts, and they must be hidden from people's sight according to the consensus. As for the obligation to cover up one's private parts when in the toilet or when alone, there are two judgments

The ṣalāt

The correct judgment within the madhhab is that it is obligatory to cover, in agreement with them, except that there is a difference of opinion as to whether one repeats the *ṣalāt* – if one performed it with one's private parts exposed – within the prescribed time, or within the time and after it.

The 'awrah of a man

It extends from the navel to his knees, in agreement with the two, while there is a difference of opinion as to whether the actual navel and knees are included and must be covered as well; and it has also been said that the *'awrah* is specifically the private parts of a man or woman. The minimum acceptable clothing in the *ṣalāt* is that which covers the private parts and the best is to cover the rest of the body, even with one cloth from the shoulders; and the most complete is the addition of a loose outer robe, and this is emphasized in the case of the *imām*.

The free woman

All of her body is *'awrah* except for her face and hands, while Abū Ḥanīfah has included her feet in the exception, and Ibn Ḥanbal has not made this exception. The minimum acceptable for her is clothing which covers her body to where the feet show and a head covering on her head.

The female slave

Her *'awrah* is like a man's except that her thighs are *'awrah*, according to the agreed judgment, so *ṣalāt* is permitted for her without the head covering and she covers the rest of her body; and like her, the *mukātabah* – the female slave who has a contract to purchase her freedom, the *mudabbarah* – the female slave who is to be set free on the death of her master, and the woman who is partly freed, contrary to the *umm walad* for she is as the free woman.

The covering

It is obligatory that it be thick closely-woven cloth and if what lies beneath is visible, then it is as if there is no covering; and if it is decorated, then this is *makrūh*; and it is prohibited to cover oneself with one single cloth, without any sleeves such that his arms can only be put out from below. Whoever does not find any clothing then he performs the *ṣalāt* alone naked – standing, bowing and prostrating; while Abū Ḥanīfah has said that he performs it sitting; and if clothing becomes available for him, then there is a difference of opinion as to whether he covers himself and carries on or interrupts the *ṣalāt* and begins anew; and if several naked persons gather in the darkness then they perform the *ṣalāt* like those covered; and if in the light, then they move off and perform it individually – otherwise they perform it sitting, although it has also been said standing while lowering their gaze. If someone only finds clothing which is *najas* – ritually impure, then he makes the *ṣalāt* in it; if he only finds clothing of silk then there are two judgments; and if he only finds two items of clothing, one *najas*, and one of silk, then there is a difference of opinion as to which he uses for the *ṣalāt*.

A supplementary note

The ruling governing a woman looking at a woman is the same as the ruling governing a man regarding looking at a man such that looking at their respective *'awrah*s is prohibited while other than this is permitted.

The ruling governing a woman with respect to looking at those who are *maḥram* for her, i.e. being related such that marriage is not permitted, is the same as the ruling governing a man regarding his looking at a man, and the ruling pertaining to her regarding her looking at someone not *maḥram*, i.e. outside the above mentioned degree of consanguinity is the same as the ruling governing a man with respect to those who are *maḥram* for him, this being looking at the face and hands only, according to the most correct judgment, although it has also been said that it is the same as the ruling for a man looking at a woman who is not *maḥram* for him.

And it is permitted a male slave to see that of his mistress which may be seen by those who are *maḥram* for her; and she may eat with him unless he is an imbecile, of weak, low or wretched status; nor shall a eunuch look at a woman unless he is her slave although one group have said that it is permitted because he is one of *the male attendants who have no sexual desire* (Sūrat an-Nūr 24:31), and according to Mālik such persons are the stupid, or the infirm or disabled.

Anyone who is prohibited from looking at a woman is not permitted to be alone with her; and it is not permitted for two women or two men to be together naked under the same bed-covering; and young lads are separated at the age of seven with respect to their place of sleep, although it has also been said from the age of ten, and Allah knows best.

7. Facing the Qiblah,

This contains three sections

1. Facing the qiblah

It is a condition of the *farḍ ṣalāt*s, except the *ṣalāt* 'of the contending with swords', i.e. that performed during the actual battle, and the person mounted while travelling who does not dismount for fear of thieves or wild animals – in which case *ṣalāt* mounted on the riding beast is permitted towards the *qiblah* and in other directions.

It is also a condition for the *nāfilah ṣalāt*s, except that of travelling whereby he performs it in whatever direction the beast turns and he performs the bowing and the prostration by mere indication, making the prostration by means of a lesser inclination than the bowing, and he neither talks or takes notice of his surroundings – and this is on condition that the journey is a long one and that he is mounted.

A passenger on a boat performs the *ṣalāt* facing the *qiblah* and if the boats shifts direction then he does too, while Ibn Ḥabīb has narrated that he does *nāfilah ṣalāt*s in the direction which the boat takes, as if he was mounted on a riding beast.

2. The three possible states of the person performing the ṣalāt

Mutayaqqin – someone who is certain of the *qiblah*, the *mujtahid* – someone who exerts himself using *ijtihād* (reasoned judgment) to find it out, and the *muqallid* – someone who follows someone else. These different states are in order of importance and it is not permitted to change from one to the other after it unless the previous one is impossible.

Absolute certainty is possessed by the person who performs the *ṣalāt* in Makkah, and the *miḥrab* of the Prophet ﷺ in Madīnah is on a par with the Ka'bah in Makkah.

The one who strives using *ijtihād* pertains to anyone who performs the *ṣalāt* in any other place on earth – if he is able.

The one who accepts *taqlīd* (imitation of another person) pertains to the person who is incapable of making *ijtihād*, in which case he asks another Muslim of sane mind, who has knowledge of the *qiblah* and then follows him; if there is no one to follow, then it is said that he should perform the *ṣalāt* in whatever direction he wants, while it is also said that he should make four different *ṣalāt*s in the four different directions.

Three subsidiary matters

1. The fard obligation is to face the Ka'bah, the Bayt al-Harām

Some say the Ka'bah itself, while others the direction of the Ka'bah. The *qiblah* of the people of the west is to the east and vice-versa. The *qiblah* of the people of Madīnah, Sham – Greater Syria, and Andalusia is towards the spout of the guttering of the Ka'bah, this being between the east and the south, while some of those with knowledge of the equinoctial line and the corners of the House say that the *qiblah* of Cordoba and its surroundings is at three degrees from the east-south quarter.

2. The qiblah may be ascertained by the rising and setting of the sun

While it has also been said by means of the direction in which the shadow begins to get larger at the time the sun passes its zenith. At night it may be ascertained by means of the moon, the two tips of it facing the east at the beginning of the month, and the west at the end of the month, while in the middle of the month it faces the east during the first part of night and during the last part the west. Moreover on occasion it may also be ascertained by mountains, the winds or other things.

3. Someone who performs the ṣalāt then it becomes clear to him that he has made a mistake regarding the qiblah

Then he performs the *ṣalāt* again if still within the prescribed time, according to the well known judgment, while Ṣaḥnūn has said he performs it both within the time and after it, in agreement with the two.

3. The sutrah i.e. anything set up as a screen in front of the person performing the ṣalāt

This is commanded in the case of the *imām* and the person who performs the *ṣalāt* alone. The *sutrah* of the *imām* also serves as a *sutrah* for those making the *ṣalāt* behind him, and the smallest size possible is something the length of one's forearm with the width of a spear. It is also stipulated that it be something which stands firmly, is clean and does not distract one's heart – so one does not have a boy as a *sutrah* if he does not stay still, or a woman, or in the direction of people talking, while it is permitted to take a camel, cow, goat or sheep as a *sutrah*. One does not face the *sutrah* directly but rather turns to the right or left slightly keeping at a distance which would permit a sheep to pass by between one and it, while three cubits has also been said. If one does not take a *sutrah* then one performs the *ṣalāt* without one, and one does not draw a line on the ground and face towards it, contrary to Ibn Ḥanbal. The *ṣalāt* is not interrupted by something passing in front of the person performing the *ṣalāt*, according to the three – contrary to those who say that it interrupted by a woman, donkey or dog; but it is not appropriate that someone expose himself to passers-by, nor that one should pass in front of anyone performing the *ṣalāt* – and if this happens then one should gently push him away.

8. The intention and the takbīratu-l-iḥrām

1. The intention

It is obligatory in the *ṣalāt* according to the consensus, and the most perfect manner is that the person performing *ṣalāt* be filled with *īmān* and make the intention to come closer to Allah by means of the *ṣalāt*, convinced of its obligation and that it should be performed on the particular day in question; and he is conscious of the particular *ṣalāt* he intends and makes the intention for the number of *rak'ah*s, and makes the intention to be the *imām*, or one of the persons making the *ṣalāt* behind him or to make it alone as the case may be, and then he makes the intention for the *takbīratu-l-iḥrām*.

Four subsidiary matters

1. The intention is obligatory

To be *ma'mūm*, i.e. one who is going to perform the *ṣalāt* behind the *imām*, or the intention that one is going to perform it alone, while it is not obligatory for the *imām* to make the intention that he is going to lead the *ṣalāt*, except for the *jumu'ah*, at Jam' (Muzdalifah), the *ṣalāt* of fear and in the case where the *imām* leaves the *ṣalāt* and indicates someone else to take his place – given that the presence of an *imām* is stipulated in such prayers, and Ibn Rushd added the *janāzah ṣalāt*.

2. There is a difference of opinion as to the obligation of an intention for the number of rak'ahs

Based on this the difference as to the validity of the *ṣalāt* for the person who begins it with the intention of shortening it and then completes it with the full number of *rak'ah*s and vice versa, and the person who begins the *jumu'ah ṣalāt* thinking it is *ẓuhr* or vice versa.

3. It is obligatory that the intention is conjoined to the takbīratu-l-iḥrām

For if the intention is done afterward or is made a considerable time beforehand, then the *ṣalāt* is invalidated according to the agreed judgment.

4. The locus of the intention is the heart

And there is no need to express it out loud in words, indeed not saying it out loud in words is preferable, contrary to ash-Shāfi'ī.

2. The takbīratu-l-iḥrām

It is obligatory, contrary to Abū Ḥanīfah, while other *takbīr*s are not obligatory according to the majority, and it consists of saying '*Allāhu akbar*', nothing else being acceptable, contrary to ash-Shāfi'ī who permits *Allāhu-l-akbar* and Abū Ḥanīfah who permits anything which contains the saying of the *takbīr* or *ta'ẓīm*, i.e. the extolling of Allah using the word '*aẓīm*.

Two subsidiary matters

1. Someone who is incapable of saying the takbīr

If he is dumb, then he commences the *ṣalāt* by means of the intention; and if ignorant of the language, then he does likewise, according to the most valid judgment, although it has also been said that he expresses the *takbīr* with his tongue.

2. Whoever says Allāhu akbār, i.e. with a long 'a' vowel [on akbār]

Then it is not accepted of him; and whoever says *Allāhu wakbar*, i.e.

changing the initial *hamzah* of the *akbar* into a '*waw*' then this is valid.

3. Raising one's hands

This is recommended according to the majority, either as a *sunnah* or as an aspect of excellence – and this is the well-known judgment; while the Ẓāhirīs have made it an obligation. One raises them when saying the *takbīratu-l-iḥrām* in particular according to Ibn al-Qāsim, in agreement with Abū Ḥanīfah, and when bowing and coming up from the bowing according to Ashhab, in agreement with ash-Shāfi'ī. And his hands are held vertically according to the majority, while Ṣaḥnūn has said outstretched with their backs facing the sky, like the form adopted by a monk; and he holds them on a level with his ears, although it has also been said on a level with his shoulders, and it has also been said on a level with his breast. One may combine the three judgments by saying that the elbow is on a level with the breast, the lower end of his palm on a par with his shoulders and the end of his fingers on a level with his ears.

9. The Standing

This consists of two sections

1. The proper form of this standing

One stands on both feet together, keeping them apart; one does not raise one's gaze to the sky; one does not place one's hands on one's hip; one looks to the place of prostration, according to them, although Mālik deems this *makrūh*; that one place one's right hand on one's left, although he deemed it *makrūh* in the *Mudawwanah*, and it has also been said that it is *makrūh* for the *farḍ ṣalāt* or if one does it to support oneself.

2. The ṣalāt of the sick person

This contains various states: that the person makes the *ṣalāt* standing up without support, but if he is unable or only able with great difficulty, then he should make the *ṣalāt* while supporting himself, then sitting without support, then sitting with support, then reclining on his right side with his face turned towards the *qiblah*, then lying on his back facing the *qiblah* with his feet, although it has also been said that this lying on one's back takes precedence over reclining on one's side; then, if still unable, to lie on his left side; and he indicates by motion or gesture the bowing and prostration while reclining or lying on his back. If he is unable to do any of this, then he makes the intention in his heart, in agreement with ash-Shāfiʿī, although it has also been said that the obligation to make the *ṣalāt* is annulled for him, in agreement with Abū Ḥanīfah.

Five secondary matters

1. Whoever abandons a position of the *ṣalāt* when capable of it must repeat it, and the obligation to repeat it remains until he fulfils it.

2. If he sits instead of standing, then he sits cross legged according to the well-known judgment, although it has also been said he should sit as he would during the *tashahhud*, while ash-Shāfiʿī has said sitting with one's legs drawn up wrapped in one's garment.

3. Whoever suffers from ophthalmia, if he is only rid of it by lying on his side, then he should make the *ṣalāt* on his side; and there is a difference of opinion as to the one whose eye has been couched for a cataract and the depression of the lenses of his eyes have become watery.

4. If the state of the person doing *ṣalāt* changes, then he should continue on the basis of what he has already done and complete it according to the new situation.

5. There is a difference of opinion as to whether it is permissible for someone to perform *nāfilah* – optional prayers – sitting if he is capable of standing: if he began the *ṣalāt* sitting then he is permitted to complete it sitting or standing; while if he began it standing, there is a difference of opinion as to whether he may complete it sitting, and Allah knows best.

10. The recitation

Comprising three sections

1. The Umm al-Qur'ān

This consists of three matters

1. Its ruling, namely that it is obligatory

Contrary to Abū Ḥanīfah, and it is obligatory in every *rak'ah* in agrement with ash-Shāfi'ī, although it has also been said in one single *rak'ah*, and it has also been said in half of the *ṣalāt* or more. And anyone who cannot recite well, then if he is dumb, then none of it is obligatory for him, while if he is still learning then he must continue learning or perform the *ṣalāt* behind someone who recites well and if he does not find anyone then it is said that he should make *dhikr* of Allah, and it has also been said that he should remain silent; and it is not permitted to translate it, contrary to Abū Ḥanīfah.

2. No du'ā is made before the recitation

Nor the expression of one's aim to concentrate one's attention on Allah, contrary to ash-Shāfi'ī in his preceding it with the words from the *ḥadīth* 'I have turned my face to the One who has created the heavens and the earth...' and contrary to Abū Ḥanīfah in his preceding it with the words 'Glory and praise be to You, O Allah, may Your name be blessed and your greatness be exalted, and there is no god except You'; nor does one seek refuge, contrary to the two; nor does one say the *bismillāh*, neither silently or aloud, contrary to ash-Shāfi'ī who has it said silently for the silent recitation and aloud for the aloud, and contrary to Abū Ḥanīfah who has it recited silently always, although there is no harm in saying the *bismillāh* for the voluntary *ṣalāt*s according to the four. And the *bismillāh* is not an *āyah* of the Fātiḥah, nor of any other *sūrah* other than an-Naḥl – the Bee, contrary to ash-Shāfi'ī.

3. SAYING 'AMĪN'

It is permitted to say '*amīn*' with an elongation of the initial 'a' vowel sound (*āmīn*), and also to pronounce it with a shorter vowel sound and a lightening of the following *mīm* consonant; and it is recommended for the person alone and in the case of anyone standing behind the *imām* in all cases, and for the *imām* if he is reciting softly according to the agreed judgment, and if aloud, in agreement with ash-Shāfi'ī; while the well-known judgment is that he does not say the *amīn* when the recitation is aloud, in agreement with Abū Ḥanīfah and he says the *amīn* softly contrary to ash-Shāfi'ī.

2. THE SŪRAH

As for the *sūrah* after the Fātiḥah, it is recited in the first two *rak'ah*s according to the consensus, but is not read in the third and fourth, contrary to ash-Shāfi'ī, and it is read in the voluntary *ṣalāt*s other than the two *rak'ah*s of *fajr* according to the well-known judgment. It is recommended to recite a long *sūrah* for the *ṣubḥ ṣalāt* – such that one reads a long *sūrah* of the *mufaṣṣal*, the fourth and last division of the Qur'ān, or what is longer than those contained in it, and a shorter *sūrah* for *ẓuhr*, a yet shorter one for *'ishā'*, yet shorter for *'aṣr* and still shorter one for *maghrib*.

Subsidiary matter

It is recommended to complete the *sūrah,* and to read the *sūrahs* in their order in the Qur'ān, and that the *sūrah* in the first *sūrah* be longer than the second, and it is permitted to repeat the *sūrah* in the second *rak'ah,* although it is *makrūh* to repeat it in one single *rak'ah.*

3. Concerning the recitation softly and aloud

The ruling regarding the *farḍ ṣalāts* is well known; as for the voluntary ones then one recites aloud for the two *'Īds* and the rain *ṣalāt,* while one recites softly for all the others during the day, and one has the option during the night of aloud or softly. Softly means one can hear oneself, and aloud one can hear oneself and those immediately next to one can also hear; a woman's reciting aloud is quieter than a man's. The *ma'mūm,* i.e. the person behind the *imām,* recites [in the prayers where the recitation is done] softly, but if he does not recite then he is not held to account within the madhhab; however he does not recite [in the prayers where] the recitation is done aloud, irrespective of whether he hears the recitation of the *imām* or not, while ash-Shāfi'ī has said he recites if he cannot hear, and Abū Ḥanīfah that he should not recite under any circumstances; and if the *ma'mūm* finishes before the *imām* then he has the option of making an additional recitation, a *du'ā* or remaining silent, and Allah knows best.

11. The Qunūt Supplication

1. Its words

What is chosen in the madhhab is:

اللَّهُمَّ إِنَّا نَسْتَعِينُكَ وَنَسْتَغْفِرُكَ وَنُؤْمِنُ بِكَ وَنَتَوَكَّلُ عَلَيْكَ وَنَخْنَعُ لَكَ
وَنَخْلَعُ وَنَتْرُكُ مَنْ يَكْفُرُكَ. اَللَّهُمَّ إِيَّاكَ نَعْبُدُ وَلَكَ نُصَلِّي وَنَسْجُدُ وَإِلَيْكَ

نَسْعَى وَنَحْفِدُ. نَرْجُو رَحْمَتَكَ وَنَخَافُ عَذَابَكَ الْجِدَّ. إِنَّ عَذَابَكَ
بِالْكَافِرِينَ مُلْحِقٌ.

Allāhumma innā nasta'īnuka wa nastaghfiruka wa nu'minu bika wa natawakkalu 'alayka wa nakhna'u laka wa nakhla'u wa natruku man yakfuruk. Allāhumma iyyāka na'budu wa laka nuṣallī wa nasjudu wa ilayka nas'ā wa naḥfid. Narjū raḥmataka wa nakhāfu 'adhābaka l-jidd inna 'adhābaka bi l-kāfirīna mulḥiq

'Allah We seek Your help and we seek Your forgiveness. We have *īmān* in You, we rely upon You, and we submit to You, and we leave and abandon whoever rejects You by covering up the Truth. O Allah You alone we worship, to you we make the *ṣalāt* and prostrate and to You we strive and hurry, we hope for Your mercy and we fear Your severe punishment, surely Your punishment shall strike the *kuffār*.'

'We submit (*nakhna'u*)': we humble ourselves. 'Leave and abandon (*nakhla'u*)': is a synonym for *natruku* – we forsake. Both are words referring to 'whoever rejects You'. And *naḥfid* 'we hurry' means either we act, or we walk to the mosque. The word in Arabic *jidd* 'severe' (also meaning serious in the sense that it is) not a joke, not a jest. The word *mulḥiq* 'strike' means 'to overtake them'; and it can also be written *mulḥaq*. Ash-Shāfi'ī opted for:

اَللَّهُمَّ اهْدِنَا فِيمَنْ هَدَيْتَ، وَعَافِنَا فِيمَنْ عَافَيْتَ، وَتَوَلَّنَا فِيمَنْ تَوَلَّيْتَ،
وَبَارِكْ لَنَا فِيمَا أَعْطَيْتَ، وَقِنَا شَرَّ مَا قَضَيْتَ، فَإِنَّكَ تَقْضِي وَلَا يُقْضَى
عَلَيْكَ، وَإِنَّهُ لا يَذِلُّ مَنْ وَالَيْتَ، وَلَا يَعِزُّ مَنْ عَادَيْتَ، تَبَارَكْتَ
رَبَّنَا وَتَعَالَيْتَ.

Allāhumma-hdinā fī-man hadayt, wa 'āfinā fī-man 'āfayt, wa tawallanā fī-man tawallayt, wa bārak lanā fī-mā a'ṭayt, wa qinā sharra mā qaḍayt, fa-innaka taqḍī wa lā yuqḍā 'alayk, wa innahu lā yadhillu man wālayt, wa lā ya'izzu man 'ādayta, tabārakta Rabbanā wa ta'ālayt.

'O Allah guide us – making us among those You have guided, spare us – making us among those You have spared and take us in charge – making us among those You have taken in charge, and bless us – in whatever You have granted us and protect us from the evil which You have decreed for You it is Who decrees for others and no one decrees for You, You do not bring low whomever you have taken in Your charge nor do you raise in honour anyone who is inimical towards You, O how blessed and sublime You are Our Lord!'

2. Four subsidiary matters

1. One says the *qunūt* during the *ṣubḥ ṣalāt*, contrary to Abū Ḥanīfah, and it is permitted before the bowing – this being the best – and after it.

2. The *qunūt* is not said in the *witr ṣalāt*, contrary to ash-Shāfi'ī and Ibn Ḥanbal, and contrary to Ibn Nāfi' during the *witr* of the last half of Ramadan, and contrary to Abū Ḥanīfah in the Sunnah *witr*.

3. The *qunūt* is recommended, according to the well-known judgment, although it has also been said that is is *sunnah*.

4. The *imām*, the *ma'mūm* and the person alone say the *qunūt* softly, and there is no harm in raising ones hands during it, although it has also been said this should not be done.

12. The bowing

Comprising four matters

1. Its form

The least is that the person inclines such that his palms reach his knees or near to them, and its most perfect form is that he inclines such that his back and neck are straight. This and the prostration are acceptable if the slightest pause is made during them, while for them and for the rest of the fundamental elements of the *ṣalāt* it is obligatory to perform them properly and distinctly (*i'tidāl*), in agreement with ash-Shāfi'ī, while it has also been said that this is a *sunnah,* in agreement with Abū Ḥanīfah. *I'tidāl* is the completion and perfection of the form or pose of every essential element, than a short moment of coming to rest. There is a difference of judgment within the madhhab as to whether it is obligatory or recommended.

2. Its refined aspects or courtesies

These are five in number: putting one's hands onto one's knees; separating the elbows from one's sides; not raising or lowering one's head; not saying any *du'ā* or reciting any Qur'ān during this or the prostration.

3. What is said during it

It is recommended to say three times:

سُبْحَانَ رَبِّيَ الْعَظِيمِ

Subḥāna rabbiya-l-'aẓīm

'Glory be to my Lord the Magnificent'

and the Ẓāhirīs deemed it obligatory, while Ibn al-Mubārak deemed it recommended for the *imām* five times. It has also been narrated in the *ḥadīth*:

اَللَّهُمَّ لَكَ رَكَعْتُ، وَبِكَ ءَامَنْتُ، وَلَكَ أَسْلَمْتُ، خَشَعَ لَكَ سَمْعِي وَبَصَرِي وَلَحْمِي وَمُخِّي وَعَظْمِي وَعَصَبِي.

Allāhumma laka raka'tu, wa bika āmantu, wa laka aslamtu; khasha'a laka sam'ī wa baṣarī wa laḥmī wa mukh-khī wa 'aẓmī wa 'aṣabī.

'O Allah to You I have bowed, in You I have trust, to You I have submitted. and my hearing, my sight, my flesh, my brain and marrow, my bones and my nerves are in humble submission to You'

and in it and in the prostration

سُبُّوحٌ قُدُّوسٌ رَبُّ الْمَلَائِكَةِ وَالرُّوحِ.

Subbūḥun quddūsun rabbu-l-malā'ikati wa-r-rūḥ

'The One Whose praises are always sung, the Most Pure, the Lord of the Angels and the Rūḥ – the Spirit'

has been narrated.

4. The rising from the bowing

This is an obligatory fundamental element; the *imām* says

سَمِعَ اللَّهُ لِمَنْ حَمِدَهُ.

Sami'a-llāhu li-man ḥamidah.

'Allah hears the one who praises Him'

and the *ma'mūm* says:

رَبَّنَا وَلَكَ الْحَمْدُ

Rabbanā wa laka-l-ḥamd

'Our Lord! and to You belongs all praise'

– or without the 'and', while the person alone combines the two, and it has also been said that the *imām* combines the two; and whoever wants to may add:

حَمْداً طَيِّباً مُبَارَكاً فِيهِ

Ḥamdan ṭayyiban mubārakan fīh

'with much good and blessed praise in it' or

مِلْءَ السَّمَوَاتِ وَالأَرْضِ وَمَا بَيْنَهُمَا، وَمِلْءَ مَا شِئْتَ مِنْ شَيْءٍ بَعْدُ

Mil'a-s-samāwāti wa-l-arḍi wa mā baynahumā,
wa mil'a mā shi'ta min shay'in ba'd

'enough to fill the heavens and the earth and what is between them both and enough to fill whatever you wish after this.'

13. The Prostration

This contains four matters

1. Its form

One is instructed to make the prostration resting on seven points of the body, namely the face, both hands, both knees, both feet. As for the face and hands, this is obligatory according to the consensus; as for the knees and feet, it has been said that it is obligatory and also that it is a *sunnah*.

One places one's nose and forehead firmly on the ground, and if one restricts oneself to just one of them, then it is said that this is acceptable, although it is also said that it is not just on the forehead, contrary to on the nose, and this is the well-known judgment, in agreement with ash-Shāfi'ī. If someone has a wound or ulcer on the forehead which hurts him if he prostrates, then he makes a gesture according to Ibn al-Qāsim, and prostrates on his nose according to Ashhab.

2. It is permitted to cover the knees and feet with one's clothes, according to the consensus

However, as for the hands, it is recommended to have them uncovered so that one has direct contact with the earth; as for the face it is obligatory to have it uncovered so that one has direct contact with the earth; and it is permitted to prostrate on cloth or clothing when the weather is hot or cold, contrary to ash-Shāfiʿī; and it is permitted on one or two folds of one's turban, contrary to ash-Shāfiʿī.

3. The finer aspects or courtesies

They are eight in number: one keeps one's knees apart and separates between one's elbows and one's sides, and between one's belly and one's thighs, but this parting or gap is not made by a woman; one lifts one's arms clear of the ground and makes the prostration between one's hand; one places one's hand on the ground before one's knees, contrary to them; and one supports oneself on one's hands when rising; and one moves from the second prostration without making a sitting, contrary to ash-Shāfiʿī.

4. What one says in it

It is recommended to say three times:

سُبْحَانَ رَبِّيَ الأَعْلَى

Subḥāna rabbiya-l-aʿlā

'Glorious is my Lord the Highest',

while the Ẓāhirīs have deemed it obligatory, and Ibn al-Mubārak has deemed it recommended for it to be said five times in the case of the *imām*. The following has also been transmitted in the *ḥadīth*:

اَللّٰهُمَّ لَكَ سَجَدْتُ، وَبِكَ آمَنْتُ، وَلَكَ أَسْلَمْتُ، سَجَدَ وَجْهِي لِلَّذِي خَلَقَهُ

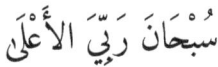

فَصَوَّرَهُ، وَشَقَّ سَمْعَهُ وَبَصَرَهُ، تَبَارَكَ اللَّهُ أَحْسَنُ الخَالِقِينَ.

Allāhumma laka sajadtu, wa bika āmantu, wa laka aslamtu, sajada wajhī li-lladhī khalaqahu fa ṣawwarah, wa shaqqa sam'ahu wa baṣarah, tabāraka-llāhu aḥsanu-l-khāliqīn

'O Allah to You I prostrate, and in You I trust, and to You I submit, my face prostrates to the One Who has created and formed it and Who has opened up its hearing and sight, may Allah be blessed, the best of the Creators.'

It is also recommended to make *du'ā* during it, and it has also been said that one say between the two prostrations:

رَبِّ اغْفِرْ لِي، وَارْحَمْنِي، وَاجْبُرْنِي، وَاهْدِنِي ، وَارْزُقْنِي

Rabbi-ghfir lī, wa-rḥamnī, wa-jburnī, wa-hdinī, wa-rzuqnī

'O Allah forgive me, have mercy on me, be charitable to me, guide me and provide for me'.

And it is permitted to make *du'ā* during the *ṣalāt* using the *du'ā* of the Qur'ān and any other *du'ā*, contrary to Abū Ḥanīfah with respect to *du'ā*s other than those of the Qur'ān

1. 4 – The sitting

This consists of two sections

1. Its form

One sits resting on one's left buttock on the ground and extends both legs out from underneath to the left setting one's right foot upright while keeping the inside of the toes on the ground, and keeping one's left foot flat under the right leg; Abū Ḥanīfah instructs one to sit on one's left foot, and ash-Shāfi'ī is like Mālik regarding the final sitting and like Abū Ḥanīfah regarding the middle one.

As for one's hands, one places them on one's thighs according to the agreed judgment, clenching the middle finger, the 'ring finger', and the little finger together of the right hand, extending the index finger with its side facing upwards with the thumb resting on the middle finger, and there is a difference of opinion as to whether one moves the index finger or not. And one spreads out flat the left hand – this applies to all of the sittings except that between the two prostrations, when one places one's hands near to one's knees spreading out both the fingers of the right and left hand alike, according to the well-known judgment, although it has also been said that it is like the sitting for the *tashahhud.*

Subsidiary matter

Iq'ā' – squatting on one's feet – is *makrūh* according to the four, contrary to Ibn Abbās, that is sitting on one's buttocks while raising one's thighs like a dog sitting on its haunches, although it has also been said that it is sitting on the front part of one's feet with one's buttocks on one's heels.

2. Its ruling

The sitting between the two prostrations is obligatory according to the consensus, while the sitting for the *tashahhuds* is *sunnah*, and within the madhhab the last sitting is obligatory, although the most correct judgment is that what is obligatory is only the amount necessary to say the final *salām*.

1. 5 – The tashahhud

This consists of three matter

1. What is said

Mālik has opted for the *tashahhud* of 'Umar, namely:

اَلتَّحِيَّاتُ لِلّٰهِ اَلزَّاكِيَّاتُ لِلّٰهِ اَلطَّيِّبَاتُ الصَّلَوَاتُ لِلّٰهِ اَلسَّلَامُ عَلَيْكَ أَيُّهَا النَّبِيُّ وَرَحْمَةُ اللّٰهِ وَبَرَكَاتُهُ، اَلسَّلَامُ عَلَيْنَا وَعَلَى عِبَادِ اللّٰهِ الصَّالِحِينَ. أَشْهَدُ أَنْ لَآ إِلَهَ إِلَّا اللّٰهُ وَحْدَهُ لَا شَرِيكَ لَهُ، وَأَشْهَدُ أَنَّ مُحَمَّدًا عَبْدُهُ وَرَسُولُهُ

At-taḥiyyātu lillāh, az-zākiyātu lillāh, aṭ-ṭayyibātu-ṣ-ṣalawātu lillāh, As-salāmu 'alayka ayyuha-n-nabiyyu wa raḥmatu-llāhi wa barakātuh. As-salāmu 'alaynā wa 'alā 'ibādillāhi-ṣ-ṣāliḥīn. Ash-hadu al-lā ilāha illa-llāhu waḥdahu lā sharīka lah, wa ash-hadu anna Muḥammadan 'abduhu wa rasūluh.

'Greetings are for Allah, all pure things are for Allah, good praise is for Allah, peace be on you O Prophet and the mercy and blessings of Allah, peace be on us and the slaves of Allah who are right acting, I bear witness that there is no god, only Allah alone without partner and I bear witness that Muḥammad is His slave and Messenger';

Ash-Shāfi'ī has opted for the *tashahhud* of Ibn Abbās and the difference between them is that he said: 'blessed greetings and good praise are for Allah' and he added 'and His blessing' after 'His mercy', and he said 'and that Muḥammad is the Messenger of Allah'; while Abū Ḥanīfah opted for the *tashahhud* of Ibn Mas'ūd in which he says 'greetings are for Allah as well as praise and good things' and he has added 'his blessing' and the rest is the same.

The meaning of '*taḥiyyātu*' is on-going, eternal life (*baqā'*), although it has also been said that it refers to the kingdom, and it has also been said it means '*Salām* – greetings of peace'.

2. Its ruling

The two *tashahhuds* are *sunnahs* in agreement with Abū Ḥanīfah while Ibn Ḥanbal deemed them obligatory, and ash-Shāfi'ī made the second one obligatory.

3. The sending of praise and blessings of Allah to the Prophet ﷺ

After the last *tashahhud* it is a *sunnah* according to the well-known judgment, although it has also been said that it is obligatory, in agreement with ash-Shāfi'ī, and it has also been said that it is an aspect of excellence. The form of it is as the full form for the sending of such praise and blessings as transmitted in the *ṣaḥīḥ*. The *du'ā* after it is recommended while the Ẓāhirīs have deemed it obligatory to seek refuge from four things: from the torment of the grave and that of Jahannam, from the trial of the raising to life and death and the trial of Masīḥ ad-Dajjāl; but there is no sending of praise and blessings nor *du'ā* during the first *tashahhud*, contrary to ash-Shāfi'ī and Allah knows best.

1. 6 – The Salām

The saying of the *salām* 'peace' is obligatory and it may not be substituted by something other than this blessing, contrary to Abū Ḥanīfah. The form of it is '*as-salāmu 'alaykum* – peace be on you' and there is a difference of opinion as to whether the indefinite form *salāmun 'alaykum* is acceptable or not.

The *imām* and the person alone say the *salām* once to the front while turning the face slightly to the right, according to the well-known judgment, although it has also been said it is said twice in agreement with them; and the *ma'mūm* says it three times, the one whereby he leaves the *ṣalāt*, the next in reply to the *imām* and the third if there is someone to his left, he replies to him according to the well-known judgment, although it has also been said two in particular. Exit from the *ṣalāt* is achieved by one single *salām* according to the agreed judgment, while there is a difference of opinion as to whether one has to renew one's intention for the *salām* or not.

A CONCLUDING REMARK

It has been recorded in the *ḥadīth* that one says 'سُبْحَانَ اللّٰه – *subḥāna-llāh* – glory be to Allah' thirty three times after the *ṣalāts*, 'اَلْحَمْدُ لِلّٰه – *al-ḥamdu lillāh* – praise be to Allah'' thirty three times and 'اللّٰهُ أَكْبَرُ – *Allāhu akbar* – Allah is greater' thirty three times and then completes the hundred with:

لَآ إِلَٰهَ إِلَّا اللّٰهُ وَحْدَهُ لَا شَرِيكَ لَهُ، لَهُ الْمُلْكُ، وَلَهُ الْحَمْدُ، وَهُوَ عَلَىٰ كُلِّ شَيْءٍ قَدِيرٌ، اللَّهُمَّ صَلِّ عَلَىٰ سَيِّدِنَا مُحَمَّدٍ وَعَلَىٰ ءَالِهِ

Lā ilāha illa-llāhu waḥdahu lā sharīka lah, lahu-l-mulk, wa lahu-l-ḥamd, wa huwa 'alā kulli shay'in qadīr. Allāhumma ṣalli 'alā sayyidinā Muḥammadin wa 'alā ālih

'There is no god, only Allah, alone without partner, to Him belongs the kingdom and to Him the glory, and He has power over all things, O Allah bless our Lord Muḥammad and his Family.'

It has also been transmitted that one says 'glory be to Allah', 'praise be to Allah' and 'Allah is greater' ten times each; and the saying has been reported of 'أَسْتَغْفِرُ اللّٰه – *astaghfiru-llāh* – I seek forgiveness of Allah' three times – then:

اَللّٰهُمَّ أَنْتَ السَّلامُ وَمِنْكَ السَّلامُ، تَبَارَكْتَ يَاذَا الْجَلاَلِ وَالْإِكْرَامِ.

Allāhumma anta-s-salāmu wa minka-s-salām, tabārakta yā dha-l-jalāli wa-l-ikrām

'O Allah You are Peace, from You is Peace, may You be blessed, O You Master of Majesty and Generosity'

and there is also transmitted:

اَللّٰهُمَّ أَعِنِّي عَلَى ذِكْرِكَ وَشُكْرِكَ وَحُسْنِ عِبَادَتِكَ.

Allāhumma a'innī 'alā dhikrika wa shukrika wa ḥusni 'ibādatik.

'O Allah help me to remember You and thank You and worship you well.'

1. 7 – The role of the imām and the jamā'ah – the ṣalāt in a group

The consists of four sections

1. The attributes of an imām

There are four kinds: those which are obligatory, which prevent from being the *imām*, which are *makrūh* and which are recommended.

The obligatory within the madhhab

They are seven in number:

1. Islam;

2. That he is of sane mind, in agreement with the two;

3. That he is of age, and this is stipulated with respect to the *farḍ ṣalāt*s according to the well-known judgment although it has also been said that it is not stipulated other than for the *jumu'ah,* in agreement with ash-Shāfi'ī;

4. That he is male, while ash-Shāfiʿī has said that a woman may be an *imām* for women;

5. That he have the quality of equity, there being a difference of opinion within the madhhab and outside it, thereby excluding the person who deviates from the right course, who is dissolute or acts unlawfully – about whom there are five judgments: permissibility in all cases, prohibition in all cases, and it has been said that it is permissible for such a person to be *imām* if his corruption is with respect to something other than the *ṣalāt*, and it has also been said as long as he is not entrenched in his deviance; and it has also been said as long as his deviance may be explained by a particular interpretation such as his deeming *nabīdh* the fermented date drink *ḥalāl*.

As for the person who innovates in aspects of *ʿaqīdah*, then there are four judgments as to his being an *imām*, [one that his imamate is completely acceptable and one that it is completely unacceptable and] one singles out the governor in the third, for it is permitted for him to be the *imām* but not other than him; and it has also been said that if we deem them *kuffār*, then it is not permitted, contrary to any deviance with respect to derivative rulings, in which case it is permitted according to the agreed judgment.

6. Knowledge of what is necessary to know of *fiqh* and recitation. As for the person ignorant of the rulings regarding the *ṣalāt*, it is not permitted for him to be an *imām*, according to the agreed judgment, and likewise in the case of someone who is unable to recite the Fātiḥah and the dumb person, but not someone who merely stutters or stammers. As for the person who pronounces the Arabic incorrectly and makes grammatical mistakes then there are four judgments, whereby one distinguishes in the third between the person who recites the Fātiḥah and other *sūrahs* incorrectly, and in the fourth between

the person who alters the meaning such as pronouncing *an'amta* – 'You have blessed', and *un'imta* – 'You were blessed', and those who do not alter the meaning.

7. The capacity to fulfil the essential elements – such that someone who can merely indicate by gesture bowing and prostration does not make the *ṣalāt* as the *imām* before someone who can bow and prostrate, but he may make it with someone whose state is like his, contrary to the person who is incapable of standing – he does not lead the *ṣalāt* sitting with someone who is capable of standing, within the madhhab, while ash-Shāfi'ī and Abū Ḥanīfah have said he may make it sitting while they are standing, and Ibn Ḥanbal said that he leads them in prayer but they must be sitting.

The qualities which prevent someone being the imām

They are the opposites of those qualities which are obligatory.

The makrūh qualities

They are that the person be a slave or a bastard – if they are engaged as full time official *imāms*, contrary to those who permit both, a eunuch or hermaphrodite, and it is also said if someone is uncircumcised, a blind person, lame or one armed.

The recommended qualities

They are knowledge, scrupulousness, esteem and distinction, age, good behaviour and fine stature, virtue, with a pleasant voice, nice clothes and any other praiseworthy aspect.

Subsidiary matter

Regarding who of various *imāms* should be given preference: preference is accorded the one who possesses some distinction after the obligatory conditions have been fulfilled – thus a governor and the owner of the house in which one is performing the *ṣalāt* have more right than others; and the *faqīh* takes precedence over a reciter, contrary to Abū Ḥanīfah; and the person who has more knowledge takes preference over someone who is more right acting; and if they are of equal standing from every aspect and they are at odds as to who should be *imām* – without any pride, then lots are drawn between them.

2. The ṣalāt al-jamāʿah i.e. the five daily ṣalāts performed in a group

This contains three matters

1. Its ruling

Namely it is one of, it being a *sunnah mu'akkadah*, i.e. of particular importance with respect to the *farḍ ṣalāt*s [therefore excluding for example the rain, eclipse and *tarāwīḥ ṣalāt*s], while the Ẓāhirīs have deemed it obligatory. It is permitted not to perform it in a group for a valid excuse, like in the case of rain, storm at night, illness, looking after someone who is ill, fear of the Sultan or a creditor when one is in straightened circumstances, or fear of retaliation when one hopes to be spared and when hungry in which case one should eat some food.

2. Repeating the ṣalāt

Whoever performs the *ṣalāt* in one group does not repeat it with another, contrary to Ibn Ḥanbal; and whoever performs it alone then it is permitted him to repeat it with a group, except for *maghrib ṣalāt*; and Abū Ḥanīfah has also made an exception of the *ʿaṣr ṣalāt*, while Abū Thawr has added the *ṣubḥ ṣalāt* as well, and ash-Shāfiʿī has made no exception. Whoever makes the *ṣalāt* alone or in a group in one of the three mosques i.e. of Makkah, Madīnah or al-Quds, then he does not repeat it in another. The *jamā'ah* is not performed twice in a single mosque, contrary to Ibn Ḥanbal. An official full-time *imām* who performs alone is as the group.

3. Whoever is making a ṣalāt alone in a mosque then the iqāmah is called

If he fears he will miss a *rak'ah* with the *imām*, he interrupts his *ṣalāt* with the *salām*; but if he does not fear this, then if he has begun a *rak'ah*, he completes two *rak'ahs* – otherwise he does not.

3. The form of following the imām

It consists of three matters

1. This is conditional upon the intention of the imām and the ma'mūm being the same in one of the farḍ ṣalāts

So one does not perform the *ẓuhr* after someone as *imām* who is performing *'aṣr*, contrary to ash-Shāfi'ī. It is permitted for someone performing a *nāfilah* to follow an *imām* performing a *farḍ ṣalāt* according to the agreed judgment, but vice versa is not permitted, contrary to ash-Shāfi'ī.

The *ma'mūm* is commanded to follow the *imām*, and so he does not do anything until the *imām* does it, and if he does the *takbīratu-l-iḥrām* or the *salām* before him, then his *ṣalāt* is invalidated; if he does them at the same time then there are two judgments, while if he does something other than these two before him then he has done it incorrectly but it does not invalidate it.

3. If the imām performs the ṣalāt while in a state of janābah ritual impurity or without wuḍū'

Then his *ṣalāt* is invalidated according to the consensus, both when done deliberately and out of forgetfulness, while the *ṣalāt* of the *ma'mūm* is invalidated if done deliberately but not in the case of forgetfulness; while ash-Shāfiʿī has said that it is not invalidated in either case. It is deemed an offense when done deliberately according to the agreed judgment, and Abū Ḥanīfah has said that it is invalidated in both cases.

4. There are four recommended positions for the ma'mūm

In the case of a single man he stands to the right of the *imām*; when two then they stand behind him, while Abū Ḥanīfah says they stand at his side to his right and left; and three or more stand behind him; and a woman, if alone, stands behind him and behind men if they are present.

5. The rows

The first row is the best, and the people of excellence are closest to the *imām*; and whoever does not find a place in a row then he makes the *ṣalāt* behind it and he does not draw a man to join him from the row in front, contrary to ash-Shāfiʿī; and whoever makes *ṣalāt* alone behind a row, then his *ṣalāt* is valid, contrary to Ibn Ḥanbal; and if the person making *ṣalāt* sees a gap in front of him, then he goes to it if it is near, and nearness is two or three rows.

Subsidiary matters

Ṣalāt between two pillars is *makrūh*; and the *imām* should not make the *ṣalāt* in a place which is higher than the *ma'mūm* unless it is insignificant and is not done out of pride.

Passengers on various boats make the *ṣalāt* together with one *imām* from one of the boats, and if the wind drives the boats apart then they are subject to the same ruling as those whose *imām* is prevented from continuing in the *ṣalāt* because of something untoward which happens, such as his losing *wuḍū'* for example.

And the *ṣalāt* of the person who can only hear the *imām* is permitted according to the most sound judgment.

The *imām* does not wait for the person who has just entered – to permit him to catch his bowing – according to the three; and whoever arrives while the *imām* is bowing then there is a difference of opinion as to whether he should also bow where he is or only when he reaches the row; if he does bow where he is, then he advances slowly still bowing, although ash-Shāfi'ī deemed it *makrūh*.

4. The imām's indicating someone should replace him during the ṣalāt

If something untoward happens to the *imām* while in the *ṣalāt* which prevents him from leading the *ṣalāt*, like his incapacity to perform one of the essential elements, or something which prevents him from performing the whole *ṣalāt*, such as his losing his *wuḍū'* or remembering a past *farḍ ṣalāt* he has not performed, then he must leave immediately, and have someone come out from the *jamā'ah* to take his place, either by making an indication or saying something, and complete it for them – on condition that the substitute had joined the *ṣalāt* before the impediment to the *ṣalāt* happened. However, if he does not have someone take his place, then the *jamā'ah* puts someone from among them forward, and if they do not put anyone forward, then one of them goes forward of himself; if no one goes forward then they make the *ṣalāt* individually and their *ṣalāt* is valid, except in the case of the *jumu'ah*. The substitute carries on from where the first *imām* left off. Ash-Shāfi'ī however does not permit this appointing of a substitute. And Allah knows best.

1. 8 – Completing the Ṣalāt after coming late

Whoever misses some of the *ṣalāt* of the *imām* should complete it, and there are three judgments as to the manner in which this should be done:

Banā' 'building upon'

i.e. making the part he caught with the *imām* the first part of his own *ṣalāt* and then completing the *ṣalāt* from there, in agreement with Abū Ḥanīfah;

Qaḍā'

i.e. making the part he caught with the *imām* the final part of his *ṣalāt* and then doing what he had missed, as the *imām* had done, in agreement with ash-Shāfi'ī and Ibn Ḥanbal.

Banā' is observed with respect to movements and *qaḍā'* with respect to the spoken elements according to the well-known judgment, and the explanation of this is to be found in the section on the *ṣalāt*.

Ṣubḥ and the Jumu'ah

If he misses a *rak'ah* of them then he stands up and recites the Umm al-Qur'ān and a *sūrah* according to all judgments. The difference of opinion has an effect on the *qunūt*: when *banā'* takes place then then the *qunūt* is recited but not when *qaḍā'* takes place.

Ẓuhr and 'Aṣr

If one misses a *rak'ah* or two *rak'ah*s from either of them, then if there is *banā'*, one reads the Umm al-Qur'ān alone, while in the case of *qaḍā'* then one also recites a *sūrah* with it – and this is how it is done according to the well-known judgment.

If one misses three, then on the basis of *banā'* one stands up and makes a *rak'ah* with the Umm al-Qur'ān and a *sūrah*, then one sits and says the *tashahhud*, then makes two *rak'ah*s with the Umm al-Qur'ān alone; while on the basis of *qaḍā'* one gets up and makes two *rak'ah*s with the Fātiḥah and a *sūrah* in each *rak'ah,* then one sits and then makes a *rak'ah* with the Fātiḥah; and according to the well known position, one gets up and makes a *rak'ah* with the Umm al-Qur'ān and a *sūrah,* then sits and then makes another with the Umm al-Qur'ān and a *sūrah,* then gets up and continues the *ṣalāt* with just the Umm al-Qur'ān.

'Ishā'

It is like *ẓuhr* except that the Fātiḥah and *sūrah* are recited aloud.

Maghrib

If one misses a *rak'ah,* then on the basis of *banā'* one reads the Fātiḥah alone; while on the basis of *qaḍā'* and according to the well known position, then with a *sūrah.*

If one misses two *rak'ah*s of it, then on the basis of *banā'* one gets up and makes a *rak'ah* with the Umm al-Qur'ān and a *sūrah* aloud, then one sits, then one makes a *rak'ah* with just the Umm al-Qur'ān alone; while on basis of *qaḍā'* one makes two *rak'ah*s aloud with the Umm al-Qur'ān and a *sūrah,* but one does not sit between them; while on the basis of the well known position one makes two *rak'ah*s with the Umm al-Qur'ān and a *sūrah* aloud and one sits between them.

Three subsidiary matters

1. Whoever bows and places his hands down on his knees before the *imām* raises his head from his bowing has caught the *rak'ah* according to the four, and if he doubts as to whether the *imām* has raised his head or not, then he does not count this *rak'ah,* nor does he count it if he catches the prostration.

2. If the person who comes after the *imām* has begun does not catch

the bowing of the last *rak'ah* and then joins in the prostration or the sitting, then he has missed the whole of the *ṣalāt* and so he gets up and performs the whole of the *ṣalāt*; and if this happens to him during the *jumu'ah* then he performs it as the *ẓuhr ṣalāt* with four *rak'ah*s, although Abū Ḥanīfah has said that he does two *rak'ah*s aloud.

3. If the person who comes after the *imām* has begun stands after the *salām* of the *imām*, then he stands up saying *Allāhu akbar* if his sitting with the *imām* coincided with his sitting – this occurring when he makes two *rak'ah*s with him; if not then he gets up without saying the *takbīr* this occurring when he makes one *rak'ah* or three *rak'ah*s with him, although it has also been said that he does say the *takbīr*.

1. 9 – Qaḍā' – Making up Missed Ṣalāts

Comprising three sections

1. Making up missed ṣalāt

It is performing after its time and it is obligatory for the person who has slept or forgotten, according to the consensus, as well as in the case of the person who deliberately misses it, contrary to the Ẓāhirīs.

The form of it is the same as the *ṣalāt* missed when it was performed in its time, that is said aloud or silently, shortened or in its full form, contrary to Abū Ḥanīfah.

2. The order

This consists of four matters.

1. It is obligatory to observe the order of the current ṣalāts

The one followed by the other, according to the consensus in all circumstances, and likewise with respect to a *ṣalāt* part of whose *ḍarūrī* time still remains.

2. It is obligatory to observe the order with respect to missed ṣalāts

The one followed by the other, when one remembers, but not if one forgets.

3. It is obligatory to observe the order of the current ṣalāts together with the missed ṣalāts

That is when one remembers and they are few in number, according to the well known position: thus if the missed *ṣalāt*s are few in number then one begins with them, even if it means missing the current one; and if one remembers them while performing a *ṣalāt*, then one interrupts the latter. If however the missed *ṣalāt*s are numerous, then one begins with the current *ṣalāt* and does not interrupt it once started. Four counts as a few and six counts as numerous, while there is a difference of opinion as to five. Ibn Maslamah has said that one does the missed ones first in all circumstances, while Ibn Wahb and ash-Shāfiʿī have said the current ones first, and Ashhab allows one to choose.

4. The order of missed ṣalāts together with ṣalāts which have been done

If, for example, one performs *ẓuhr* and then remembers *ṣalāt*s which have been missed, then if one finishes doing the latter before the *ḍarūrī* time elapses, i.e. before *maghrib*, then it is recommended to repeat *ẓuhr* because the order of the *ṣalāt*s which have been done is to be respected.

3. Doubt

This may be conceived as occurring in three situations.

1. DOUBT ABOUT THE NUMBER OF ṢALĀTS

In which case one must do what frees one with certainty from any further obligation, as for example someone who doubts as to whether he has missed doing one or two in which case he must do two.

2. DOUBT ABOUT WHICH SPECIFIC ṢALĀT ONE MUST DO

In which case one must do whatever frees him with certainty from any further obligation, as for example someone who has forgotten a *ṣalāt* and does not know which of the five it was, in which case he makes five *ṣalāt*s, such that if he has forgotten a *ṣalāt* belonging to the daytime then he makes *ṣalāt*s of *ṣubḥ*, *ẓuhr* and *'aṣr*; if a *ṣalāt* belonging to the night, then he makes the *ṣalāt*s of *maghrib* and *'ishā'*.

3. DOUBT ABOUT THE ORDER BUT KNOWING THE NUMBER

This is in the case of someone who has forgotten a *ẓuhr* and an *'aṣr ṣalāt*, one of them from a Saturday and the other from a Sunday, and he does not know which one is from the Saturday and which from the Sunday, in which case the well known position *(mashhūr)* is to observe the order, such that he makes three *ṣalāt*s consisting of *ẓuhr* between two *'aṣr ṣalāt*s, or three *ṣalāt*s consisting of *'aṣr* between two *ẓuhr ṣalāt*s in order to achieve with certainty the required order. The calculation in this regard is that you multiply the number of *ṣalāt*s missed by a number which is one less than this number and then you add one to the result, such that if a person has forgotten three, then he makes seven *ṣalāt*s and if four, then thirteen and if five, then twenty one; and whichever *ṣalāt* he begins with then he finishes with it also.

2.0 – Omissions, additions or mistakes in the ṣalāt

There are two sections in it

1. Prostrations

There are six matters

1. When the extra prostrations to make good a mistake are made

One prostrates before the final *salām* for an omission and after it for an addition; if one makes both an omission and an addition then it is made before the *salām*; while ash-Shāfi'ī has said it is made before in all instances; and Abū Ḥanīfah said afterwards in all instances; and Ibn Ḥanbal before when the instance has been recorded in the *ḥadīth* and afterwards in all other instances; and within the madhhab if one does the prostration that is normally made afterwards before the *salām* then it is acceptable, although it has also been said that one should repeat it afterwards; and if one does the prostration normally made before afterwards then this is more correct.

2. The ruling on the prostrations of negligence

It is obligatory, in agreement with Abū Ḥanīfah, while it has also been said that it is a *sunnah*, in agreement with ash-Shāfi'ī; and it has also been said that in particular the one before is obligatory.

If one misses the prostration to be made afterwards, then one has to make the prostration whenever he remembers it, even if this is after a month; and if one misses the prostration to be done before, then he should make the prostration if the time elapsed is not long or he has not lost his ritual purity; if however a long time has elapsed or he has broken his *wuḍū'*, then his *ṣalāt* is invalidated according to the well known *(mashhūr)* judgment, although it has also been said that it is invalidated on account of an omission of one of the movements of the *ṣalāt* but not because of omission of a spoken element. If, while actually performing a *ṣalāt,* one remembers a prostration that ought to ought to have been made after the *salām,* then one carries on and makes the prostration after this *ṣalāt*; if one remembers a prostration that ought to have been made before the *salām,* then he is as someone who has remembered a *ṣalāt* during the *ṣalāt* he is actually performing.

3. The form of the prostrations

One says the *takbīr* at the beginning of each prostration and when raising oneself from them; and there is a difference of opinion as to whether the prostration done afterwards needs to be accompanied by the *niyyat al-iḥrām* – the initial intention made to open the inviolate state of *ṣalāt.* And one makes the *tashahhud* for the prostration made afterwards and then says the final *salām*; as for the prostration before, then the *salām* of the actual *ṣalāt* being made is enough and covers for it, while there are two narrations as to whether one makes the *tashahhud* for it.

4. If the imām or the person making the ṣalāt alone is negligent

Then they make the prostration of negligence; while if the *ma'mūm* behind the *imām* makes a mistake necessitating the prostration of negligence, he does not make the prostration as the *imām* bears the responsibility for the acceptability of his *ṣalāt* and removes his negligence; but he does not bear responsibility for any omission of one of the essential elements of the *ṣalāt* on his part other than the Fātiḥah. The *ma'mūm* makes a prostration for some negligence of his *imām,* even if he has not forgotten to do it with him as long as he has caught one *rak'ah*; but if he did not, then he does not make the prostration, although Ṣaḥnūn has said that he does.

5. If the person who comes late makes a mistake after the final salām of the imām

Then he makes the prostration, but as for some negligence on the part of his *imām*, then if it is such that it requires the prostration beforehand then he makes the prostration with him, but if one which requires the prostration afterwards, then he delays it until he has finished making up what he has missed. And Abū Ḥanīfah and Ibn Ḥanbal have said that he makes the prostration with him in all instances, while Ṣaḥnūn has said that he makes it after having finished making up what he has missed in all instances, and ash-Shāfi'ī has said that he makes it with him then prostrates after he has finished making up, and within the madhhab there is a difference of opinion as to whether after the *imām* has made the final *salām*, he gets up to make up what he has missed or he waits until he has finished making his prostration.

6. Whoever makes a mistake then 'subhāna-llāh!' is said to him

And ash-Shāfi'ī has said that the saying of '*subhāna-llāh*' is for the men whereas women clap; and it is permitted for the *imām* and the *ma'mūm* to speak, to ask something or to repeat something in order to put the *ṣalāt* right, according to the well known position (*mashūr*), although Ibn Kinānah has said that it invalidates the *ṣalāt*, and Ṣaḥnūn has said that it is permitted in the case of saying the final *salām* after only two *rak'ahs* of a four *rak'ah ṣalāt* as described in the *ḥadīth* known as that of [the Companion called] Dhū Yadayn ['The person of the two hands'].

2. WHAT MAKES PROSTRATIONS NECESSARY

IT IS EITHER AN ADDITION, AN OMISSION OR DOUBT.

1. AN ADDITION

THERE ARE FIVE MATTERS

1. An addition of a physical action during the *ṣalāt.* If there has been a lot of movement – even if necessary, like the killing of a snake or scorpion, saving a blind person or anyone else from danger, or securing something of value from being lost or stolen – it invalidates the *ṣalāt* in all cases; and the definition of a lot, with regard to movements which are not of the same kind as those of the *ṣalāt,* is an amount which equals the *ṣalāt,* while it has also been said an amount equal to a half of it;

And if quite insignificant then it may be overlooked, like swallowing something caught in one's teeth or turning away even if with the whole of one's cheek – unless he turns his back on the *qiblah,* or moving ones finger to scratch;

And anything more than what is insignificant, then if it is of the kind like the physical movements of the *ṣalāt* such as the *sajdah,* then if done intentionally it invalidates, and if done in negligence one makes the prostration; and if not of the kind pertaining to the *ṣalāt* but is done out of necessity then it may be overlooked, such as when a beast escapes, or when one walks to something which may serve as a *sutrah* or to a gap in the row in front; but with respect to other than this, then if intentional it invalidates, and in the case of negligence one makes a prostration.

2. An addition concerning something spoken – if unintentional and of the kind of utterance pertaining to the spoken elements of the *ṣalāt* then it may be overlooked; and if not pertaining to the *ṣalāt* then

one makes a prostration for it, while Abū Ḥanīfah has said that the *ṣalāt* is invalidated. If intentional and of the kind of speech pertaining to the *ṣalāt* then it may be overlooked; and if said in order to put right something in the *ṣalāt* then this is permitted, contrary to Ibn Kinānah. And other than this invalidates – even if necessary.

SUBSIDIARY MATTERS

If the *imām* stops during the recitation and asks [implicitly to be made aware], the *ma'mūm* informs him; whoever recites with the intention of instructing him then there is no harm in this, like his saying [the words of the Qur'ān] *'Enter them in peace, in complete security!'* [when the *imām*, having stopped is hesitant and undecided regarding the recitation]; the *ma'mūm* does not seek refuge from Shayṭān and does not make any *du'ā* when reciting an *āyah* about punishment or mercy, and it is *makrūh* for the *imām* and the person making the *ṣalāt* alone to do so, contrary to ash-Shāfi'ī; whoever sneezes during the *ṣalāt* does not say *al-ḥamdu lillāh* – unless it is to himself, nor does he bless someone else who sneezes, contrary to Ibn Ḥanbal; and it is permitted to say *as-salāmu 'alaykum* to the person doing the *ṣalāt* and this person may reply with a gesture, while al-Lakhmī has said that he says it silently to himself.

3. That which is similar to expressing something: blowing out air from one's mouth or nose does not invalidate, although it has also been said that it does when done intentionally, and one makes the prostration when done in negligence; weeping, when done in humility, is good, otherwise it is deemed to be like speaking; and moaning or groaning is deemed as speech unless it is necessary; and guffawing invalidates in all instances, although it has also been said [only] when done intentionally; and smiling may be overlooked, although it has

also been said that one makes the prostration for it after the final *salām,* as it is an addition, while it has also been said before the *salām,* as it is a lack of humility; clearing one's throat when necessary does not invalidate, while there are two judgments with regard to when it is unnecessary; and reading a book, if one moves one's tongue in doing so, is deemed to be like speaking, otherwise it may be overlooked unless it goes on for a long time.

4. Whoever gets up to do an additional *rak'ah* in a *farḍ ṣalāt,* should return when he remembers and make the prostration after the *salām*; and likewise he makes the prostration if he does not remember until he has made the final *salām*; if he is the *imām,* then those among the people who are aware of the addition but who follow him, then their *ṣalāt* is invalidated; while those who follow him unawares or in a state of doubt, then their *ṣalāt* is valid; and those who follow him and are ignorant or who make some interpretation for the addition, then there are two judgments; and whoever does not follow him and sits down, then his *ṣalāt* is valid. If his standing up was for some necessary reason, like a *rak'ah* being null and void such that one has to make it up, then whoever is certain of the reason or is doubtful about it must follow the *imām,* and if he does, then his *ṣalāt* is invalidated, but whoever is sure that there is no reason, it is invalid for him to follow the *imām* and if he does so, his *ṣalāt* is invalid.

5. Whoever stands up for a third *rak'ah* in a *nāfilah ṣalāt* and remembers before the bowing, then he returns and makes the extra prostration after the *salām*; and if he remembers after straightening up from the bowing, then he adds an additional *rak'ah* to the *ṣalāt* and makes the final *salām* after four *rak'ah*s, and makes the extra prostration after the *salām* on account of having made two extra *rak'ah*s, although it has also been said beforehand because of the omission of the *salām* in its

proper place; and if he remembers while he is bowing then there are two judgments based on how one decides as to what makes a *rak'ah*, that is, whether it is the bowing or straightening up from it.

2. An omission

It may be categorised as either an omission of an essential element, or of a *sunnah* or an aspect of excellence.

If he has omitted an essential element deliberately, then his *ṣalāt* is invalidated; if inadvertently, then he makes it good as long as he has not carried on past the place of the omission, but if he has gone beyond it, then he regards the *rak'ah* as being annulled and makes it up – but without making another intention or saying the *takbīratu-l-iḥrām*.

If he has omitted a *sunnah* inadvertently, then he makes extra prostrations for it, and if deliberately then he also makes the extra prostrations for it, in agreement with ash-Shāfi'ī, while Ibn al-Qāsim has said that he does not have to do anything extra, in agreement with Abū Ḥanīfah, although it has also been said that it is invalidated on account of his disparaging the Sunnah.

As for the ignorant person, there is a difference of opinion with regard to all the matters: that is as to whether he is to be included with the person who forgets or the one who deliberated omits something.

If he omits an aspect of excellence then he has nothing to make up. This then is a summary and we shall now go into the details:

Omission of one of the essential elements

There are five matters

1. The iḥrām

If someone forgets the *takbīratu-l-iḥrām* or has doubts regarding it and he is alone or he is the *imām,* then he interrupts [the *ṣalāh*] as soon as he remembers, makes the *takbīratu-l-iḥrām* and begins again.

If he is a *ma'mūm,* then there are three possible circumstances in his regard: if he says the *Allāhu akbar* for the bowing while making the intention by it for the *iḥrām,* then this is acceptable, contrary to ash-Shāfi'ī, but if he says the *Allāhu akbar* for the bowing without making the intention by it for the *iḥrām*, then he continues – bearing in mind the difference of opinion – then repeats the *ṣalāt*; if he neither says the *Allāhu akbar* for the bowing or the *iḥrām*, he interrupts [the *ṣalāh*], says *Allāhu akbar*, begins anew and does not take into account what has passed.

2. With regard to the Fātiḥah

Whoever forgets the Fātiḥah and is a *ma'mūm,* then he has nothing to make up; if he is the *imām* or alone, and forgets to recite it for the whole of the *ṣalāt*, then his *ṣalāt* is invalidated, contrary to Abū Ḥanīfah; and if he forgets it for a *rak'ah* or more, then it is said that he repeats the *ṣalāt*, while it is also said that he annuls the *rak'ah* and then makes it up, and it is also said that he makes the prostrations of negligence.

3. The bowing and the prostration

In the case of the *imām* or someone praying alone who forgets a bowing or a prostration, then if the person has passed beyond the point where they should be done, he annuls the *rak'ah* and makes it up in its entirety; if he catches the point where it should be done then he does it – and what counts as 'catching it' according to the madhhab is if he has not put into effect the *rak'ah* following – this being subject also to a difference of opinion based on whether one deems it to be put into effect with the bowing or the straightening up from it; and one 'catches' it according to the two, i.e. ash-Shāfi'ī and Abū Ḥanīfah, even if the bowing of the following *rak'ah* has been completed.

If he is a *ma'mūm,* then he should do them and catch up with the *imām* as long as the latter has not stood up for the second *rak'ah*, while it is also said that he catches him as long as he has not raised his head from the second bowing, and it has also been said that he annuls it; and if the *ma'mūm* omits to make the prostration in the final *rak'ah,* then he should catch it as long as the *imām* has not made the final *salām.*

Remark

This is the ruling when the *ma'mūm* omits the bowing or the prostration out of negligence, or because of drowsiness which overpowers him, or when it is so crowded that he does not find space to make the bowing or the prostration; and ash-Shāfi'ī and Ibn Ḥanbal have said that in crowded circumstances he prostrates on the back of his brother – but this is not permitted within the madhhab.

Six subsidiary matters

1. If he remembers a prostration during the final *tashahhud,* then if it was in the last *rak'ah,* then he prostrates there and then; if it was in another place, then he makes up a *rak'ah*; if he is in doubt as to whether it is from it or from another place, then he prostrates and makes a *rak'ah* according to Ibn al-Qāsim, and in particular makes a *rak'ah* according to Ashhab.

2. If he remembers a prostration in the last *rak'ah* after his saying the *salām*, then he prostrates, alt hough it has also been said that he makes another *rak'ah* as the *salām* is a the defining separation from the *ṣalāt.*

3. Whoever forgets four prostrations from four *rak'ah*s, then he makes a prostration by which he makes good the fourth *rak'ah*, then makes

up three *rak'ah*s, according to the well-known position (*mashhūr*), while it has also been said that the *ṣalāt* is invalid on account of the large amount of negligence, and Abū Ḥanīfah has said that he makes four prostrations one after the other, and ash-Shāfi'ī has said he counts the four as the prostrations of two complete *rak'ah*s, and then he stands up and makes up two *rak'ah*s. If he forgets eight prostrations from four *rak'ah*s, then he makes two prostrations to make good the fourth *rak'ah,* then he makes up three *rak'ah*s – although invalidation in this case is preferable.

4. If one fails to fulfil the bowing in a *rak'ah* or the prostration in another – or vice versa, one does not piece together the prostration of one with the bowing of another, according to the well-known position (*mashhūr*).

5. If one makes the bowing and omits straightening up, then Ibn al-Qāsim has said that he annuls the *rak'ah,* although he has also said that he returns as long as he has not effected another *rak'ah.*

6. Whoever omits to straighten up in the standing position prostrates on the basis of the judgment that it is a *sunnah,* or annuls the *rak'ah* on the basis of the judgment that it is obligatory.

4. THE SALĀM

Whoever forgets the *salām* and a long time has elapsed or he has broken his *wuḍū',* then his *ṣalāt* is invalidated, contrary to Abū Ḥanīfah; if a long time has not elapsed and he has not broken his *wuḍū',* then he returns to his sitting position and says the *salām* and prostrates after the *salām,* if had stood up or faced away from the *qiblah;* and he goes back to the sitting position while saying *Allāhu akbar* according to the well-known position (*mashhūr*) – but there are two opinions as to whether one says *Allāhu akbar* sitting or standing, and there are two judgments as to whether one says the *tashahhud* before this saying of the *salām*. And if he has doubt as to the *salām*, he makes the *salām* and he does not have to make a prostration.

5. Whoever deliberately says the salām before completing his ṣalāt

Then his *ṣalāt* is invalid. If done inadvertently, then he returns and completes his *ṣalāt* and makes the prostrations on account of the negligence – and his return is without any *takbīr* if only a short time has elapsed; if not, then there are two judgments. And if he does say *Allāhu akbar,* there are two judgments as to whether he does it standing or sitting; and if he says the *takbīr* standing, then there are two judgments as to whether he sits and then gets up to continue the *ṣalāt,* or he does not sit. And if he doubts as to whether he has completed the *ṣalāt* and says the *salām,* then it is invalidated; and if he thinks that it has been completed and then makes the final *salām,* then he returns to complete it; and whoever makes the *salām* before his *imām* has completed it, then his *ṣalāt* is invalidated; but if done inadvertently or thinking that the *imām* had said the *salām,* then he returns and says the *salām.*

As for the omission of sunnahs

There are five matters

1. Whoever forgets the *sūrah* that is recited with the Umm al-Qur'ān, then he prostrates before the *salām* according to the well-known position (*mashhūr*); and it has also been said that he does not prostrate based on the question as to whether one should prostrate for the *sunnah*s which are elements of speech or not – this in the case of the *imām* and the person alone; as for the *ma'mūm* he does not have to make any prostration.

2. There is a difference of opinion as to whether there are prostrations in the case of the person who omits a *takbīr* other than the *tabīrat al-iḥrām* or the '*sami'a llāhu liman ḥamidah* – Allah hears the one who praises', or who says *al-ḥamdu lillāh* instead of *Allāhu akbar* or vice versa – on the basis of the question as to whether one prostrates in the case of the spoken elements or not; although one does not prostrate for one single instance of all this because of its insignificance according to the well-known position (*mashhūr*).

3. Whoever recites silently that which is to be recited aloud prostrates before the *salām* according to the well-known position (*mashhūr*), although it has also been said after it; and whoever recites aloud what is to be recited silently prostrates after the *salām* according to the well-known position (*mashhūr*), although it has also been said before it – and this is with respect to what is done inadvertently. If however one deliberately omits the reciting aloud or silently then there are three judgments: invalidation, prostration and that it is accepted without the prostration. And it is pardonable if – having reciting at least one *āyah* or the like aloud – one does not recite any further aloud. Ash-Shāfi'ī has said that one does not have to make anything up if one omits to discriminate between the recitation aloud or silently.

4. Whoever forgets the middle sitting, prostrates for it before the final *salām*; if he remembers before his hands leave the ground, then he is instructed to return to the sitting position – if he does return, then he does not have to prostrate, according to the well-known position (*mashhūr*) on account of the slightness of the mistake; if he does not return, then he prostrates; and if he remembers after getting up for the standing position, then he does not return and prostrates on account of the mistake – and if he does return, then he would have acted wrongly, but it does not invalidate his *ṣalāt,* according to the well-known position

(*mashhūr*), although there is a difference of opinion as to whether or not he prostrates after the *salām* on account of the additional standing or beforehand on account of the combination of the additional standing and the omission of the sitting in its proper place.

5. Whoever forgets the two *tashahhud*s or one of them, but had made the sitting for it, then he makes the prostrations before the *salām*, according to the well-known position (*mashhūr*), although it has also been said afterwards, on account of the fact that the spoken element is not deemed so significant. And it has also been said that one does not prostrate, on the basis of the ruling that there is no prostration for the spoken elements.

And there is no prostration in the case of the person who omits the sending of blessings on the Prophet ﷺ according to the well-known position (*mashhūr*), whereas ash-Shāfi'ī said that the person who forgets this in the first *tashahhud* prostrates, but the *ṣalāt* of the person who omits it in the second *tashahhud* is invalidated.

As for doubt, if it is the whisperings of Shayṭān then one acts in accordance with one's first thought – and there are two judgments as to whether one prostrates or not: on the basis of the judgment that one should prostrate, then there are two judgments as to whether one should make the prostration before the *salām* or afterwards; and if [the doubt is] authentic, then if he has doubts as to some omission – then he would be as someone who has made one; and if he has doubts as to the number of *rak'ah*s – like someone who does not know whether he has made three or four – then he continues on the basis of the lesser of the two, and does what he has doubts about, according to the two Imāms, and prostrates after the *salām* according to the well-known position (*mashhūr*), while it has also been said before it, in agreement with ash-Shāfi'ī.

Subsidiary matter

If the person performing *ṣalāh* has doubts, then he accepts the word of two just persons, and it has also been said of one just person, and if he is certain, then he does not have recourse to any other person, unless it is a group by means of whom one may arrive at certainty.

2.1 – The Jumu'ah

1. The obligation of the ṣalāt al-jumu'ah

It is a *farḍ 'ayn* according to the majority, and the conditions of its obligation are ten in number – which are also those of the other *ṣalāt*s, and to these are added four others: that one be male; free, according to the agreed judgment; the saying of the *iqāmah,* contrary to the Ẓāhirīs; and proximity of three miles to its location or less, while six has also been said, and twelve has also been said, and Abū Ḥanīfah has said that it is obligatory for the person living in a town or city, but not for someone outside of it, while Ibn Ḥanbal has said that it is obligatory for anyone who hears the call to it, and ash-Shāfi'ī has said it is obligatory for whoever is in the town or city, irrespective of whether he hears the call, and obligatory for anyone outside the town or city who hears it.

Six subsidiary matters

1. The obligation is removed for seven reasons: illness; taking care of a relative or a slave who is ill – if there is no one to take care of them or one fears they may die; or being occupied with a dead person if one fears a change for the worse in their condition; or someone who has been imprisoned; or if a blind person no longer has anyone to guide him; or when one fears a creditor; while there is a difference of opinion as to whether it is removed in the case of rain or mud; and it

is not removed in the case of a bridegroom during the first seven days of his marriage, according to the well-known position (*mashhūr*).

2. Whoever attends the *jumu'ah* from amongst the persons for whom it is not obligatory, then it does instead of the *ẓuhr*; and if a traveller arrives and has not made *ẓuhr*, then he makes the *jumu'ah*, but if he has made *ẓuhr*, then there is a difference of opinion as to whether he has to do the *jumu'ah* if he is there on time for it; and if [the traveller] acts as the *imām* for the *jumu'ah*, then there is a difference of opinion as to whether it is valid.

3. It is permitted to travel on the day of *jumu'ah* before the sun has gone past its zenith, although it has also been said that it is *makrūh*, in agreement with ash-Shāfi'ī and Ibn Ḥanbal; and it is prohibited after the sun has passed its zenith and before the *ṣalāt*, according to the agreed judgment.

4. Those who miss the *jumu'ah* for a valid reason are permitted to make the *ṣalāt* in the form of *ẓuhr* in a group, if their excuse is evident, although it has also been said that it is not permitted, in agreement with Abū Ḥanīfah.

5. Whoever does not do the *jumu'ah* without an excuse and makes *ẓuhr* in the form of four *rak'ah*s, then if this is after the *jumu'ah*, it suffices – although accompanied by his disobedience; if before it, then he is obliged to perform the *jumu'ah*.

6. It is recommended for the person who hopes that his [valid] excuse will cease to be that he delay the *ẓuhr* until he has almost given up hope of catching the *jumu'ah*; if his excuse ceases to exist after having finished making *ẓuhr*, then he makes the *jumu'ah* if he catches it; and likewise in the case of a young boy who comes of age after having made the *ẓuhr ṣalāt*.

2. With respect to the conditions for its validity

They are the same ten in number as all the other *ṣalāts*, with the addition of four others, they being: the *imām*; the *jamā'ah*; the mosque and taking up a settled place of abode (*istīṭān*) in either a town (*balad*) or a village settlement (*qaryah*). The truth with respect to these four is that they are both conditions of obligation and conditions of validity.

As for the *imām*, it is not a stipulation that he be a governor, contrary to Abū Ḥanīfah; and it is not permitted that the *imām* be a slave, contrary to the two and Ashhab.

As for the *jamā'ah*, it must consist of a sufficient number of persons able to ensure the independence and safety of a settlement – without a specific number according to the well-known position (*mashhūr*); but three or four persons would not suffice according to the well-known position (*mashhūr*), while Ibn Ḥanbal has narrated that the minimum is thirty, and fifty has also been said, and ash-Shāfi'ī said forty and Abū Ḥanīfah two with the *imām*. It is also stipulated that the *jamā'ah* should remain until the *ṣalāt* has been completed, according to the well-known position (*mashhūr*).

As for the mosque, al-Bājī has stipulated that it be covered with a roof and that people gather in it continuously, while Ibn Rushd thought that improbable. *Ṣalāt* is permitted in the courtyard of the mosque and the ways leading to it, although it is *makrūh* when there is no need; but it is not permitted on the roof of the mosque or in enclosed areas like rooms or shops, according to the well-known position (*mashhūr*).

As for the *jumu'ah ṣalāt* in two mosques in one single town there are three judgments, [that is not permitted, that it is permitted and] the third making the distinction as to whether or not the two are separated by a river – or some other similar obstacle. If we accept it being restricted to one mosque, then the *jumu'ah* of the oldest *jāmi'* mosque is the valid one. And ash-Shāfi'ī has said that whoever performs the *jumu'ah* first of all, his *ṣalāt* is valid.

3. The jumu'ah has two fundamental elements – the ṣalāt and the khuṭbah

As for the *ṣalāt* it consists of two *rak'ah*s done aloud, according to the consensus, and it is preferable to recite in the first the Sūrah al-Jumu'ah and in the second the Munāfiqūn – the Hypocrites or *Sabbiḥ* – Glorify! [also known as al-A'lā – the Most High].

The earliest time for it is after the sun has passed its zenith, according to the three, while Ibn Ḥanbal has said that it is permitted to do it before this, and the latest time is at sunset according to the well-known position (*mashhūr*), and it has also been said at the paling of the sun towards sunset, and it has also been said when the shadow of a thing attains the length of that thing.

The *adhān* for it is made from the minarets, while ash-Shāfi'ī has said the group of *mu'adhdhin*s call it in front of the *imām* – calling it three times, and twice is also said, while once suffices.

As for the *khuṭbah* it is obligatory, contrary to Ibn al-Mājishūn, and it is a condition for the validity of the *jumu'ah,* according to the most correct judgment; and the shortest speech deemed to be a *khuṭbah* is what is deemed to be a *khuṭbah* by the Arabs, while it is also said it consists of: *ḥamd* – praise, sending blessings on the Messenger, advice and admonition, and Qur'ān.

And it is recommended to keep it short. There are two judgments as to the obligation of the second *khuṭbah*; and there are two judgments as to the obligation of being in a state of ritual purity; and there are two judgments regarding the obligation to sit before the two *khuṭbah*s and between them; and there are two judgments as to the obligation to stand for the two *khuṭbah*s; and there are two judgments as to the stipulation there be a *jamā'ah* for the two *khuṭbah*s.

No one other than the person who makes the *khuṭbah* should lead the *ṣalāt* unless there is a valid excuse; and he should make the *khuṭbah* on the minbar leaning on a staff or bow, and the people should be facing him; and he does not say *as-salāmu 'alaykum* to them on entering, contrary to ash-Shāfi'ī.

And it is obligatory for those present to listen silently to the *khuṭbah,* according to the agreed judgment, and to remain silent even if one cannot hear, contrary to Ibn Ḥanbal. One does not say *as-salāmu 'alaykum*, or bless someone who has sneezed, nor does one reply to the one who greets with *as-salāmu 'alaykum*, contrary to Ibn Ḥanbal; and one does not make the *ṣalāt* of greeting the mosque if the *imām* has come out to the minbar, contrary to as-Sayūrī, ash-Shāfi'ī and Ibn Ḥanbal. It is however permitted to seek refuge when mention is made of the Fire, and to ask for blessings when mention is made of the Prophet ﷺ, and to say *amīn* quietly when *du'ā*s are being made, while there are two judgments in this matter as to whether one may say it aloud; and one does not instruct people to be silent by speaking, but rather by indicating to them.

4. There are special duties that pertain to the jumu'ah

1. That one makes haste to go to it, and that is obligatory if the *khaṭīb* has sat down, and it is recommended to set off for it before the beginning of its time, contrary to ash-Shāfi'ī.

2. It is forbidden to buy or sell, to conclude a marriage contract or any other contract from the time the *khaṭīb* sits down to the end of the *ṣalāt*; if it does occur, then there is a difference of opinion as to

whether is nullifies such contracts.

3. The *ghusl* for it is a *mu'akkad sunnah,* while the Ẓāhirīs deemed it obligatory; and it does not suffice if made before *Fajr*, nor when it is not made immediately before setting off, contrary to ash-Shāfi'ī.

4. It is recommended to wear perfume, to use the *siwāk* tooth-stick, to wear one's finest clothes and to make the acts of grooming known as the *khisāl al-fiṭrah,* i.e. clipping nails, trimming one's moustache, shaving one's armpits and pubic hair.

2.2 – Joining two Ṣalāts together

It is permitted to join *ẓuhr* and *'aṣr*, and *maghrib* and *'ishā'* for specific reasons: when at 'Arafah and Muzdalifah, according to the agreed judgment, this being a *sunnah*; and when one is travelling or when it is raining, contrary to Abū Ḥanīfah with respect to the last two reasons; and when one is ill, contrary to the two; and when one is afraid – there being a difference of judgment within the madhhab regarding this; and the Ẓāhirīs and Ashhab have permitted the joining without any reason.

As for travel, it is conditional upon the difficulty of the journey, according to the well-known position (*mashhūr*), and contrary to ash-Shāfi'ī, but it is not conditional upon distance.

As for rain, one may join *maghrib* and *'ishā'* according to the two Imāms, but not *ẓuhr* and *'aṣr*, contrary to ash-Shāfi'ī; if rain, mud and darkness combine or two of them, or there is just rain, then joining is permitted – there being a difference of opinion when there is just darkness; if there is just mud then there are two different judgments; and if the rain ceases after having joined the *ṣalāts*, then one may carry on.

As for the time of the joining in the case of rain, there are three judgments: the first, that it is at the time of *maghrib*, or to delay it slightly after this, or to delay it until the end of the prescribed time; for each of the two *ṣalāt*s there is an *adhān* and an *iqāmah*, according to the well-known position (*mashhūr*), while it has also been said that it suffices to say the *adhān* for the first while making the intention of the joining; and there is a difference of opinion as to whether it suffices if one makes the intention for it at the second. And on the basis of this there are two subsidiary matters if one makes the first *ṣalāt*, then there occurs a reason for the joining. And whoever has made just the first and catches the second, then there are two judgments as to whether joining is permitted. One does not have to move [or occupy oneself with something other than the *ṣalāt* – as would normally be necessary – to avoid performing the second *ṣalāt* immediately after the first] between the two *ṣalāt*s, when joined at night, or after them, in the mosque, nor does one perform the *witr* until the redness has disappeared from the sky.

As for the sick person, then he joins if he fears he might lose consciousness, or when it would be comfortable for him; and the time for it is at the beginning of the prescribed time for the first *ṣalāt*, although it has also been said that it is at the end of the prescribed time of the first and at the beginning of the time for the second.

2.3 – Fear

There are two kinds of fear

1. That which prevents one from completing the ṣalāt in its proper form

This is during the fighting and violence of war, in which case one delays the *ṣalāt* until one fears one will miss its prescribed time, and then one makes the *ṣalāt* as one is able – walking, riding or running

– while making gestures for the bowing and prostration, towards the *qiblah,* or in another direction, and he does not have to stop saying or doing anything he might need to say or do [in this exceptional situation].

2. The fear which arises when one expects to be molested or harmed by the enemy if all of the Muslims become occupied with the ṣalāt

In this case it is permitted them to make the *ṣalāt* individually, or for one group to make it with one *imām* and another group with another *imām*; and it is permitted for them to make the fear *ṣalāt* – laid down in the *sharīʿah* – which is permitted by the majority, contrary to Abū Yūsuf who stated that it was particular to the Prophet ﷺ.

It has various forms

1. The well-known position (*mashhūr*) in the madhhab, is that the *imām* and leader divides the army into two, one group with him and the other busy guarding against the enemy, then he makes the *ṣalāt* with the first group that is with him by making one *rakʿah* in a *ṣalāt* consisting of two *rakʿah*s and two *rakʿah*s in the *ṣalāt*s consisting of three or four *rakʿah*s, then they carry on and complete the *ṣalāt* by themselves, and then they stand and take up guard, and the second group comes and he makes the *ṣalāt* with them by making one *rakʿah* in the *ṣalāt* consisting of two *rakʿah*s and two *rakʿah*s for those consisting of four and for *maghrib* just one *rakʿah,* and then says the final *salām,* and they then make up the rest after his *salām.*

2. The second form is like it, except that the *imām* does not say the final *salām* after completing his *ṣalāt,* but rather waits until the second group has made up what they have to make up, then says the final *salām* with them. This is the madhhab of ash-Shāfiʿī, while it has also been narrated from Mālik.

3. That the first group moves away before completing their *ṣalāt* and they do not say the final *salām*, then they stand and take up guard and the second group comes and [the imām] makes the *ṣalāt* with them, then after he has said the final *salām* the two groups make up what they have to make up together, this being the madhhab of Ashhab.

4. This is like the third except that the first group makes up what it has to make up after the second group has finished making what they have to make up, this being the madhhab of Abū Ḥanīfah.

Secondary matters

The fear *ṣalāt* is permitted while travelling and resident, according to the well-known position (*mashhūr*), and an *adhān* and *iqāmah* are made for it; and if it is the *ṣalāt* with two *rak'ahs*, the *imām* waits for the second group while standing, whereas if it is a *ṣalāt* with three or four, there is a difference of opinion as to whether he waits for them standing or sitting; and while waiting he has the option of making *du'ās* or remaining silent. And if the fear ceases to exist after the *ṣalāt* of the first group, then there is a difference of opinion as to whether the second group should join him or not.

2.4 – Travel

This has four sections

1. The ruling of shortening the ṣalāt

There are five judgments within the madhhab, that it is: obligatory, in agreement with Abū Ḥanīfah; *sunnah* – and this is the well-known position (*mashhūr*); recommended; licit; and the ruling of 'licence' to do so which is deemed of less excellence than doing the full *ṣalāt,* in agreement with ash-Shāfi'ī.

Two secondary matters

1. If the traveller makes the *ṣalāt* in full, then there is a difference of opinion with respect to the shortening: if this latter is obligatory for the traveller in question, then he repeats the *ṣalāt* both within the prescribed time and after it; if a *sunnah* or recommended, then he repeats it within the time; while if there is licence or it is licit for him, then he does not repeat it.

2. If the resident makes the *ṣalāt* behind the traveller, then he completes his *ṣalāt* after the final *salām*; if the traveller makes it behind the resident, then there are four judgments: invalidity; doing it in full with the *imām*; saying the *salām* after two *rak'ah*s; and waiting after two *rak'ah*s until the *imām* says the final *salām*.

2. The conditions for shortening

They are six in number

1. The length of the journey, that is forty-eight miles, according to the well-known position (*mashhūr*) and in agreement with ash-Shāfi'ī and Ibn Ḥanbal, while forty has also been said; and Abū Ḥanīfah has said a journey of three days; and the Ẓāhirīs have said the minimum which people deem to be a journey, even if he merely goes out to his orchard. And the distance of the return journey is added to the journey itself, each being reckoned separately.

2. That one resolves unequivocally to cover the whole distance from the very beginning.

3. That he has a specific destination – so the person who is wandering aimlessly does not shorten, nor someone who has gone after a runaway slave, who will return from the place he finds him in.

4. That the travel be licit – so the person who is disobedient does not shorten his *ṣalāt*, such as bandits and runaway slaves, contrary to Abū

Ḥanīfah; and it is not stipulated that the journey be an act of *qurbah* – of coming closer to Allah, contrary to Ibn Ḥanbal.

5. That the person goes beyond the town limits and any adjoining buildings, orchards or inhabited areas, according to the majority, while Ibn Mājishūn has said after the distance of three miles.

6. That he does not decide to be stationary for four days and four nights during his journey; and Ibn Ḥanbal has said more than four days, while Abū Ḥanīfah has said fifteen days, and if he remains stationary with the intention of further travel then he does not stop shortening; and if he enters a town in which he has family (a wife) and it is one of his abodes, then he does not shorten; and if he intends to be resident there, then he sets off again, there is a difference of opinion as to the effect of his intention; and if he intends to take up residence after entering into a *ṣalāt*, then there is a difference of opinion as to whether he completes the four; and if he makes the intention for this after finishing it, he does not repeat it, and Allah knows best.

2.5 – THE TWO ʿĪDS

THIS CONSISTS OF THREE SECTIONS

1. THE RULING OF THE ṢALĀT FOR THE TWO ʿĪDS

It is *sunnah*, according to the majority. Those for whom the *jumuʿah* is an obligation are also instructed to do it, while there is a difference of opinion as to those who are not obligated, that is women, slaves and travellers.

The location of it is in the *muṣallā*, not in the mosque, unless in the case of necessity, and one does not perform it in two places.

The time for it is from after the sunrise until the sun has passed its zenith. Whoever misses it, does not make it up, while ash-Shāfiʿī has said that he makes it up according to its form, while Ibn Ḥanbal has said that one makes four *rak'ah*s; and if a group of people only learn of the *'Īd* after the sun has passed its zenith, they do not make it the next day. And it does not do instead of the *jumu'ah ṣalāt*, contrary to ash-Shāfi'ī.

2. Its form

It is two *rak'ah*s with the recitation aloud, without an *adhān* or *iqāmah*. And it is recommended to recite in it '*Glorify...*', that is al-A'lā – 'The Most High' (Sūrah 87), and the like, while ash-Shāfi'ī and Ibn Ḥabīb have deemed the *sūrah* Qāf and al-Qamar – 'The Moon' recommended. One says the *takbīr* seven times, including the *takbīratu-l-iḥrām*, in the first *rak'ah*, while ash-Shāfi'ī has said in addition to it; and in the second one says the *takbīr* six times including the *takbīr* said while standing up from the first *rak'ah*, according to the two Imāms; and one does not raise one's hands during the *takbīr*s, according to the well-known position (*mashhūr*), contrary to ash-Shāfi'ī and Ibn Ḥanbal; nor does one make any dhikrs or express any other things between the *takbīr*s, contrary to ash-Shāfi'ī and Ibn Ḥanbal; and if the *imām* forgets a *takbīr*, then he returns to say it, and there are two judgments regarding the repetition of what has been recited, and there are two judgments as to whether one makes the prostrations of negligence when a *takbīr* has been omitted.

And the *khuṭbah* is made after the *ṣalāt*, according to the agreed judgment, and it consists of two *khuṭbah*s – the *imām* sits before the two of them and between the two of them; and one utters the *takbīr*s just before them and during them without limit, while it has also been said one says it seven times just before them, and one instructs people concerning what they need that day.

3. The duties of the 'Īd

Which are *ghusl* after the dawn *ṣalāt,* while it suffices before this; perfume; wearing one's finest clothes; the acts of grooming known as the *khisāl al-fiṭrah*, i.e. clipping nails, trimming one's moustache, shaving one's armpits and pubic hair; walking to the mosque on foot; saying the *takbīr*s on the way there; breaking the fast before going out for the *'Īd al-Fiṭr*, and afterwards in the case of the *'Īd al-Aḍḥā* – such that one eats of the sacrificial animals; walking there by one route and taking another for the return; saying the *Allāhu akbar*s for the days of Minā after each of the prescribed *ṣalāh*s from *ẓuhr* of the day of slaughtering to *ṣubḥ* of the fourth day, while it has also been said up to *ẓuhr* of that day, and Ibn Ḥanbal has said from *ṣubḥ* of the day of 'Arafah to *'aṣr* of the fourth day after the *'Īd*, and Abū Ḥanīfah has said from *ṣubḥ* of the day of 'Arafah to *'aṣr* of the fourth day after the day of slaughtering.

One says the *Allāhu akbar*s in a group, according to the agreed judgment, and when alone, contrary to Abū Ḥanīfah and Ibn Ḥanbal, and one does not say them after the voluntary *ṣalāh*s, contrary to ash-Shāfi'ī; and it is said in the following manner: *Allāhu akbar Allāhu akbar Allāhu akbar* while it has also been said that one says *Allāhu akbar Allāhu akbar Allāhu akbar lā ilāha illa-llāh wa-llāhu akbar wa lillāhi-l-ḥamd*, and Allah knows best.

26. Istisqā' – the ṣalāt for rain

1. The rulings for the rain ṣalāt

It is a *sunnah*, according to the agreed judgment, the reason for it being the need for rainfall or groundwater for crops or to water animals whether one is on land or at sea. And it is repeated for as long as there is a need.

Women and children are not commanded to go, according to the well-known position (*mashhūr*), contrary to ash-Shāfiʿī.

Beasts do not go out for it. As to the going out of the Jews and the Christians there are two judgments, and on the basis that it is permitted, then there is a difference of opinion as to whether they do it on a different day or they go out with the people to one side of them.

And the time for it is after sunrise up to when the sun has passed its zenith, and its location is the *muṣallā*.

2. As for its form

It consists of two *rakʿah*s said aloud without *adhān* or *iqāmah*, in which '*Glorify...*' (Sūrah 87) is recited and the like, as in the case of the other *nāfilah ṣalāt*s; and ash-Shāfiʿī has one make the *Allāhu akbar*s in it as on the *ʿĪd*, and Abū Ḥanīfah has said that one may make *duʿā* to seek rainfall without any *ṣalāt*.

It has a *khuṭbah* delayed until after the *ṣalāt*, according to the majority, and in it the *imām* repeatedly seeks forgiveness from Allah and admonishes and advises, then he makes a *duʿā* facing the *qiblah* and the people say *amīn* and he turns his cloak about after the two *khuṭbah*s – while it has also been said between the two *khuṭbah*s – placing the left side on the right and the right to the left, while there is a difference of opinion as to whether it is turned upside down such that the top is placed at the bottom; and all the people turn their cloaks about – they being seated when the *imām* turns his about – according to the majority, but the women do not turn theirs about, nor anyone who has no cloak.

3. The duties of the rain ṣalāt

Among them are the turning to Him in *tawbah* and seeking forgiveness of Him, and putting right any wrongs done to others.

People are not commanded to fast before it, contrary to Ibn Ḥanbal and ash-Shāfiʿī.

Its *sunnahs* are to give generously, to be humble in one's clothing and other matters.

One does not say *Allāhu akbar* on the way there, according to the well-known position (*mashhūr*), and one makes *nāfilah ṣalāts* before and after it, according to the well-known position (*mashhūr*).

27. Eclipses

1. The ṣalāt for eclipses

It is a *sunnah* in the case of an eclipse of the sun, according to the consensus, and those people for whom the *jumuʿah* is an obligation are commanded to it, according to the consensus; and with regard to other than these persons there are two judgments.

The time for it is up to the time the sun passes its zenith, while it has also been said as long as the time for *ʿaṣr* has not arrived, while it has also been said as long as the sun has not begun to turn deep yellow, and it has also been said up to *maghrib*, in agreement with ash-Shāfiʿī. If the sun appears during the *ṣalāt* then there is a difference of opinion as to whether one completes it in the form of the eclipse *ṣalāt* or in the form of all the other *nāfilah ṣalāts*.

The location for it is the mosque, according to the well-known position (*mashhūr*).

As for the eclipse of the moon then people make the *ṣalāt* for it individually like all the other *nāfilah ṣalāts*, while ash-Shāfiʿī and Ibn Ḥanbal said one makes it in the group as in the case of the eclipse of the sun.

People are not commanded to make a particular *ṣalāt* for earthquakes or other natural phenomena, contrary to Ibn Ḥanbal.

2. Its form

It consists of two *rak'ah*s according to the two Imāms, each *rak'ah* consisting of two bowings, two standings and two prostrations; and in the first standing *sūrah* al-Baqarah or the like is read, and in the second a *sūrah* less than this, and in the third less than this, and in the fourth less than this, and one repeats the Umm al-Qur'ān for each standing, according to the well-known position (*mashhūr*), and one recites silently contrary to Ibn Ḥanbal, and one lengthens the bowing but one does not recite during it, and as for lengthening the prostration there are two judgments; while Abū Ḥanīfah has said that it is two *rak'ah*s as in the case of the other *nāfilah ṣalāt*s.

And within the madhhab there is no *khuṭbah*, but rather the *imām* admonishes and advises the people, and commands them to make *du'ā* and give *ṣadaqah*, while ash-Shāfi'ī has said that he makes two *khuṭbah*s after it.

Secondary matter

If the person who comes late catches the second bowing, then he has caught the *rak'ah*.

28. The witr

1. Its ruling

It is a *sunnah*, while Abū Ḥanīfah has made it an obligation.

The time for it is after the *'ishā' ṣalāt*, when done in its normal time – excluding thereby a night when there is a joining of *maghrib* and *'ishā'* [at the time of the former] – up to the break of dawn, and if the dawn breaks, then one makes the *witr* afterwards, contrary to Abū Ḥanīfah. If one remembers the *witr* during the *ṣubḥ ṣalāt*, then there are two judgments as to whether one carries on or interrupts.

And there is no *witr* after the *ṣubḥ ṣalāt.* And the best *witr* is that done at the end of the night for the person who has the strength for this; and whoever makes the *witr* at the beginning of the night and later makes *nāfilah ṣalāt*s, then he does not repeat the *witr,* according to the majority, contrary to those who say that one repeats it and those who say one makes it an even number by making a single *rak'ah* [and then does the *witr* again after the *nāfilah ṣalāt*s].

2. Its form

It consists of one *rak'ah*, preceded by the *shaf'* – i.e. the couple of *rak'ah*s – and one separates [the *shaf'* from the *witr*] by saying the *salām*, whereas ash-Shāfi'ī said that the *shaf'* is not stipulated, while Abū Ḥanīfah said that the *witr* is three *rak'ah*s with no *salām* between them; and on the basis of the madhhab there is a difference of opinion as to whether making the *shaf'* beforehand is a condition of validity or of perfection; and whether it is permitted or not for time to elapse between it and *witr,* and whether [the *shaf'*] is characterised by a particular intention or any *nāfilah ṣalāt* suffices for it

It is recommended to recite in it 'The Most High' and 'The Rejecters' or the *sūrah Ikhlāṣ* 'Sincerity' in the two *rak'ah*s, and in the *witr* the *Ikhlāṣ* 'Sincerity' with the two *sūrah*s of seeking refuge and Allah knows best.

29. The remaining voluntary ṣalāts

This consists of two sections

1. The two rak'ahs of fajr

The time for it is after the break of dawn, and if one does it before this or does one *rak'ah* of it before it, then one must repeat it.

One recites silently in it Umm al-Qur'ān alone, while it has also been said in the first 'The Rejecters' and in the second 'Sincerity', in agreement with ash-Shāfi'ī.

Whoever comes to the mosque and has already made the *fajr* at home, then there is a difference of opinion as to whether or not he does the two *rak'ahs* of greeting the mosque; and if he has not done the *fajr* at home, then he does it in the mosque but does not do the *ṣalāt* of greeting; if he finds people making the *ṣubḥ ṣalāt* he does not make the *fajr* in the mosque nor in the courtyard adjoining it.

Lying down after the two *rak'ahs* of *fajr* is not sanctioned, contrary to the Ẓāhirīs.

2. The rest of the nāfilah ṣalāts

The *qiyām al-layl* – 'the standing in the night' – is desirable, and the most excellent is at the end of the night, and there is a difference of opinion as to whether the best is to make a large number of *rak'ahs* or to prolong the standing.

Its desirability in the nights of Ramadan is stressed more, and it is recommended to stand in it for thirty-six *rak'ahs* apart from the *shaf'* and the *witr*, while twenty has also been said, in agreement with the two.

Nāfilah ṣalāts in people's houses are better; and one does not gather for them in *jamā'ah* outside of Ramadan, unless the places are private and the gathering small.

And *nāfilah ṣalāts* by day or night each have two *rak'ahs*, and one makes the *salām* after each pair of *rak'ahs*, contrary to those who say after four or six.

And whoever misses a *nāfilah* then he does not make it up, according to the madhhab, unless one has missed the two *rak'ahs* of *fajr* in which case he makes them after sunrise in agreement with the two.

30. The prostrations of the Qur'ān

This contains two sections

1. Its rulings

It is not obligatory, contrary to Abū Ḥanīfah. The reciter and anyone who listens to it are instructed to do it, but not the person who just hears it without paying attention. One says the *Allāhu akbar* when bending down for it and rising from it. It is subject to the conditions of the *ṣalāt,* but there is no*takbīratu-l-iḥrām* or final *salām* for it, according to the four. It is permitted in the *nāfilah ṣalāt*s, according to the agreed judgment, and in the *farḍ* ones, as long as it does not confuse people. One says *subhāna-llāh* in the prostration and makes *du'ā,* and it has been narrated in the *ḥadīth*:

اَللَّهُمَّ اكْتُبْ لِي بِهَا عِنْدَكَ أَجْراً، وَضَعْ عَنِّي بِهَا وِزْراً، وَاجْعَلْهَا لِي
عِنْدَكَ ذُخْراً، وَتَقَبَّلْهَا مِنِّي كَمَا قَبِلْتَهَا مِنْ عَبْدِكَ دَاوُدَ.

Allāhumma ktub lī 'inidaka ajran, wa ḍa' 'annī bihā wizran, wa j'alhā lī 'indaka dhukhran, wa taqabbalhā minnī kamā qabiltahā min 'abdika Dāwūd.

'O Allah, record a reward for me by it and take a burden off me and store it up for me with You and accept it of me just as You accepted it from your slave Dāwūd'

2. The number of places of prostration in the Qur'ān

There are eleven according to the well-known position (*mashhūr*): in al-A'rāf – the Ramparts, ar-Ra'd – Thunder, an-Naḥl – the Bee, al-Isrā' – the Night Journey, Maryam – Mary, at the beginning of al-Ḥajj – the Pilgrimage, al-Furqān – Discrimination, an-Naml – the Ant, Alif Lām Mīm as-Sajdah – Prostration, in Ṣād, and Fuṣṣilat – Made Plain.

Ten are according to the consensus, ash-Shāfi'ī omitting the one in Ṣād, and he, Ibn Ḥanbal and Ibn Wahb adding those at the end of al-Ḥijr, an-Najm – the Star, al-Inshiqāq – the Bursting and Iqra' – Recite (Blood-clots).

The places of the prostrations in the *āyat*s are well-known, except there is a difference of opinion regarding the one in Ṣād as to whether it is at His words '*and repented*' [*āyah* 23] or '*and a good homecoming*' [*āyah* 24]; and there is a difference of opinion in Fuṣṣilat – Made Plain as to whether it is at His words '*if you worship Him*' [*āyah* 36] or '*and never grow tired*' [*āyah* 37], and in al-Inshiqāq – the Bursting whether it is at His words '*they do not prostrate*' [*āyah* 21] or at the end of the *sūrah*.

3 – The Ṣalāt over the dead

Consisting of an introduction and five chapters

Introduction

The person who is dying is urged to say *lā ilāha illa-llāh* – there is no god, only Allah; and one asks for good for him by making *du'ā*; and he should have a good opinion of Allah so that his hope dominates; there are two judgments as to whether one recites Yāsīn or something else, the one being that it is recommended and the other that it is *makrūh*; and likewise in turning him to the *qiblah*. When he passes away, one closes his eyelids and he has four rights: that he be given a *ghusl*, be covered in a shroud, that one makes the *ṣalāt* over him and that one buries him. There are five chapters in this part.

1. The ghusl

This is a *farḍ kifāyah*, although it has been said that it is a *sunnah*.

There follows an examination of the form of the *ghusl* and the person who performs it, consisting of two sections:

1. The form of the ghusl

It is as the *ghusl* made in the case of *janābah* – ritual impurity – and he is undressed, contrary to ash-Shāfi'ī, although his *'awrah* – private parts are covered; and *wuḍū'* is performed on him, contrary to Abū Ḥanīfah.

What is required is that the whole of his body is washed, while it is recommended to do more an odd number of times; and that one applies camphor during the last washing or some other perfume; and one gently applies light pressure to his belly if this is necessary, but one does not cut his hair or his nails, contrary to ash-Shāfi'ī.

2. The person who makes the ghusl

A man washes a man and a woman a woman, according to the agreed judgment; if this is not possible then a man makes *tayammum* on a non-*maḥram* woman up to her wrists, and a woman does *tayammum* on a man up to his elbows.

A man makes the *ghusl* for women who are *maḥram* for him while keeping them covered with a cloth, while it has also been said that he makes *tayammum* for them; and likewise a woman makes the *ghusl* for those men who are *maḥram* for her,; while it is said that the clothing is removed and the *'awrah* is covered. A man and wife make *ghusl* of each other if the bond of marriage remained intact up to death, while Abū Ḥanīfah has said that a man does not make the *ghusl* of his wife. As for those who are divorced finally, then they are like un-related non-*maḥram* persons; whereas in the case of a wife of a revocable divorce there are two judgments. And women make the *ghusl* for a boy of six or seven years, and there is a difference of opinion as to a man washing a girl.

Secondary matter

There is a difference of opinion as to the *najāsah* (ritual impurity) of a human being if he dies, and on this basis there is a difference of opinion as to the ritual impurity of his *ghusl* water and bringing it into a mosque, the most correct judgment being that it is not *najas*.

2. Shrouding

Consisting of two sections

1. The cost of the shroud

It is taken from the money of the dead person, and if he has none then from the *Bayt al-Māl* of the Muslims; and if there is none in it then it is the responsibility of the Muslims. The master is responsible for shrouding his slave; and there is a difference of opinion as whether the father is under an obligation to shroud his son or the son his parents. With regard to the wife, there are three judgments: the cost is taken from her money; from her husband's money; and from her money if she is of means, and from her husband's if she is not.

2. Its form

The person is shrouded with cloth that is permitted; as for silk there are three judgments: permitted, prohibited and permitted particularly with respect to women.

It is recommended to use white for it and an odd number of cloths, the minimum being one and the maximum seven, while one group has said that it is not to be less than three.

One fixes cotton to the orifices, the eyes, nostrils and the ears; and one places balm of camphor or musk or other than these on the places of prostration and in the folds of the body [in particular between the thighs and in the armpits etc.] and in his shrouds; and one treats the person who is in the state of *iḥrām* just as one does the person who is out of this state, while ash-Shāfi'ī has said that one does not cover the dead person's head or apply any perfume.

Secondary matter

If a pregnant woman dies and the foetus moves in her womb, then there is a difference of opinion as to whether or not one cuts her belly open and takes it out.

3. Ṣalāt over the dead person

Consisting of three sections

1. Regarding the person over whom the ṣalāt is made

Such a person has five characteristics

1. That he was clearly living beforehand, for one does make the *ṣalāt* over the new-born baby or miscarried foetus, unless it manifests it is living by suckling, moving or starts crying, contrary to Abū Ḥanīfah.

2. That the person be a Muslim, for one never makes the *ṣalāt* over a *kāfir*. And the *dhimmī*, i.e. the people of the book living under the protection of the Muslims, are buried and there is no harm in the Muslim burying his relatives who are *kāfir*.

As for the children of the *mushrikūn*, if they are with their parents and have not been taken prisoner and none of them have become Muslim, then one does not make the *ṣalāt* over them, according to the consensus; if the father has become Muslim, then the child is accorded the status of a Muslim, contrary to the mother according to the well-known position (*mashhūr*); and if they were captives who were bought by a Muslim, then they are not deemed to be Muslims until the sign of Islam is manifest in them, according to the well-known position (*mashhūr*).

3. That the body or most of it exists; one does not make it over a body-part, contrary to ash-Shāfi'ī.

4. That the person is not a *shahīd* (martyr), for if he dies in the battlefield while making *jihād*, then no *ghusl* is made on the *shahīd* nor is he shrouded and no *ṣalāt* is made over him, but he is buried with

the clothes he has on him, and his weapon is taken from him, but Abū Ḥanīfah said that he is not given the *ghusl,* but the *ṣalāt* is made over him

If he was killed unjustly outside the battle, or he was taken away from the battlefield while still alive and his vital organs had not been pierced, but then he dies, he is given a *ghusl* and the *ṣalāt* is made over him, according to the well-known position (*mashhūr*), in agreement with ash-Shāfi'ī.

Whoever is killed in the battlefield during fighting between Muslims is given a *ghusl* and the *ṣalāt* is made over him. If the *shahīd* is in a state of *janābah,* there is a difference of judgment as to whether the *ghusl* is made.

5. That the body of the dead person be physically present, for one does not make the *ṣalāt* over someone who is absent, according to the majority.

And any person over whom the *ṣalāt* is not made is not given a *ghusl* either.

2. The persons who lead the ṣalāt

Priority is given to the person who was stipulated in the testament of the deceased, then the governor, then the male relatives according to their degree of proximity if needed as guardians for marriage, while ash-Shāfi'ī said that a relation takes precedence over the governor. And the *imām* (the leader of the community) does not make the *ṣalāt* over someone who has been put to death for a *ḥadd* punishment or in retribution (for murder), but makes it for any others.

Persons of excellence ought to stay away from *ṣalāt* done over an innovator or someone who has clearly committed major wrong actions – in order to deter their like.

3. The nature of the ṣalāt

There are four essential elements: the intention; four *takbīr*s – with no more or less than four, while one group have said three, another five, and yet another six; *du'ā;* and the final *salām*; while ash-Shāfi'ī, Ibn Ḥanbal and Ashhab have added the recitation of the Fātiḥah after the first *takbīr*s. One raises one's hands only for the first *takbīr,* according to the well-known position (*mashhūr*), and for the others, according to Ibn Wahb

The most complete form of *du'ā* is to begin with *al-ḥamdu lillāh*, then the sending of blessings on the Messenger of Allah ﷺ, then one makes a *du'ā* for the dead person. This does not have a specific wording, but one of the best is that mentioned by Ibn Abī Zayd al-Qayrawānī in the *Risālah.*

Secondary matter

If a person who comes late catches the *imām* while doing a *takbīr,* then he joins him, according to the agreed judgment, while there are two narrations regarding his joining him other than during the *takbīr*s: it is said that he joins him and makes the *takbīr*s, in agreement with ash-Shāfi'ī, and it is said that he remains standing until the *imām* makes a *takbīr*, then says it with him in agreement with Abū Ḥanīfah. Then when the *imām* makes the *salām*, he makes up for what he has missed of the *takbīr*s by making *du'ā* – if the deceased is still present; but if the body has already been removed, then he says *takbīr*s in an orderly and unbroken manner [i.e. without *du'ā*s].

Four secondary matters

1. The conditions stipulated for the *janāzah ṣalāt* are those stipulated for the *ṣalāt*;

2. The *ṣalāt* is not made over the deceased in the mosque, unless the street is narrow, contrary to ash-Shāfi'ī;

3. The *ṣalāt* is not made over someone who has been buried, if the *ṣalāt* has already been made over him, contrary to ash-Shāfi'ī; if the *ṣalāt* has not been made over him, then the body is taken out, and the *ṣalāt* performed over him as long as the time has not elapsed; if it has, then one makes the *ṣalāt* over the grave, contrary to Ṣaḥnūn. 'The time having elapsed' is deemed to be when the burial has been completed, while it has also been said that it is when one fears that the body has begun to decompose.

4. The *imām* stands at the middle of a man and at the shoulders of a woman, while it has also been said at the middle of her person.

5. If there are several *janāzah*s, then it is permitted for each to have a separate *ṣalāt* or for the *ṣalāt* to be made over them all in one *ṣalāt* – in which case one presents first to the *imām* whoever was the most excellent of them, and then one gives precedence to men before women, the free before slaves, and one gives precedence to adults of any kind over those of a young age, and one gives precedence to those who have a particular distinction in the *dīn* – and if equal, then one give precedence by age, and if equal, then one takes lots to decide precedence, or the choice is made to the satisfaction of the parties present.

4. THE CARRYING OF THE CORPSE AND ITS BURIAL

COMPRISING TWO SECTIONS

1. THE CARRYING OF THE CORPSE

There is no particular order or arrangement for it, according to the well-known position (*mashhūr*), while it is said that it is recommended to carry it at the four corners. Those on foot walk in front of the *janāzah* and those mounted go behind, according to the well-known position (*mashhūr*), while it has also been said that all follow behind in all circumstances, in agreement with Abū Ḥanīfah. Women follow last in all circumstances, and those women whom one fears shall cause a disturbance are prevented from coming out for it, while it is *makrūh* for other women unless they are very close relations.

One does not stand for the *janāzah,* according to the majority, as this has been abrogated.

There is no harm in transporting the corpse from one place to another, as long as it has not been buried.

2. The burial

There is no harm in putting the corpse into its grave from any direction, although the *qiblah* is preferred.

The men place the corpse in its grave, and there is no prescribed odd or even number of them in this. If it is a woman, then this is done by her husband from underneath her, while her *maḥram* relatives undertake it from above; if there are none, then it is done by the right acting *mūminūn,* but if there is a woman who can undertake that, then this is preferable to non-relatives.

The corpse is placed on its right side facing the *qiblah,* and his right arm is extended along his body, and the knot of the shrouds is undone at his head and feet, and one adjusts his head and feet until he is resting level.

It is recommended to make *du'ā* at this point, and it is recommended for all who are near to throw handfuls of earth, while it has also been said that it is not recommended. And a woman is covered with a cloth until she is covered in earth.

Whoever is buried without a *ghusl* or in a manner which is not that of a normal burial – and has begun to decompose – then he is not taken out; and if he has not begun to decompose, then there are two judgments.

Whoever dies at sea is given a *ghusl*, shrouded and the *ṣalāt* is made over the person, and one waits until one reaches land if this is to be expected within a day or so, in order to bury the corpse there. If land is far off, or one fears lest the corpse will decompose, one ties up the shrouds firmly, and throws it in the sea facing the *qiblah*, while turning him on his right side. There is a difference of opinion as to whether one weighs him down with stones or not, and Allah knows best.

5. THE FORM OF THE GRAVES

CONSISTING OF TWO SECTIONS

1. THE FORM OF GRAVES

The excavated space with a niche for the corpse in the lateral wall being better than the furrow or trench kind [in the bottom of the grave] if this is possible, and that it be facing the *qiblah*. And it is recommended that the grave not be deep.

It is *makrūh* to make a construction of the grave and plaster it, contrary to Abū Ḥanīfah. If this is done out of ostentation then it is *ḥarām*, but if the intention is to make it distinct, then there are two judgments.

The grave is not to be raised more than the height of a handspan. There is a difference of opinion as whether it is permissible to form it into a mound.

One does not bury two corpses in one grave unless necessary. Then they are arranged in order of excellence in the excavated space, the most excellent being to the fore.

The best thing to close up the vault with is unbaked brick, then something flat of slate, metal or wood, then tile or plaster, then fired brick, then stone, then cane – all of this being better than moulding earth and moulding earth is better than a coffin.

When the corpse has been buried, then the location is *ḥabs* (*waqf*), i.e. inviolable, inalienable.

And there are two judgments about burying miscarried foetuses in houses.

2. Respect for graves

Graves are to be respected – one does not dig up the bones of the dead when digging graves, or remove them from their location, and one takes care not to break their bones, one does not walk on what is manifestly a grave, nor does one squat on it to urinate or to defecate, according to the madhhab, contrary to those who forbid sitting on them in all circumstances.

Conclusion

Wailing is forbidden, as is slapping one's cheeks, or a woman tearing the front of her garment, as opposed to weeping out of mercy.

It is recommended to express one's condolences and make *du'ā* for the dead person and for the people who are bereaved, and to exhort them to be patient; and to prepare food for the family of the dead person.

And the dead person will not be punished for the weeping of his family unless he has instructed this to be done.

4 – Zakāt

Zakāt is a *farḍ* obligation and one of the foundations of Islam. Whoever denies its obligation is a *kāfir*, and whoever prevents it from being taken from him then it is taken by force and if he still refuses then he is fought until he pays it. This book contains ten chapters.

1. Conditions for the obligation of zakāt

There are two types of *zakāt*, the *zakāt* of wealth and the *zakāt* based on persons, this being the *zakāt al-fiṭr*, which shall be explained later.

As for the *zakāt* of wealth, there are six conditions for its obligation.

1. Islam

There is no *zakāt* on the *kāfir*, as he is not amongst the people of purity – except in two cases

1. When a tenth is taken from the traders of the *dhimmī*s and those at war, i.e. non-Muslims not under truce or safe-conduct, if they conduct trade to one of the territories of the Muslims other than their own territory, even if this is repeated several times during the year, irrespective of whether what they possess reaches the *niṣāb*, i.e. the minimum amount on which *zakāt* is to be paid, or not, while Abū Ḥanīfah stipulates the *niṣāb*, and he has said that half of a tenth is to be taken specifically from *dhimmī*s, and a tenth from the enemy,

whereas Mālik has said a half of a tenth is only taken from them, from the wheat and oil in particular that they carry to Makkah and Madīnah and their outlying villages, while ash-Shāfi'ī has said that nothing is taken from them.

2. That ash-Shāfi'ī and Abū Ḥanīfah have said that twice the amount of *zakāt* is to be paid by the Christians of Banī Taghlab in particular, while there is no recorded text from Mālik in this regard.

2. Freedom

In the madhhab it is not obligatory on the slave or on the slave who still has payments to make before he is freed, nor on his master, in agreement with Ibn Ḥanbal, while ash-Shāfi'ī and Abū Ḥanīfah have said that the *zakāt* on the wealth of a slave is the responsibility of the master, and the Ẓāhirīs have said that the slave is responsible for payment on his wealth.

As for being of age or of sane mind, these are not stipulated; rather the guardian pays it from the wealth of the mad person and the child, in agreement with ash-Shāfi'ī and Ibn Ḥanbal, while Abū Ḥanīfah says that a tenth on agricultural products is paid, but no other, while some people have annulled it in all cases.

3. That the wealth be such that zakāt is obligatory on it

This is of three kinds: *'ayn* (gold and silver), agricultural produce and livestock, and whatever may be subsumed under these on the basis of its worth as in the case of trade. So it is not obligatory on jewels, personal property or real estate, nor on horses or slaves, nor on honey or milk, nor on other than these, except if they are for trade. Abū Ḥanīfah has however made it obligatory on horses for breeding that pasture at liberty, while the Ẓāhirīs have made it obligatory on honey.

4. Nisāb

That the wealth have attained the *nisāb* or its worth has attained it

5. Ḥawl (the passage of a year)

The period of a lunar year of possession should have elapsed on the gold and silver, the agricultural produce should be ripe, and the the tax collector should have arrived, together with the elapsing of the lunar year in the case of livestock.

6. The absence of debt

This is stipulated in particular in the case of gold and silver; but if the person has property that would cover the debt, then the *zakāt* is not cancelled for him, although it has also been said that it is cancelled; while Ibn al-Qāsim has distinguished between a debt – when there are personal belongings – which cancels the *zakāt* and other kinds of debt; and Abū Ḥanīfah has said that debt annuls *zakāt* other than the *zakāt* of agricultural produce; while one group has said it annuls it in all cases while still another has said the opposite of this.

2. The characteristics of zakāt

There are three conditions for the fulfilment of the characteristics of the *zakāt*:

1. Intention

There is a difference of opinion within the madhhab based on the question as to whether it discharges the obligation in the case of the person who is coerced into paying it; and the correct judgment is that it does – just as it does in the case of children or mad persons.

2. Its payment after it becomes obligatory by the elapsing of a lunar year over it, or the ripening of the crops or the arrival of the tax collector

If it is paid before its proper time, then it does not discharge the obligation, contrary to them, although it has also been said that it does if it is paid just slightly before the time – there being a difference of opinion as to the amount of time, be it a day, two days up to a month. And delaying payment when in a position to do so entails liability and denotes disobedience.

3. Payment to those who are entitled to receive it

There are three prohibitions in its regard

1. That one invalidates it by reproach or expectation of gratitude;
2. That a man buys back his *zakāt*;
3. That the person paying the *zakāt* brings together the people to the location of the *zakāt* – rather he pays them the *zakāt* where they are located.

The courtesies of it are six in number

1. That he pay it in an agreeable and friendly manner;
2. That it of the highest quality of what he has acquired;
3. And of the choicest part;
3. That he conceal it from the eyes of people, although it has also been said that to manifest it – in the case of the *farḍ* obligations – is more excellent;
4. That he appoint someone to take responsibility for it lest he be praised;
5. That the person receiving it makes a *du'ā* for the person paying it – and the Ẓāhirīs have deemed this obligatory, and Allah knows what is correct.

3. Zakāt on gold and silver

This refers to gold and silver irrespective of whether minted, made into ornaments or lumps of smelted gold or silver. There are seven matters in this regard

1. The nisāb

The *nisāb* of gold is twenty dinars of legal standard – that is each dinar is seventy two grains of barley of average size, this being about seventeen dinars of the currency in our time.

The *nisāb* of silver is two hundred dirhams of legal standard, which is five legal *ūqiyah*s, the weight of each dirham being fifty-five grains of barley of average size, this being one hundred and forty *mithqāl*s of the *mithqāl* weight in our time here in Andalusia and the Maghrib, corresponding to that dirham – ten of which make up a dinar, and for every seven dinars an *ūqiyah* of the *ūqiyah*s in use in our times.

The different kinds of gold and silver are placed together, and gold and silver are placed together, contrary to ash-Shāfiʿī and Ibn Ḥanbal. And they are placed together item by item not on the basis of worth and so the *nisāb* is attained in full by them both: thus whoever has a half of the *nisāb* of gold and a half of silver is obliged to pay the *zakāt*; and so if he has less than the *nisāb* of gold – although its worth be that of the *nisāb* of silver – he does not have to pay anything.

2. If the dinars and dirhams are deficient

If the deficient dinars and dirhams circulate numerically in exchange for [those of correct] weight, then *zakāt* is paid on them, contrary to the two; and Ṣaḥnūn has said that it is obligatory if the deficiency is slight, but if they do not circulate numerically in exchange [for those of correct] weight then no *zakāt* is payable, according to the agreed judgment, until the weight [of precious metal in the coins] attains five *ūqiyahs* [in the case of silver].

3. If the dirhams and the dinars are adulterated

If it is with copper or some other metal then it is deducted, and *zakāt* is only payable on the gold or silver content.

4. The amount payable

This is a quarter of a tenth, i.e. two and a half percent, so that on twenty dinars half a dinar and on two hundred dirhams five dirhams are payable, and any amount more than this is calculated in this way proportionately, even if this further amount is slight, contrary to Abū Ḥanīfah, who has said that nothing is payable on the extra amount until it amounts to forty dirhams.

Gold is payable on gold and silver on silver. And if one wants to pay in gold for the *zakāt* of silver or in silver for the *zakāt* on gold, then this is permitted in both cases, contrary to ash-Shāfiʿī with respect to both and to Ṣaḥnūn with respect to paying gold for the *zakāt* of silver; and on the basis of this permission, then one pays in accordance with the [market] worth it attains, according to the well-known position (*mashhūr*), while it has also been said in accordance with [market] worth as long as it is not less than ten dirhams per dinar; while it has also been said that it should be done on the basis of ten dirhams of legal standard for one dinar of legal standard.

5. Those who come into possession of wealth

If it is from a gift, bequest, sale or some other transaction, then *zakāt* does not become obligatory until one lunar year has elapsed on it; but if there is profit on money [which has been invested in trade, for example] then *zakāt* is paid on it after the year has elapsed on the original capital, irrespective of whether the capital amounted to the *nisāb* or less than it – as long as the *nisāb* is reached when the profit is reckoned with it – for the profit on money is added to the original amount of money.

If he comes into possession of two items of wealth, then if each attains the *nisāb* or more, then *zakāt* is paid after the year has elapsed on them; if the *nisāb* is completed by adding one to the other, *zakāt* is paid on the two together on the elapse of the year of the second; and if the first attains the *nisāb* alone, then *zakāt* is paid with the elapse of its year and one waits with respect to the second for the elapse of its year; and if the second alone attains the *nisāb,* then *zakāt* is paid on both at the elapse of the second year.

6. Zakāt paid on jewellery

Jewellery of gold and silver is divided into four categories:

1. Those used as permitted ornaments of attire, in which case no *zakāt* is paid on them, contrary to Abū Ḥanīfah;
2. Those used for trade, in which case *zakāt* is paid according to the consensus, and they are reckoned by weight without the cost of their manufacture into ornaments;
3. Those which are rented out;
4. And those stored up for future use – there being two judgments with respect to these two.

A secondary matter

If the ornament of gold or silver is inset with jewels that may be removed without damaging it, then the *zakāt* of articles of property is paid on the jewels while the *zakāt* of gold and silver is paid on the gold and silver; if they cannot be removed except by damaging the ornament, then each is assigned its worth, while it has also been said that the ruling is based on the material which dominates.

7. Which jewellery is permitted.

For women they are permitted in all cases;

As for men, it is permitted to ornament swords with silver, according to the agreed judgment, where there are two judgments regarding their ornamentation with gold. And there are also two judgments as to whether other instruments of war are to be included under the ruling governing swords. It is permitted to ornament a copy of the Qur'ān with gold and silver, and to have rings of silver in particular. However anything not permitted with respect to the use of gold or silver in ornaments or vessels is subject to *zakāt*.

4. Buried treasure and mined material

There is a difference of opinion as to the ruling regarding treasure, the difference being based on the land in which it is found, it being classified in four ways:

1. If it is found in the desert and its burial dates from the time of the *jahiliyyah,* then it belongs to the person who finds it, and *khums*, the 'fifth' tax, is paid on it if it is of gold or silver; if it does not consist of either, then there is nothing to pay, while it has also been said that the fifth is payable;

2. If it is found on owned land then it is said that it belongs to the person who finds it, while it has also been said that it belongs to the owner of the land;

3. If it is found on land which has been conquered by force, then it is said that it belongs to the person who finds it, while it is also said that it belongs to those who conquered it;

4. If found in land that has been acquired by reconciliation or

settlement with someone, then it is said that it belongs to the person who found it, while it has also been said that it belongs to those who negotiated the reconciliation or settlement. All the above applies if it does not pertain to the Muslims, for if it does then its ruling is the same as lost property.

As for mined material, this applies to the gold or silver extracted from the ground through physical work and purification, and this consists of two matters:

1. Ownership is divided into three sections:

First, that the land is not owned, in which case it belongs to the *imām*, i.e. the leader; and if situated in land which is owned by a particular person then it belongs to the owner, while it is also said that it belongs to the *imām*; if located in land which does not belong to a specific person, like land conquered by force or acquired by conciliation and settlement then it has been said that it belongs to those who conquered it while it has also been said that it belongs to the *imām*.

2. What is obligatory to pay is the *zakāt*, that is a quarter of a tenth if the *nisāb* is attained; if below the *nisāb* then there is nothing to pay unless anything is extracted after this which would make up the *nisāb*, then *zakāt* is paid on anything extracted after this be it a small or large amount, for as long as is obtained; if interrupted and another source of extraction is obtained, then this is not lumped together with the first and the second is subject to its own particular ruling.

The year does not have to elapse for the payment of *zakāt* on mineral wealth, rather *zakāt* is paid immediately as in the case of crops, contrary to ash-Shāfiʿī, while Abū Ḥanīfah has said that the fifth tax is paid on mineral wealth and it is deemed to be the same as treasure according to him, irrespective of whether it is gold, silver or some other mineral wealth.

5. Trade

ARTICLES OF PROPERTY ARE DIVIDED INTO FOUR SECTIONS

1. Personal acquisitions in domestic use on which no *zakāt* is payable according to the consensus;

2. Property used for trade on which there is *zakāt*, contrary to the Ẓāhirīs;

3. Personal acquisitions in domestic use and for trade on which there is no *zakāt* contrary to Ashhab;

4. And personal acquisitions in domestic use used for renting out – regarding which there are two judgments as to whether *zakāt* is applicable in the case of their sale.

Transfer of something from the category of personal acquisitions to that of trade does not occur merely by means of intention, but rather by action, contrary to Abū Thawr, while transfer from the category of trade to that of personal acquisitions occurs by intention, in which case *zakāt* is annulled contrary to Ashhab.

Trade is of three kinds, that conducted as 'managing', that based on 'storage' and that based on a *qirād* loan.

As for the 'manager (*mudīr*)', this refers to someone who buys and sells but does not wait [until a later date or season when his goods might have increased in price] and he is not regulated by the lunar year like the traders in the market – such that he determines for himself a month in the year in which he examines how much gold and silver he has and assesses the worth of the goods he has and adds this to the gold and silver and pays the *zakāt* of the whole of this if it reaches the *nisāb,* after having deducted any debt if he has any.

Those other than 'managers', i.e. those who buy goods and wait for them to increase in price, then there is no *zakāt* payable by them until they sell these goods – such that if they sell them after the lunar year has elapsed or several lunar years have elapsed then they pay *zakāt* of their worth for one single year, while ash-Shāfi'ī and Abū Ḥanīfah have said that they pay each year, even if they do not sell anything, and that they have the option according to them both of paying the *zakāt* in kind from the goods or the value of the goods.

SECONDARY MATTER

Whoever sells goods for goods and receives no gold or silver cash in the transaction does not have to pay *zakāt*, contrary to the two, unless he does this to avoid paying the *zakāt*, in which case it is not annulled in his case.

AS FOR QIRĀD

THERE ARE THREE MATTERS

1. THE OBLIGATION OF ZAKĀT ON THE OWNER OF THE CAPITAL AND THE ACTIVE PARTNER WITH IT

If they both do not have to pay *zakāt* on account of their being slaves, *dhimmīs* or in debt, then neither has to pay *zakāt*; if they do have to pay it, then they both have to pay *zakāt*; and if one of them has to pay it but not the other, then the owner of the capital should take into consideration his own financial situation, according to the agreed judgment, but as for the active partner the financial situation of the owner of the capital is taken into consideration such that if he has to pay *zakāt*, then it is also obligatory on the active partner irrespective of whether it is an obligation for him or not, so they both pay *zakāt* on the capital and the total profit, although it has also been said that one takes into consideration the ruling with respect to the active partner himself.

2. There are two judgments regarding what is taken into account with respect to the nisāb

First, that it be attained by the capital together with the total profit;

Second that it be attained by the capital and its owner's portion of and so the *zakāt* is obligatory on the share of the partner even if it does not attain the *nisāb* and each pays *zakāt* on his portion, in agreement with Abū Ḥanīfah; while it is also said that the owner of the capital pays *zakāt* on the whole, in agreement with ash-Shāfi'ī.

3. The time of paying the zakāt

If the active partner is a 'manager', he pays the *zakāt* at the conclusion of one trading year based on the worth of the trade during this year;

If he is not a manager, then he pays *zakāt* one year after the conclusion of the trading agreement, unless the owner of the capital is himself a 'manager' and what he has in his possession is more than that in the possession of the active partner – so the well-known position (*mashhūr*) is that the owner of the capital assesses what is in the possession of the active partner and pays *zakāt* on it from his wealth before the conclusion of the trading agreement, while it has also been said after it;

Then there is a difference of opinion as to whether he assesses all the wealth together with its profit every year or he assesses the capital and his portion of the profit; and Abū Ḥanīfah has said he pays *zakāt* of the money of the *qirāḍ* each year and does not wait until the conclusion of the trading agreement.

6. The zakāt of debts [returned to the lender]

This consists of two matters

1. The kinds of debt

They are four in number: a debt on an acquisition of benefit, from trade, from a loan or from something usurped.

As for a debt on an acquisition of benefit, like inheritance, gift, dowry, indemnity or blood-money, wage, rent, or price of goods, then there is no *zakāt* payable until it is taken possession of and the lunar year elapses on it after taking possession.

As for the debt of trade, its ruling is the same as that of goods of trade: the 'manager (*mudīr*)' assesses their worth, and [in the case of] someone other than a 'manager' he pays *zakāt* on them for one year after taking possession of them.

As for the debt of an advance [i.e. a loan] then someone who is not a 'manager' pays *zakāt* on it for one year after taking possession of it, while there is a difference of opinion as to whether a manager assesses its worth or not.

As for the debt of usurped goods, then the well-known position (*mashhūr*) is that *zakāt* is payable for one year immediately after taking possession of them as in the case of loans, while it is also said that one waits a year from the day of taking possession as in the case of personal acquisitions, whereas Abū Ḥanīfah has said that there is no *zakāt* payable with regard to debt until taking possession of it – such that if he takes possession of it, then he pays *zakāt* on the years which have elapsed on it, while ash-Shāfi'ī said one pays *zakāt* on debt each year even if one does not take possession of it, it being on loan for a long period.

2. If one takes possession of that of one's debt which amounts to the nisāb

Then one pays the *zakāt* on it, and one pays *zakāt* on what one takes possession of after this, be it a small or large amount;

If one takes possession of less than the *nisāb* then there is no *zakāt* payable on it, contrary to Abū Ḥanīfah, unless one has cash which would make up the *nisāb*;

If one takes possession of less than the *nisāb* then later takes possession of what would make up the *nisāb*, he pays *zakāt* on the whole of the *nisāb* on the elapse of the lunar year on the taking possession of the second amount, irrespective of whether the money – gold and silver – is still in his hands or he has spent it – although there is a difference of opinion with regard to his having spent it or lost it.

And whoever has deposited money, i.e. gold and silver, then *zakāt* is payable for each lunar year.

7. Zakāt on agricultural produce

This consists of five matters

1. The produce on which zakāt is payable

What the earth produces is of three kinds:

1. Grains, in which case *zakāt* is obligatory on wheat and barley, according to the consensus, and on other grains which are staples and are stored, according to the majority.

2. Fruits (*thimār*), in which case it is obligatory on dates and raisins, according to the consensus, and olives, contrary to ash-Shāfi'ī, but it is not obligatory on fruit (*fawākih*) like apples and pomegranates, contrary to Abū Ḥanīfah, while Ibn Ḥabīb has deemed it obligatory on figs, but there is a difference of opinion regarding leguminous

beans and seeds, crops of flax and safflower.

3. Greens and vegetables, on which there is no *zakāt,* contrary to Abū Ḥanīfah.

2. The nisāb

It is taken into account regarding produce, contrary to Abū Ḥanīfah who has a judgment contrary to the consensus – for there is no *zakāt* payable on less than five *wasq*s, a *wasq* being sixty *ṣā'*s each *ṣā'* being four cupped *mudd*s, i.e. cupped double handfuls, using the *mudd* of the Prophet ﷺ; and the amount of the *nisāb* corresponds to about twelve Andalusian *qinṭār*s.

Grapes are estimated on the basis of the amount of raisins they will yield, and fresh dates on the basis of the amount of dried dates they will yield, and there is a difference of opinion as to grapes and dates which do not ripen or are not dried as raisins. And nothing else is estimated – although if a need arises for an estimate to be made, this is not done, according to the well-known position (*mashhūr*), although it has also been said that an estimate is made, while it has also been said that that a trustworthy person is appointed.

It is an obligation for the person making the estimate be a just person who is knowledgeable of the produce, and one person is enough, according to the well-known position (*mashhūr*); and if he makes a mistake in the estimation, then there is a difference of opinion as to whether one acts in accordance with the estimation or with what actually exists.

3. How much is payable

This varies according to the way in which the land is irrigated: thus what is irrigated naturally by rain, springs and rivers, then there is a tenth payable, and what is irrigated by watering it with buckets, then half of a tenth; and if both are applicable in equal proportions, then three quarters of a tenth is payable; and if there is a difference of opinion, then there are two judgments as to whether one subordinates the lesser to the greater or assesses each in proportion to its relative amount. Ibn al-Qāsim has said that what is taken into account is what crops are produced. In the case of produce which is not pressed for oil, one takes the produce itself, and in the case of produce pressed for oil, like olives, one takes the oil.

4. Which produce may be put together with which other produce in order to attain the nisāb

Wheat, barley – and spelt, i.e. dinkel wheat, are one kind, and sorghum or maize, pearl millet and rice are a kind according to the well-known position (*mashhūr*), and pulses are one kind, they being chick peas, lentils, broad beans, leguminous seeds, other kinds of beans and cow and grass peas, while there is a difference of opinion regarding the peas from vetch as to whether it belongs to the former kind or represents a kind on its own.

Each is paid in kind according to the amount produced, and one has to pay the best of the lowest quality and not vice versa; and one does not add together anything to another kind, according to them; while produce of one kind is added together, according to the agreed judgment, like different kinds of grapes, dates and wheat; if they are all of good quality or all of low quality, then one takes from them, according to the well-known position (*mashhūr*), contrary to sheep and goats, while if of varying quality, then from the middle quality.

5. The time of its obligation

In the case of fruits, when they have ripened, in the case of grain crops, when the grains have become dry on the stalk, according to the well-known position (*mashhūr*), while it is also said at the assessing, and also said at the cutting of the harvest – the difference of opinion resulting in that when the owner dies, or the produce is sold, the *zakāt* is paid after or before one of the three times.

8. Zakāt of livestock

It is only obligatory on camels, cows, sheep and goats. This chapter contains seven matters.

1. The zakāt on camels

There is nothing payable on less than five, and one sheep or goat is payable on five to nine camels, two on ten to fourteen, three on fifteen to nineteen; four on twenty to twenty four.

Then one finishes with payment in sheep and takes camels: for twenty five camels a young female camel in its second year is paid, but if not available then a young male camel in its third year; if this is not available then a female camel in its second year is payable, contrary to their judgment that one has the option. This rate remains until thirty five. At thirty six up to forty five a female camel in its third year. At forty six to sixty female camels a female camel of four years. At sixty one up to seventy five a female in its fifth year. For seventy six up to ninety, two females in their third year. From ninety one up to one hundred and twenty, two females of four years. On one hundred and twenty one up to one hundred and twenty nine, two females of four years according to Ashhab and three females of three years according to Ibn al-Qāsim, while Mālik has given the option of two females of four years and three of three years. And on one hundred and thirty, a female of foury ears and two females of three, and any number above this then on every fifty a female of four years is paid, while for every forty a female of three. The tax collector has the option on two hundred of taking four males of four years or five females of three, while it has also been said that the owner is given the option – that is when both are available or both are unavailable – and if one kind is available this is taken. The numbers of livestock between the above fixed rates are not taken into account.

Secondary matter

The sheep or goats which are taken as *zakāt* for the camels are those of at least six months in their first year or those in their second year from those most common in the region, from either sheep or goats.

2. The zakāt on cows

There is no *zakāt* on less than thirty and on thirty to thirty nine, one pays a male or female of two years, although it is also said of one year. And on forty to fifty nine a female of four years, while three years has also been said. Any more than this, then a male of two years is payable for each thirty and a female of four years for each forty.

3. The zakāt on sheep and goats

There is no *zakāt* on less than forty and on forty to one hundred and twenty, one sheep is payable. On one hundred and twenty one up to two hundred, two sheep are payable. On two hundred and one up to three hundred and ninety nine, three are payable. On four hundred, four sheep are payable. Any more than this then for every hundred, one sheep.

4. Zakāt is obligatory on livestock

And this is irrespective of whether they graze freely or are given fodder or are used as working animals. This is contrary to the two with respect to those given fodder or used as work animals. Goats are included together with sheep, and buffaloes are included with cows, and Bactrian camels are included with dromedaries. Mothers are included with their young irrespective of whether the mothers make up the *nisāb* or not. *Zakāt* is taken from the average quality not from the best or the worst and it is not taken from the young animals. If the sheep and goats are equal in number, then the tax collector has the choice in the matter; if they are not equal then he takes from the type which are most numerous.

5. The case of two persons in a co-proprietorship

This co-proprietorship of livestock has an effect on the *zakāt,* such that the two persons pay the *zakāt* of a single owner, contrary to Abū Ḥanīfah, but it is only of effect if each person has the *nisāb* if they were to be alone; if the *nisāb* is only reached by their combined amount then there is no *zakāt* payable by them, contrary to ash-Shāfi'ī; if the total does not amount to a *nisāb* then there is no *zakāt* on the amount, according to the consensus; but if one has the *nisāb* and the other less than the *nisāb,* then only the person with the *nisāb* pays *zakāt* of a single person. Co-proprietorship is deemed a co-proprietorship with effect if there is a common shepherd, stallion, bucket, pasture and housing, while it has also been said that two of these five suffice, and it has also been said that a common shepherd suffices.

For co-proprietorship to be in effect it is subject to three conditions:

1. That the livestock of each of the co-proprietors be such that they may be combined as in the case of sheep with goats.

2. That each of the co-proprietors is subject to paying *zakāt*; if one of them is a slave or a *kāfir* then the other pays the *zakāt* alone.

3. That the elapse of the lunar year occurs at the same time for the livestock of both; if the lunar year elapses on the livestock of one of them but not the other, then the latter pays his *zakāt* as an individual person.

Sometimes co-proprietorship has the effect of lowering the amount payable, as in the case of one hundred and twenty sheep or goats between three people, for they only have to pay one sheep, while if they were individuals they would have had to pay one sheep each; and sometimes it has the effect of increasing the amount payable as for example when one of two persons has one hundred sheep and the other one hundred and one, in which case they would have to pay two sheep if individuals and three as a co-proprietorship. For this reason one does not separate what is combined or combine what is separate out of fear of *zakāt,* and if anyone does do this then his action is of no effect, and what is obligatory before this action is taken from him. If the *zakāt* is taken from one of the two co-proprietors, then he has recourse to his companion for the amount of his share.

There is a difference of opinion as to whether or not *shirākah* – partnership – has an effect on the number of head of livestock to be reckoned, as in the case of co-proprietorship. And there is no effect in the case of co-proprietorship with respect to anything other than livestock, contrary to ash-Shāfiʿī who has said that it is of effect with respect to gold and silver (*'ayn*) and agricultural produce.

6. Increase in the livestock through the birth of young

It is subject to the same ruling as the person who makes profit on gold and silver, that is, they are included with the mothers of the young. As for the birth of two young animals, if the first constitutes part of the *nisāb,* then the second is also included and *zakāt* is paid on the basis of the lunar year of the first; if however, the first does not make up the *nisāb*, then the reckoning regarding the first is delayed and *zakāt* is paid for the lunar year of the second.

7. Exchange

Someone who has the *nisāb* of gold or silver who exchanges it for the *nisāb* of livestock or vice versa, or who exchanges the *nisāb* of livestock for the *nisāb* of livestock of another sort – there is a difference of opinion as to whether *zakāt* is paid on the basis of the elapse of the lunar year of the first or of the second: if one exchanges livestock for livestock of the same kind, then *zakāt* is paid for the lunar year of the first. Whoever has livestock which are dispersed in different region then they are combined.

9. Division of the zakāt

It is divided among the eight categories that Allah mentions when He says: '*Zakāt is for: the poor, the destitute, those who collect it, reconciling people's hearts, freeing slaves, those in debt, spending in the Way of Allah, and travellers*' (Sūrat at-Tawbah 9:60).

The poor (fuqarā')

They are those who do not possess enough to live on.

The destitute (masākīn)

They are in more need than the 'poor', in agreement with Abū Ḥanīfah, although the reverse has also been said, in agreement with ash-Shāfi'ī, and it has also been said that they both mean the same, while it has still further been said that the 'poor' person is the one who is known as such, and one gives *ṣadaqah* to him while the 'destitute' person is the person who is not known to be destitute.

With regard to these two categories it is stipulated that they be

Muslim and free, according to the agreed judgment, and that they are not among those who require upkeep over a long period like family dependents. There is a difference of opinion as to whether or not a condition of eligibility regarding these two categories is that they lack the capacity to earn their living and that they do not possess the *nisāb*.

A husband does not give any of his *zakāt* to his wife, while there are two judgments, one of prohibition and the other that it is *makrūh,* as to whether she may give any of hers to him. Those to whom upkeep must be given are not given any of the *zakāt*, nor to any of one's family. As to others of one's relations there are three judgments: that it is permissible, that it is *makrūh* and that it is recommended.

Those who collect it

This refers to those who exact the tax, distribute it, and who register it, even if they themselves are free of need, contrary to Abū Ḥanīfah, and a condition of their eligibility is that they be just and that they have knowledge of the *fiqh* of *zakāt.*

Reconciling people's hearts

This refers to the *kuffār* who are given of it in order to encourage them towards Islam, while it is also said that it refers to Muslims who are given of it in order to strengthen their Islam. And there is a difference of opinion as to whether the ruling in their regard still remains or whether it has been annulled because one can dispense with them.

Freeing slaves

This refers to buying a slave and setting him free, and their relationship of clientage is to the Muslims. A condition of their eligibility is that they be Muslim, according to the well-known position (*mashhūr*); and there are two judgments as to whether those with defects fulfil this condition. And prisoners are not counted as being among them because there exists no bond of clientage, but the poor among them may be given *zakāt*; while Ibn Ḥabīb has said that they are counted as being among them.

THOSE IN DEBT

This refers to those burdened by debt to people without this having resulted from any foolish, shameless or corrupt spending, in which case the person is given the amount of his debts. There is a difference of opinion as to whether the person who has debts arising from *kaffārāt*, i.e. expiations or reparations, or from unpaid *zakāt* is given of the *zakāt*, and whether a condition of eligibility is that the debtor be in need.

SPENDING IN THE WAY OF ALLAH

This refers to *jihād* and is spent on the *mujāhidūn* even if they are without need, according to the most valid judgment, and for the instruments of war; and there is a difference of opinion as to whether it may be spent for building walls and fleets of ships; but it is not spent on hajj, contrary to Ibn Ḥanbal, unless the *ḥajjī* is someone who is in need and a traveller.

TRAVELLERS

This refers to the person who finds himself in a land which is not his home, and it is a condition of eligibility that he be in need, according to the most valid judgment, and that his journey is not for some act of disobedience.

SIX SECONDARY MATTERS

1. Its distribution is according to the decision of the Imam, such that

it is permitted him to give it all to one category and to give preference to one category, contrary to ash-Shāfiʿī who has said that it is divided equally amongst the eight categories. And whoever has two of the qualities inherent in the eight categories, then he has a right to two portions contrary to ash-Shāfiʿī.

2. It is not transferred to a place other than the place it was taken from unless there is a superfluity, contrary to Abū Ḥanīfah.

3. The family of the House of the Messenger of Allah ﷺ are prohibited from accepting both the obligatory *ṣadaqah*, i.e. the *zakāt*, and the voluntary *ṣadaqah*, although it has also been said that it is permitted them in both cases, and it has further been said that the voluntary *ṣadaqah* in particular is permitted, while vice versa has also been said. And it is permitted that they be among those who collect it, contrary to a group.

They are the Banū Hāshim, according to the agreed judgment, and there is none from among them before Ghālib ibn Fihr, according to the agreed judgment, and there are two judgments regarding those between this period, and there are two judgments regarding those connected to them by clientage.

4. *Zakāt* is not to be spent on building mosques or to bury the dead.

5. If on the basis of *ijtihād* it is spent on someone who is not in need, then there is a difference of opinion as to whether it is acceptable or not.

6. If the Imam is just, then it is obligatory to pay the *zakāt* to him, and if he is not and it is not possible to avoid paying it to him, then it is valid; if it is possible to avoid paying it to him, then the person paying the *zakāt* is to pay it to those who are entitled to it, and it is recommended that he not hand it over himself lest he be influenced by the praise of those receiving it.

10. Zakāt al-fiṭr

This is a *farḍ* obligation, according to the well-known position (*mashhūr*), in agreement with ash-Shāfi'ī, while it has also been said that it is a *sunnah*, and Abū Ḥanīfah has said that it is *wājib*, i.e. an obligation but not of the order of a *farḍ* obligation according to his legal definitions. This chapter consists of four sections.

1. Those who are commanded to give it

Namely the free Muslim who has enough food for a day together with that of the *zakāt al-fiṭr*, while it is also said anyone who is not overburdened by it, while it has also been said anyone who is not himself entitled to receive it; and Abū Ḥanīfah has said anyone who possesses two hundred dirhams.

Payment is required from a man for himself and anyone else whose upkeep he is responsible for, be it a free Muslim or slave, irrespective of whether young or old, male or female, such as children, slave girls, male slaves, a wife and her servant – even if well-to-do, and the wife of his father who is himself poor and his servant, while Abū Ḥanīfah has said that the wife pays for herself.

If the small child has wealth then it is paid from his wealth, according to the three. If the child is adult and poor for some time, then his father is responsible, contrary to Abū Ḥanīfah.

Zakāt is not paid on behalf of a *kāfir* slave, contrary to Abū Ḥanīfah.

Mukātab slaves are the same as other slaves, according to the well-known position (*mashhūr*), and the slave who has partially bought his freedom is the responsibility of his master in particular not the slave himself, according to the well-known position (*mashhūr*), while it has also been said that it is the responsibility of both; and the slave who is jointly owned is the responsibility of the two owners in proportion to their relative shares, according to the well-known position (*mashhūr*).

2. What is obligatory to pay

Namely a *ṣāʿ* of wheat, barley, spelt or dinkel wheat, dates, raisins dried cheese, rice, maize or millet, and Ashhab has said from the first six in particular.

It is paid in the most common foodstuffs of the land in question, while it is also said from the foodstuff normally consumed by the person paying, as long as he is not miserly. And if the foodstuff is pulses, figs, mealy porridge, meat or buttermilk, then these are acceptable, according to the well-known position (*mashhūr*). As to flour with its 'surplus' or 'excess' [*rayʿ* – through milling for example] there are two judgments. Abū Ḥanīfah has said one pays a half a *ṣāʿ* of wheat and a *ṣāʿ* of the other foodstuffs.

3. The time of its obligation

It is the sunset of the night before the *ʿĪd al-Fiṭr,* according to the well-known position (*mashhūr*), in agreement with ash-Shāfiʿī, while it has also been said at dawn of the day of the *ʿĪd al-Fiṭr,* in agreement with Abū Ḥanīfah, and it has also been said at sunrise. Differences have arisen regarding a child born between these times, and someone who has become Muslim, someone who has died or someone who has sold a slave between these times. It is recommended to pay it before going out to the *muṣallā,* according to the agreed judgment, while it is permitted after it, and there are two opinions as to paying it one two or three days before.

4. Those who may receive it

Are those for whom it is permitted to take the *zakāt*, while it has also been said that it is the poor person who does not take any *zakāt.*

On the basis of the first, it is permitted for a person to take *zakāt* from more than one person, and this is the well-known position (*mashhūr*); while on the basis of the second, one is not given more than that mentioned above.

It is not given to the poor from amongst the *dhimmī*s, contrary to Abū Ḥanīfah

5 – Fasting and I'tikāf

This consists of ten chapters

1. Regarding the conditions for fasting

They are six in number: islam, being of age, sane, being free of the blood of childbirth and menstruation, health and being resident.

Islam

This is a condition of its obligation, there being a difference of opinion as to whether the *kuffār* are addressed regarding the behavioural, outward elements of the *dīn*. It is a condition for the validity of its performance, according to the consensus, and also for the obligation of making it up if missed. If someone becomes Muslim during the month of fasting, then he fasts the rest of it but he does not have to make up what he has missed of it; and if he becomes Muslim during the day, then he desists from eating for the rest of the day, and it is recommended that he makes it up.

Being of age

This is a condition for its obligation and the obligation of making up the fast but not with respect to the validity of its performance, for it is permitted for the person who has not yet reached puberty to fast; and there is a difference of opinion as to whether it is recommended for him or not; and ash-Shāfi'ī has deemed it obligatory for him if he is able.

Being sane

It is a condition for its obligation, for the person who has left his senses is not required to fast for the period he loses his senses.

As for the mad person, his fasting is invalid and he must make up any missed fasting in all circumstances, according to the well-known position (*mashhūr*), while it has also been said that he does not have to make it up if many years elapse; and it has also been said that if he reaches puberty and is mad, then he does not have to make up fasting contrary to the person who reaches puberty and is of sound state of mind and then becomes mad. Ash-Shāfi'ī and Abū Ḥanīfah have said that he does not have to make up in any circumstances.

As for the person who faints, then if this lasts for a day or more, or for the greater part of a day, then he makes up; if he loses consciousness for a short while after dawn, then he does not have to make up; and if he faints during the night and this state remains until dawn, then there are two judgments as to whether he makes up. And Ismā'īl al-Qāḍī has said that fasting is invalidated in all cases if one faints, while Abū Ḥanīfah has said the opposite.

The person who sleeps never has to make up, and inebriation is as fainting except that the person must desist from eating, drinking or sexual intercourse during the day in question.

As for becoming free of the blood of menstruation or childbirth

This is a condition for the validity of the fasting and for the permissibility of making the fast, but is not a condition with respect to the obligation of making up any fasting missed, and there is a difference of opinion as to whether it is a condition for it being obligatory or not, while there is consensus that the menstruating woman or one still bleeding from childbirth are prohibited from fasting and that they must make up any fasting due during these two states.

If a woman starts to menstruate during the day, then her fast is invalidated and she must make it up, and if she becomes clean of blood during the night and she makes a *ghusl* and makes the intention to fast before dawn, then this is accepted of her, according to the agreed judgment; if she delays the *ghusl* to dawn, then this is also accepted of her, according to the well-known position (*mashhūr*), while Ibn Maslamah has said that she makes it up and Ibn al-Mājishūn has said that she makes it up if time is short and is not enough to make the *ghusl*. If she becomes free of blood during the day then she may eat during the rest of the day and makes up the missed fast, and if she becomes clean but does not know whether her becoming free of blood occurred before dawn or after it, then she fasts and makes up.

As for health and being resident

These are both conditions for the obligation of the fasting not for its validity nor for the obligation of making it up. The obligation to fast is annulled for the sick person and the traveller, but both must make up any missed fasting if they break their fast, according to the consensus, and their fasting is valid if they do fast, contrary to the Ẓāhirīs.

2. The various kinds of fasting

There are six kinds: *wājib*, *sunnah*, *mustaḥabb*, *nāfilah*, *ḥarām* and *makrūh*.

The wājib

It is the obligatory fast of Ramadan as well as making up any fasting missed, fasting on the basis of a vow taken and making it up, and fasting of the *kaffārāt*.

Sunnah fasting

It is that of 'Āshūrā' on the 10th of Muḥarram, while it has also been said the 9th.

The mustaḥabb

It is that of the *ḥarām* months, Sha'bān, the first ten days of Dhu-l-Ḥijjah, the day of 'Arafah, the six days of Shawwāl, three days of each month and Mondays and Thursdays.

The Nāfilah

It is any fasting not undertaken for a specific time or reason during days other than those in which it is obligatory or prohibited. It is not permissible for a woman to fast voluntarily without the permission of her husband.

And it is ḥarām

To fast the day of the *'Īd al-fiṭr* and that of *al-Aḍḥā*; the three days of *at-Tashrīq* following it, while there is a licence for the person doing the *tamattu'* hajj to fast the days of *at-Tashrīq*, contrary to the two, and there is licence to make the fasting on the basis of a vow taken or for *kaffārāt* on the fourth day, while there is a difference of opinion regarding the two days before it; the fasting of the menstruating woman or one still bleeding from childbirth; and fasting in the case of someone who it is feared might die as a result.

And it is makrūh

To fast every day; fasting in particular on the day of *jumu'ah,* unless one fasts the day before or after; fasting on Saturday in particular; fasting the day of 'Arafah at 'Arafah; fasting the Day of Doubt, that is the last day of Sha'bān, as a precautionary measure if the crescent moon does not appear, while it has also been said if the sky is covered then the chosen position is desisting from eating, but it is permitted to fast it voluntarily, contrary to ash-Shāfi'ī.

3. The characteristics of fasting

Its *farḍ* obligations are the intention, desisting from eating, drinking, sexual intercourse, masturbation and causing oneself to vomit.

Its *sunnah*s are the *suḥūr* breakfast, breaking the fast as quickly as possible, delaying the *suḥūr* as long as possible, guarding one's tongue and limbs, and making *i'tikāf* at the end of Ramadan.

Its aspects of excellence are to fill it with acts of worship, to give much *ṣadaqah*, to break the fast on *ḥalāl* food which is in no way dubious as to its provenance or nature, to break the fast with dates or water, to stand in *ṣalāt* during the nights and in particular the Night of the Decree.

The things which invalidate it are the opposite of the *farḍ* obligations as shall be explained, the onset of menstruation or blood of childbirth, madness, fainting as mentioned above, reneging on one's Islam.

It is *makrūh* to spend consecutive days fasting without breaking the fast between them, going into a room where there is a woman and looking at her, idle talk and behaviour, rinsing out the mouth and snuffing up water into the nose in an excessive manner, taking anything moist into one's mouth that has taste even if one spits it out, chewing gum, tasting the contents of the cooking pot and excessive sleep during the day.

4. Sighting the crescent moon

It is obligatory to fast Ramadan and to break the fast on the Day of the *'Īd al-Fiṭr* – the day of fast-breaking – on the basis of sighting the crescent moon. If the sky is covered, then one completes the fast of thirty days. The sighting of the crescent has different aspects:

1. If a person sights the crescent moon of Ramadan

Then he is obliged to fast, according to the majority, and if he breaks his fast then he must make it up and pay *kaffārah* – compensation, and there are two narrations regarding the annulling of *kaffārah* when there is a *ta'wīl* – a valid legal explanation.

If he alone sights the crescent moon of Shawwāl, then he does not break the fast for fear of suspicion [falling on him of eating during Ramadan] and in order to prevent the possibility of that, in agreement with Ibn Ḥanbal and contrary to ash-Shāfi'ī, while it is also said that he breaks the fast if he can keep this hidden, while Ashhab has said that he makes the intention to break the fast in is heart. On the basis of the madhhab, if he does break the fast then nothing is written against him with respect to what is between him and Allah, exalted is He, but if he is discovered then he is punished if suspected [of breaking the fast without a valid reason].

2. If one witness bears testimony as to the sighting

Then fasting is not obligatory because of it, and breaking the fast is not obligatory because of it, whereas Abū Thawr has said that one fasts and breaks the fast on the basis of it, while ash-Shāfi'ī has said one fasts on the basis of it but does not break the fast on the basis of it.

3. If two just witnesses testify specifically in front of the Imam

Then the fasting and the fast breaking is confirmed by this dual testimony of theirs when the sky is overcast, according to the consensus, whereas if the sky is clear and the town is large it is confirmed by their dual testimony, according to the well-known position (*mashhūr*), although Ṣaḥnūn has said that it is not confirmed by them, in agreement with Abū Ḥanīfah.

4. If a large crowd sights it together in public

Then it is confirmed even if they are not *'adūl* – just persons, i.e. of probity, equity and integrity, and no testimony is needed.

5. That the Imam informs that it has been reliably sighted in his view

6. That a just person informs that the Imam has confirmed a reliable sighting or that there has been a general sighting

7. That the people of the land informed of a public sighting

Or that the reliability of a sighting has been confirmed by their Imam.

8. That two just persons declare that they have made a sighting

9. That a just person declares having sighted it in a place where there is a no Imam to act on the matter

Four secondary matters

1. If the crescent moon is obscured by clouds

Then one completes thirty days fasting, and one does not pay attention to what the astronomers say, contrary to some people.

2. If the people of one particular land sight it

Then their judgment applies to the people of other lands, in agreement with ash-Shāfi'ī and contrary to Ibn al-Mājishūn, but this is not necessary for countries which are far apart like for example Andalusia and the Hijaz, according to the consensus.

3. If the crescent moon is seen during the day

Then it is the moon of the coming night, in agreement with the two, while Ibn Wahb and Ibn Ḥabīb have said that if it is sighted before the sun goes past its zenith then it is the moon of the previous night, while if sighted at the end of the day then it is the moon of the coming night – according to the precautionary judgment.

4. If the crescent moon is anticipated but does not appear

And then the following day it is confirmed that it had indeed been sighted, then that day should have been fasted and so it has to be made up. If the crescent moon of Shawwāl is confirmed as having been sighted during the day, then one must break one's fast.

5. The Intention

There are five matters in this respect

1. The intention for all kinds of fasting is obligatory

This is according to the majority, contrary to Zufar [ibn al-Hudhayl] in Ramadan. The form of the intention is that it is specific, made during the previous night and definitive.

As for its being specific, this is obligatory and so it is not acceptable to make an intention just to fast, contrary to Abū Ḥanīfah.

As for its being made during the night, this is obligatory, and it means making the intention to fast before the break of dawn for every fast, contrary to ash-Shāfi'ī and Ibn Ḥanbal with respect to the *nāfilah* fasts; while Ibn al-Mājishūn has said with respect to the person who as yet during the morning has not eaten or drunk anything, then realizes that it is a day of Ramadan, that he continues to desist from eating and drinking and this is accepted of him, and he does not have to make it up. And it is permissible to make the intention at the beginning of the night, but is not permitted before the onset of the night.

As for resolve, this is to exclude any wavering with respect to someone who makes the intention during the Night of Doubt to fast the following day if it is Ramadan, which and is not accepted of him – because of the absence of resolve. However, there is no harm in wavering in one's intention after having been certain with regard to a testimony of sighting or *istiṣḥāb* (i.e. assuming the continuation of the situation with regard to the continued validity of the original intention made at the beginning of Ramadan) – such as at the end of Ramadan, or with regard to the independent judgment of a captive. Whoever interrupts his intention during the day, then his fasting is invalidated.

2. One intention made at the beginning of Ramadan suffices

And likewise with respect to fasting a number of days in succession, as long as the intention is not broken, or his state is such that he is permitted to break the fast in which case he must make the intention again. And ash-Shāfi'ī and Ibn Ḥanbal have said that the intention must be renewed every night.

3. If a captive in the land of the enemy is confused as to the months

Then he fasts at the time which is correct to the best of his knowledge and if he fasts later than Ramadan, then this is accepted of him and he does not have to make it up, but if he fasts before it then it is not accepted of him – irrespective of whether this is one month or several months over several years, according to the well-known position (*mashhūr*), whereas Ibn al-Mājishūn has said that he makes up just the last of these, while the Ẓāhirīs have said that it is not accepted of him irrespective of whether he fasts after or before the correct time.

6. Desisting from eating, drinking and sexual intercourse

1. Food and drink

It is obligatory to desist from both, according to the consensus, and the fast is broken, according to the consensus, by whatever reaches the stomach – with three restrictions:

1. That it is something that one can avoid such that if it is not possible, like a fly which flies into the throat or dust of the road, then this does not break the fast, according to the consensus, but if water reaches the throat when rinsing out the mouth or snuffing up water, then this breaks the fast, contrary to Ibn Ḥanbal. However, if part of a grain between the teeth reaches the stomach, this does not break the fast, while it is also said that it only breaks the fast if one intends to swallow it, contrary to Abū Ḥanīfah.

2. That it be something edible, but [nevertheless] if it is something inedible, like a pebble or dirham, then it breaks the fast, in agreement with the two, while it is also said that it does not break the fast. And there is a difference of opinion regarding the dust that flour sellers and makers of gypsum [are exposed to].

3. That it reaches the stomach through one of the larger openings, that is the mouth, the nose and ear.

As for an enema there are three judgments: that it breaks the fast, in agreement with Abū Ḥanīfah and Ibn Ḥanbal, that it does not, and that the breaking of the fast is particular to enemas made with liquids.

As for someone who puts drops into the outer opening of the urethra, then this does not break the fast, contrary to Abū Yūsuf.

As for medicine applied to a wound which reach the stomach, this does not break the fast, contrary to the two.

As for kohl – antimony – if none of it dissolves, then it does not break the fast, but if any of it does dissolve, then it does break the fast, whereas Abū Muṣ'ab has said that it does not break the fast under any circumstances, in agreement with the two, while Ibn al-Qāsim has prohibited it absolutely, in agreement with Ibn Ḥanbal.

As for the *miswāk* stick used as a toothbrush, it is permitted before or after the sun has passed its zenith as long has nothing detaches itself from it, although ash-Shāfi'ī and Ibn Ḥanbal have deemed it *makrūh* after the sun has passed its zenith, and if it is such that bits break off from it, then it is *makrūh,* and if they reach the throat then this breaks the fast.

2. Sexual intercourse and that subsumed with it

The disappearance of the glans of the penis into the vagina or anus, of a human being or animal, breaks the fast, according to the consensus, irrespective of whether there is ejaculationn or not; as a result the fast must be made up and *kaffārah* paid, according to the consensus – other than Abū Ḥanīfah who has said that *kaffārah* is not obligatory in the case of anal intercourse.

As for ejaculation which occurs by sexual contact but without penetration of the vagina or by physical contact or kissing, then the fast has to be made up and *kaffārah* paid, in agreement with Ibn Ḥanbal but contrary to the two.

As for ejaculation as a result of looks or thoughts of an arousing nature, then if this is prolonged, one has to make up the fast and the *kaffārah*, contrary to the two; while if it is not prolonged then it is just to be made up, contrary to the two also. And if semen is emitted without reason then this is of no consequence.

As for the thin white pre-seminal fluid excreted after experiencing sexual pleasure (*madh-y*), then if it is excreted as a result of physical contact, kissing or prolonged looking or thinking – or without these two latter – then the fast is also to be made up, in agreement with Ibn Ḥanbal but contrary to the two, while there is a difference of opinion as to whether this is obligatory or recommended. If looking or thinking is not prolonged then this is of no consequence.

As for an erection without the thin white pre-seminal fluid excreted after experiencing sexual pleasure (*madh-y*), if as a result of physical contact or kissing, then it has been said that it is obligatory to make up the fast, as well as that this obligation is null and void in this case, in agreement with them; and if as a result of just looking or thinking, or without these two latter, then it is of no consequence. As for kissing there is a difference of opinion within the madhhab as to whether it is *ḥarām* or *makrūh*, while the judgment that it is *makrūh*, according to them, is particular to the young, strong person, whereas Ibn Ḥanbal has permitted it in all circumstances.

Two secondary matters

1. Whoever has a wet dream during the day in Ramadan, then this does not invalidate his fast according to the consensus.

2. Whoever becomes in a state of ritual impurity during a night of

Ramadan (*junub*) then awakes fasting, his fasting is valid and he does not have to make up, according to the majority.

3. Vomiting and cupping

As for vomiting, whoever is overcome by vomiting, then it does not break one's fasting, according to the majority, but whoever vomits intentionally, then it is obligatory for him to make up but he has no *kaffārah* to pay, according to the well-known position (*mashhūr*), and according to the majority, if the vomit returns to the throat or he belches and eructs vomit on the tongue after it happens, then he must make up.

As for cupping, it does not break the fast, contrary to Ibn Ḥanbal, Isḥāq and Ibn Mundhir, and it is *makrūh* lest one expose oneself to the increased possibility of vomiting, contrary to Abū Ḥanīfah.

4. The time for refraining from food

It begins at the true, 'white' dawn, according to the majority, and it ends at sunset, according to the consensus.

Whoever doubts whether dawn has broken, then it is *ḥarām* for him to eat, whereas it has also been said that it is *makrūh,* while Ibn Ḥabīb, ash-Shāfi'ī, Abū Ḥanīfah and Ibn Ḥanbal have said that it is permitted; and if he does eat, then it is obligatory for him to make up, according to the well-known position (*mashhūr*), while it has also been said that it is recommended.

And if one has doubts as to the sunset, then one does not eat, according to the agreed judgment, and if one eats, then one has to make up and pay *kaffārah,* while it has also been said that one just has to make up.

And if it becomes clear to someone after eating, that he has broken the fast after dawn or before sunset, then he must make up, according to the majority contrary to Isḥāq.

If dawn breaks while one is having sexual intercourse and one continues, then one has to make up, while it is also said one pays *kaffārah*; and if one stops, then there is a difference of opinion between Ibn al-Mājishūn and Ibn al-Qāsim as to whether it is necessary to make up or not, the reason for this being the question as to whether or not withdrawal from intercourse counts as sexual intercourse or not.

7. The things which permit one to break the fast

They are seven in number: travel, illness, pregnancy, breastfeeding, old age, being overcome by hunger and thirst, and coercion.

As for travel

It is preferable to fast during it, although Ibn al-Mājishūn has said that it is better to break the fast, in agreement with ash-Shāfiʿī and Ibn Ḥanbal, while it has also been said that they are both equally valid; and if the travel is for a military expedition (*ghazwah*) and meeting the enemy draws near, then breaking the fast is better in order to maintain one's strength.

Breaking one's fast is permitted on four conditions:

1. That the travel is licit;

2. That the journey is a long one – in the sense mentioned above regarding breaking the fast – in the light of the judgments regarding shortening the *ṣalāt* within the madhhab, contrary to the Ẓāhirīs and others;

3. That one does not intend to stay in a place for four days during the journey;

4. That during the night prior to the journey one has the intention to fast the following day, as travel does not permit shortening the *ṣalāt* or breaking the fast except by means of the intention *and* action,

contrary to when one resides in a place – for this renders the fast and its completion obligatory without the action.

As for the traveller, either he travels before dawn and intends to break the fast, in which case this is permitted him, according to the consensus; or he travels after dawn in which case, it is not permitted for him to break the fast, according to the three, because setting out unexpectedly in travel during the day is other than the onset of illness, although Ibn Ḥanbal has permitted it.

If one breaks the fast before setting out, then there are three judgments as to the obligation of paying *kaffārah*, the distinction in the third being that one travels, in which case it is annulled, or one does not travel, in which case it is obligatory; and if one breaks one's fast after setting out, then there is no *kaffārah* to pay, according to the well-known position (*mashhūr*), contrary to Ibn Kinānah.

Secondary matter

Whoever is on a journey and enters upon the morning or wakes up in the morning with the intention of fasting, then it is not permitted for him to break the fast except with an excuse like strengthening oneself for engaging the enemy, but is permitted without excuse by Abū Muṣ'ab Muṭarrif ibn 'Abdallāh, while according to the well-known position (*mashhūr*), if he breaks his fast there are three judgments as to the obligation of *kaffārah*, where a distinction is made in the third as to whether one breaks the fast through sexual intercourse, in which case it is obligatory, or for some other reason, in which case it is not.

As for the ill person

There are various states in his respect:

1. That he is unable to fast or fears death as a result of the illness

and weakness if he were to fast, in which case the breaking of the fast is obligatory for him.

2. That he is able to fast with difficulty, in which case breaking the fast is permitted, while Ibn al-'Arabī has said that it is recommended.

3. That he is able to fast with difficulty and fears an aggravation of the illness, in which case there are two judgments as to the obligation of breaking the fast.

4. That it is not difficult for him but he fears an aggravation of the illness, in which case he does not break the fast, according to the majority contrary to Ibn Sīrīn.

FIVE SECONDARY MATTERS

1. If he wakes up in the morning ill or on a journey with the intention of fasting but then the excuse for not fasting ceases to exist, it is not permitted him to break the fast; and if he wakes up in the morning with the intention of breaking the fast and then the excuse for not fasting ceases to exist, then it is permitted him to break the fast for the rest of the day, and likewise in the case of the person who wakes up breaking the fast on the basis of a valid excuse, then the excuse for not fasting ceases to exist for the rest of the day, contrary to Abū Ḥanīfah. Thus on the basis of the madhhab, whoever arrives home and is breaking the fast and finds his wife has become free of menstrual blood, it is permitted to have sexual intercourse with her.

2. It is not valid for the sick person or the traveller to make a voluntary fast in Ramadan.

3. If the sick person or traveller fasts in Ramadan this is accepted of them, while the Ẓāhirīs have said that they both have to make up.

4. It is not stipulated that one has to make up consecutively the days

missed, according to the majority, contrary to Ḥasan al-Baṣrī and the Ẓāhirīs.

5. Whoever had to make up a fast, then dies before he can make it up, no one fasts instead of him, according to the three, while Ibn Ḥanbal has said someone may fast instead of him; and one does not provide food for anyone on this person's account, according to the madhhab, while ash-Shāfi'ī and others have said that one feeds a destitute person for every day to be made up.

Old age

1. As for the old and decrepit unable to fast, it is permitted them to break the fast, according to the consensus, and they do not have to make it up.

The pregnant woman

If she fears for herself or for the foetus, then she breaks the fast and makes up.

The breastfeeding mother

She breaks the fast if this is necessary for her child if no other wet nurse accepts it or she is unable to pay the fee to the wet nurse, and she must make up. We shall discuss below the *fidyah* compensation to be paid by such persons.

Someone who is overcome by hunger and thirst

He may break the fast and make it up; and if one fears for one's life then it is prohibited to fast, and the same applies to the pregnant woman or the breastfeeding mother if they fear for their life or their children. As for the person overcome by thirst or hunger who fasts there is a difference of opinion as to whether he desists from eating for the rest of the day or may eat.

Someone who is obliged to break the fast against his will

He must make up, contrary to ash-Shāfiʿī, and if a woman is compelled to have sexual intercourse or it is had with her while she is asleep, then she must make up.

8. The requirements attached to breaking the fast

These are seven in number: making up, the major *kaffārah*, the minor *kaffārah*, i.e. the *fidyah* compensation, desisting from food, drink and sexual intercourse, the interruption of consecutiveness, penalty, interruption of the intention.

1. Making up

Whoever deliberately breaks a *farḍ* fast must make it up, and likewise anyone who breaks it with a valid excuse such as the sick person or traveller, and anyone who breaks it out of forgetfulness must also make it up, contrary to the two.

There are two judgments as to whether someone who deliberately breaks his fast when making up [for an obligatory fast] must make up the original only or the latter together with making up the fast he was making up.

Whoever breaks his voluntary fast must make it up, according to the consensus, but if he breaks if with a valid excuse he does not have to make it up.

2. The kaffārahs

This is considered with respect to the causes of payment and their various kinds.

As for the causes, this is in particular to deliberately and intentionally render the fast of Ramadan defective – because he is violating the sanctity of the fast without there being a valid excuse for breaking the fast. Thus there is no *kaffārah* payable for the person who breaks the fast when making up a Ramadan fast, according to the majority, nor any payable by the person who breaks the fast out of forgetfulness, or who is coerced into breaking it; nor is it obligatory in the case of kissing, nor for the menstruating woman or the woman bleeding after childbirth, or the mad person, the person who faints, for this is all beyond their control; nor for the sick person, the traveller, the person overcome with hunger and thirst, or the pregnant woman, on account of the valid excuse they all have; nor for the renegade, for he violates the sanctity of Islam not that of the fast.

FOUR SECONDARY MATTERS

1. *Kaffārah* is obligatory if sexual intercourse is had deliberately, irrespective of whether with his wife or a woman outside of marriage; if the woman consented willingly then *kaffārah* is incumbent on both him and her, while ash-Shāfi'ī and Dāwūd have said that one *kaffārah* suffices for both of them; and if he has intercourse with her while she is sleeping or coerces her he pays *kaffārah* for himself and her; but if he has intercourse while forgetting, there is no *kaffārah* required of him, according to the well-known position (*mashhūr*), contrary to Ibn Ḥanbal, but he must make it up, contrary to the two; and whoever is coerced into having intercourse, then he has no *kaffārah* to pay, contrary to Ibn al-Mājishūn and Ibn Ḥanbal.

2. *Kaffārah* is obligatory if food or drink is taken deliberately, contrary to ash-Shāfi'ī and the Ẓāhirīs, or anything else is ingested and it reaches the throat by way of the mouth in particular, it is considered subject to the same judgment, but it is not obligatory in the case of anything that reaches [the throat] from other than the mouth, like the nose or ear, contrary to Abū Muṣ'ab alone.

3. *Kaffārah* is obligatory if one enters into the morning with the intention of breaking the fast even if one makes the intention to fast after this, according to the most correct judgment, and if one abandons the intention to fast during the day, according to the most correct judgment.

4. There is a difference of opinion as to its obligation for the person who vomits and the person who deliberately swallows something inedible and in the case of the person subject to recurring or periodic fever who says that 'today is the day it will come to me', then breaks his fast and it does indeed come to him, and in the case of the woman who says 'today I will have my menstruation' and she breaks her fast and does indeed have her menstruation; and if one intentionally breaks the fast without an excuse, then falls ill or sets out on a journey or a woman begins to menstruate, the person must pay *kaffārah*, according to the well-known position (*mashhūr*) – on the basis of the actual state of the person, while it has also been said that *kaffārah* is cancelled on the basis of the outcome.

Kinds of kaffārah

They are three in number: setting free a slave, feeding people and fasting.

As for setting free, it refers to freeing a male or female slave who is *mūmin* and free of defects and who is not subject to any other contract entailing manumission and whose manumission is not necessitated for another reason.

As for fasting, this refers to two consecutive months.

As for feeding people, this refers to feeding sixty destitute persons a *mudd* for each person, using the *mudd* of the Prophet ﷺ, while Abū Ḥanīfah has said two *mudd*s.

The type used to carry out the *kaffārah* is optional, as in the *kaffārah*s used to compensate for unfulfilled oaths, although the best of them is feeding people, according to the well-known position (*mashhūr*), while it has also been said the order mentioned above is to be respected, as in the case of the kind of divorce known as *ẓihār*, in agreement with the two.

Two subsidiary matters

1. Regarding repeatedly breaking the fast: if someone breaks the fast then pays the *kaffārah* then breaks it again on the same day, he has to pay another *kaffārah,* according to the consensus; and whoever repeatedly breaks the fast on a single day has to pay one *kaffārah*; and whoever breaks the fast and does not pay the *kaffārah* until he has broken the fast on a second day has to pay a second *kaffārah,* contrary to Abū Ḥanīfah.

2. Whoever is unable to pay the *kaffārah*, then it remains his liability, and what is taken into account is his state at the moment of intending the *kaffārah* – on the basis of the judgment that one should respect the order of the three kinds of *kaffārah.*

Summary

With respect to the judgment of the madhhab regarding the making up and the *kaffārah*: as for the person who deliberately breaks the fast, irrespective of the kind of fast, he has to make it up but only has to pay *kaffārah* in the case of the fast of Ramadan; and whoever breaks the fast out of forgetfulness, irrespective of the kind of fast, has to make it up but without *kaffārah* except in the case of a voluntary fast, in which case there is neither making up or *kaffārah.*

3. As for the fidyah compensation

It is giving a *mudd* of food to a destitute person for every day missed, and it becomes obligatory in four cases:

1. Whoever delays making up days of Ramadan, despite the fact that he is able to make them up, until the next Ramadan occurs, contrary to Abū Ḥanīfah, and [the *fidyah*] is not repeated even if the making up is missed repeatedly over the years, and [the *fidyah*] is paid when one begins to make it up, while Ashhab has said when one is unable to make up.

2. The *fidyah* becomes obligatory for the pregnant woman according to the narration of Ibn Wahb, in agreement with ash-Shāfi'ī, whereas Ashhab has said that it is a recommendation in her case, while Ibn al-Mājishūn said that if she fears for her health or life then she does not have to feed a destitute person as she is considered to be ill, but if she fears for her child then she does feed a destitute person.

3. In the case of the sick person there are two narrations as to the obligation to pay the *fidyah*.

4. In the case of the senile or decrepit person there is no liability to pay *fidyah*, according to the well-known position (*mashhūr*), although it has also been said that it is an obligation for this person, in agreement with the two, while it has also been said that it is a recommendation.

4. As for desisting from food, drink and sexual intercourse for the rest of the day

This is prescribed in particular in the case of the person who either deliberately or our of forgetfulness breaks fast in Ramadan but not for someone who breaks it for a legitimate excuse.

5. As for the punishment

This is for the person who violates the sanctity of Ramadan and the amount of the punishment is determined by the leader-*imām* and the state of the person in question.

6. As for interrupting the continuous and successive nature of the months to be fasted

In the case of someone who breaks the fast deliberately with respect to a fast undertaken on account of a vow and the continuous fasts undertaken for the *kaffārahs* for killing and the *ẓihār* divorce, the person in question must begin the fast from the beginning again, contrary to someone who has interrupted his continuous fasting out of forgetfulness or on account of an excuse or because he has made a mistake when reckoning up the number of days – for this person carries on fasting where he interrupted.

7. As for interrupting one's intention

This occurs when the fasting is invalidated or when it is completely abandoned on account of an excuse or without an excuse or the removal of the necessity of fasting as in the case of travel – even if one fasts during it – for the intention is broken by the judgment associated with the travel.

9. I'tikāf

An examination of its judgment, where and when it may take place, its conditions and those things which invalidate it

Its judgment

It is an act of *qurbah*-drawing nearer, which is desirable for both men and women, in particular in the last ten days of Ramadan; and it becomes obligatory if a vow is made to do it. And there occurs something from Mālik from which apparently he regarded it as *makrūh* on account of its difficulty.

ITS LOCATION

It may be made in all mosques, according to the majority contrary to one group who have restricted it to the three mosques, and contrary to Ibn Lubāba who permitted it in places other than mosques. If someone makes the intention for *i'tikāf* for a period during which the *jumu'ah* would become incumbent on him then a *jāmi'* mosque becomes incumbent, for if he were to leave for the *jumu'ah*, then his *i'tikāf* would be invalidated, contrary to Abū Ḥanīfah and Ibn al-Mājishūn.

The person is not to leave the place of *i'tikāf* other than for four reasons: his bodily needs, what he must buy in the way of food and drink, in the case of illness, in the of menstruation – and if someone leaves for one of these then he is deemed still to be in the state of *i'tikāf* until he returns.

ITS TIME

The minimum is a day and a night while what is preferred is that one does not do less than ten days, although there is no minimum according to the two.

It is recommended that someone enter it before sunset of the night preceding the day he commences it and if he does this then it is accepted of him, according to the agreed position, while if he enters between *maghrib* and *'ishā'* then there are two judgments as to its validity or invalidity.

As for his leaving it, if he leaves after sunset of the last day then it is acceptable, but if he makes the *i'tikāf* at the end of Ramadan then he is instructed in the madhhab to remain until going out for the *'Īd ṣalāt*; and there is a difference of opinion as to whether this is deemed an obligation or recommendation – and on the basis of this there is the question of whether the *i'tikāf* is invalidated for the person who leaves before it or not.

Its conditions

They are three in number: the intention, according to the agreed judgment, fasting, contrary to ash-Shāfi'ī, and occupying oneself with worship as much as one is able during the day and night – in the form of *ṣalāt*, *dhikr*, and recitation in particular according to Ibn al-Qāsim, and with all the other acts of the *Ākhirah* – i.e. the Next World, according to Ibn Wahb: thus on the basis of the first he may not witness any *janāzah*, visit a sick person or impart knowledge, while on the basis of the second he may do this.

The things which invalidate it

They are six in number: sexual intercourse, according to the agreed judgment, setting about this act even if there is no emission, contrary to Abū Ḥanīfah, reneging on one's Islam, intoxication and leaving his place of *i'tikāf* for any other reason than what has been permitted him to leave it for, even if obligatory, such as a *jihād* that is incumbent on him individually and imprisonment for a debt, or committing a major wrong action like a slanderous false accusation of fornication – although there is a difference of opinion in this regard.

Perfume does not invalidate it, according to the madhhab, nor concluding a marriage contract neither for oneself or another; and it is of no benefit that the person stipulate that he is going to do something which *i'tikāf* prohibits, contrary to ash-Shāfi'ī.

10. The Night of the Decree

This refers to the night about which Allah, exalted is He, has said: '*on a blessed night*' and '*better than a thousand months*', that is any action undertaken during it is better than the action undertaken in a thousand other months – and this remains valid and has not been abrogated according to the majority; and the *'ulamā'* have three different judgments in its respect:

1. That it is specific but not known, indeed hidden

And those who hold to this have four differing judgments:

1. That it has been hidden in the whole year; and in Ramadan; and in the middle ten days of it; and in the last ten days.

2. That it is specific and known

These have four differing judgments – the night of the 21st, 23rd 25th, 27th and this latter is the most well-known and the most obvious.

3. That it is not specific nor known

Rather that it changes – and Ibn Rushd said 'this is what Mālik, ash-Shāfi'ī and Ibn Ḥanbal held to and is the most correct judgment'. On the basis of this its moving takes place in the middle ten days of Ramadan and in the last ten, and the most likely within the middle is that it is the night of the 17th and the 19th and within the last ten days on one of the odd nights.

6 – Hajj

CONSISTING OF TEN CHAPTERS

1. The Introductory Aspects

THIS COMPRISES THREE SECTIONS

1. Its judgment

It is obligatory for the person who is able, once in a lifetime – an obligation in the widest sense by which a certain latitude of time is permitted, in agreement with ash-Shāfi'ī, although it has also been said that it becomes immediately obligatory, in agreement with Abū Ḥanīfah, and if we hold to this permission for a certain latitude then it becomes obligatory for someone who reaches sixty years of age. It is *makrūh* for someone to make a *nāfilah* hajj, i.e. a supererogatory one, before he has carried out the *farḍ* one, and if he does, then it is not transformed into a *farḍ* one but rather is counted on the basis of the intention he made.

2. Its conditions

As for the conditions of its obligation they are that one is of age and sane of mind, according to the agreed judgment, and that one is free, contrary to the Ẓāhirīs, that one has capacity, and there is a difference of opinion as to the condition of Islam – as to whether it is a condition of obligation or of validity, based on the difference of opinion as to whether the *kuffār* are addressed with respect to the applied aspects of the *sharī'ah*.

And the only condition for its validity is Islam, given that it is valid for the legal guardian to forbid the child and the mad person. And the only condition for the validity of its practice is Islam and discrimination – for if the child with discrimination makes the hajj with the permission of its guardian then this is permitted, contrary to Abū Ḥanīfah, and likewise the slave.

As for the capability that is necessary for the hajj it refers to the ability to reach Makkah – by three means: physical strength, either in walking or riding, safety of the road one takes there, and having enough provision to reach there – and this is assessed in accordance with a person's state and varies according to their custom and habit.

Ibn Ḥabīb said that capability refers to provision and the riding beast, in agreement with them; and according to the madhhab it is obligatory for anyone able to walk, even if there is no riding beast, and likewise the blind person if he finds someone to guide him.

And whoever only finds a way by sea then the hajj is not annulled for him, contrary to ash-Shāfiʿī, unless fear overwhelms him or he knows that he will not be able to perform the *ṣalāt* on account of the rolling of the ship and subsequent nausea, and if he considers that he will not find a place to prostrate because of the constricted circumstances, except on the back of his brother [in the *dīn*] then he does not embark, according to the madhhab.

The enfeebled or crippled person who cannot keep a firm hold on his riding beast does not have to pay someone else to make the hajj for him, contrary to the two.

The obligation of the hajj is cancelled if the enemy are on the road seeking out people and money.

The obligation on women is the same as that on men if a guardian accompanies her; and if there is no guardian but safe company is available then it is also obligatory for her, contrary to Abū Ḥanīfah, and there is a difference of opinion as to the obligation for her if the sea route or travel on foot becomes necessary.

As for provision, if someone has no dirhams or dinars then he is required to sell his belongings and assets – i.e. that which would be sold for cash in the case of debt – and to make the hajj with it; and whoever usually asks of others then he is also obligated to perform the hajj if he thinks it likely that he will find someone who will give him what he needs, while it is also said that he is not obligated.

3. Delegating someone to perform one's hajj

The correct judgment is that it is not permitted with respect to the *farḍ* hajj, while it is *makrūh* with respect to the voluntary one irrespective of whether for a fee or not; and it is valid to employ someone to do the hajj, contrary to Abū Ḥanīfah, on the basis that it is *makrūh,* and it has two aspects:

1. Whereby a specific fee is assigned to employ someone – which belongs to the person employed as in the case of all other kinds of payment for employment – in which case any deficiency in the required amount he makes up from his own money and any extra belongs to him.

2. Whereby [the emphasis is on] fulfilling the hajj, in which case the person employed is paid money to go on hajj instead of him and if he needs more then he takes it from the person who has employed him while if there is any excess then he returns it to him.

If a deceased person has left instructions that someone make the hajj on his behalf from his wealth and he had not performed the hajj, then his testament is carried out from the third of his wealth not automatically distributed to his relations, but if he has not instructed anything then it lapses in his regard, while ash-Shāfi'ī has said that someone makes the hajj instead of him using his capital and the person employed makes the intention of the hajj for the person he is making the hajj for; and it is permitted for the person employed for the hajj not himself to have performed the *farḍ* hajj, contrary to ash-Shāfi'ī

2. THE VARIOUS ELEMENTS WHICH MAKE UP THE HAJJ

Its *farḍ* elements are the fundamental elements which may not be put right by sacrifice: the intention, the *iḥrām*, the standing at 'Arafah, the *ifāḍah ṭawāf* and the *sa'y* between Ṣafā and Marwah, although Abū Ḥanīfah said that the *sa'y* may be put right by sacrifice, and 'Abd al-Mālik has added the stoning of the final *jamrah*, i.e. the 'place of pebbles'.

THE OBLIGATORY SUNNAHS WHICH ARE NOT FUNDAMENTAL ELEMENTS AND WHICH MAY BE PUT RIGHT BY SACRIFICE

They are ten in number: doing the hajj as *ifrād*, i.e. the hajj alone without the *'umrah*; the *iḥrām* from one of the five *mīqāt*, i.e. the boundary locations; declaring *labbayk* 'at Your service'; the *ṭawāf* of arrival; spending the night at al-Muzdalifah on the night prior to the day of sacrifice; stoning the *jamrah*s; shaving one's head; cutting off some of one's hair; the two *rak'ah*s prior to the *ṭawāf*; spending the night in Minā during the nights of the stoning; and joining the *ṣalāt* at 'Arafah and al-Muzdalifah.

THE ASPECTS OF EXCELLENCE

They do not require sacrifice to put right and entail no wrong if omitted, they are twenty in number: *iḥrām* in the month of hajj; wearing white for the *iḥrām*; *ghusl* prior to the *iḥrām* and for the *ṭawāf* of arrival and for 'Arafah and for the *ifāḍah ṭawāf* – making four *ghusl*s in all; two *rak'ah*s before *iḥrām*; kissing the Black Stone; greeting the Yemeni Corner; going at a jog-trot for three of the *ṭawāf* circumambulations and a walking pace for the rest; going at a jog-trot between the two markers on *sa'y*; making haste at the place known as the Wādī Muḥassir between al-Muzdalifah and Minā; leaving al-Mash'ar al-Ḥarām the morning of the Day of Sacrifice; the farewell *ṭawāf*; *ṣalāt* in al-Muḥaṣṣab after the great dispersal from Minā towards Makkah; delaying one's leaving until the second dispersal on the last of the days of Tashrīq, i.e. the 11th 12th and 13th of Dhu-l-Ḥijjah; voluntarily bringing a sacrificial animal; standing, i.e. being present, at 'Arafah on its plain not the heights or hills; and beginning the stoning at the last *jamrah* then making the sacrifice then shaving or cutting some of one's hair.

3. The mawāqīt

Mawāqīt refers to the times and locations

The time

It is Shawwāl, Dhu-l-Qa'dah and the first ten days of Dhu-l-Ḥijjah, and whoever makes the *iḥrām* before this time then it is valid but on the basis of its being *makrūh*, in agreement with Abū Ḥanīfah, and it has also been said that it is without effect and consequence, in agreement with Dāwūd, while ash-Shāfi'ī has said his hajj is annulled and it changes to an *'umrah*.

And it is recommended for the people of Makkah when the crescent moon of Dhu-l-Ḥijjah appears, while ash-Shāfi'ī has said on the day of *tarwiyah*, i.e. the 8th , the day of watering when the hajjis see to their provision of water for the coming days.

The locations

These are five in number, determined according to the directions of approach to the *Ḥarām*: Dhu-l-Ḥulayfah for the people of Madīnah, Qarn for the people of Najd, al-Juḥfah for the people of Sham, Egypt and the Greater Maghrib, Yalamlam for the people of Yemen and Dhātu 'Irq for the people of Iraq, Khurasan and the East.

It is *makrūh* to enter *iḥrām* before reaching these, but it is binding if done, while ash-Shāfi'ī has said that the most excellent is to enter the *iḥrām* from one's country. It is more fitting for the person whose *mīqāt* is al-Juḥfah but who passes by Dhu-l-Ḥulayfah that he enters the *iḥrām* at Dhu-l-Ḥulayfah as this is the *mīqāt* of the Prophet ﷺ. As for the resident of Makkah he enters *iḥrām* from Makkah.

The *mīqāt*s of the *'umrah* are from the locations of the *mīqāt*s for hajj except for someone in the *Ḥarām* in which case he must go out to the *ḥill*, i.e. the place beyond the territory of Makkah and not within the *Ḥarām*, even to its first point in order to combine the *Ḥarām* and the *ḥill* just as the *ḥajjī* combines them, and he has the option of entering the *iḥrām* for *'umrah* from al-Ji'rānah or at-Tan'īm.

And if a person's house is nearer to Makkah than the *mīqāt* then his *mīqāt* is from his house for the hajj or *'umrah.*

Section

The person who passes the *mīqāt* has one of three circumstances:

1. That he passes it for some need he has outside of Makkah in which case he does not have to enter *iḥrām*;

2. That he wants to enter Makkah for something he needs in which case he is required to enter *iḥrām* – and it is required for anyone who enters it except for the person from among its inhabitants who goes out for something he needs to do, then returns, and the person who

repeatedly comes and goes to it like the seller of firewood or fruit, while Abū Muṣ'ab has said that it is not required of him;

3. That he wants to make the hajj or *'umrah* and makes the *iḥrām* but does not go beyond it, but if he does go beyond, then he returns as long as he has not entered *iḥrām* and he does not have to sacrifice; but if he has entered *iḥrām*, then he carries on and he must sacrifice, and if he returns after entering *iḥrām*, then the obligation to sacrifice does not lapse, contrary to ash-Shāfi'ī.

4. The actions of hajj

Comprising ten sections

1. The iḥrām

This is effected by means of the intention accompanied by vocal expression of this or by an action connected to the hajj like the *talbiyah* and setting out on the way and Ibn Ḥabīb has stipulated the *talbiyah* and has said that it is not effected without it, and Abū Ḥanīfah has stipulated it and said the driving of the sacrificial animal is a substitute for it. If the intention is devoid of vocal expression or action then it is not effected, although it has also been said that it is effected in agreement with ash-Shāfi'ī.

The sunnahs of the iḥrām

They are four in number

1. The *ghusl* made to clean oneself [rather than the ritual washing], and it is a *sunnah* also for the woman who is menstruating or still undergoing post-natal bleeding, and one does not apply perfume, neither before or after – with a perfume which lasts;

2. One removes any sewn articles with respect to the lower body wrap, outer garment or sandals;

3. One makes two *rak'ah*s or more, and if one enters the *iḥrām* immediately after a *farḍ ṣalāt* then there is no harm;

4. The *talbiyah* at the moment of beginning to walk, and one repeats it at every descent and ascent on the way, when any new situation arises, after the *ṣalāt*s and on hearing anyone saying the *talbiyah*.

And it is recommended to raise one's voice without being immoderate, except for women and one does not have to excessively earnest or importune when saying it.

The form of it is:

لَبَّيْكَ اَللَّهُمَّ لَبَّيْكَ، لَبَّيْكَ لَا شَرِيكَ لَكَ لَبَّيْكَ،
إِنَّ الْحَمْدَ وَالنِّعْمَةَ لَكَ وَالْمُلْكَ، لَا شَرِيكَ لَكَ.

Labbayka-llāhumma labbayk, labbayka lā sharīka laka labbayk, inna-l-ḥamda wa-n-ni'mata laka wa-l-mulk, lā sharīka lak.

'Always at Your service, O Allah, at Your service, You have no partner, always at Your service, all praise and blessing belong to You, as does the Kingdom, You have no partner'.

If one wants one may add:

لَبَّيْكَ لَبَّيْكَ، لَبَّيْكَ وَسَعْدَيْكَ، وَالْخَيْرُ بِيَدَيْكَ، وَالرَّغْبَاءُ إِلَيْكَ وَالْعَمَلُ.

labbayka labbayk, labbayka wa sa'dayk, wa-l-khayru bi yadayk, wa-r-raghbā'u ilayka wa-l-'amal.

'Always at Your service, Always at Your service, Always at Your service, for Your contentment and help, and all good is in Your hand, seeking and imploring You with this action'.

The saying of the *talbiyah* does not stop on the hajj except on beginning the *ṭawāf*, and one carries on again after completing the *sa'y* – but one stops saying it after the sun has gone past its zenith on the day of 'Arafah, and Ibn al-Qāsim said when one sets out for the *ṣalāt*, while ash-Shāfi'ī said when one stones the *jamrah* on the Day of Sacrifice; and the person doing *'umrah* stops on entering the *Ḥarām*. And whoever stops pronouncing the *talbiyah* must sacrifice an animal, contrary to ash-Shāfi'ī.

2. Entry into Makkah

Its *sunnah*s are to make a *ghusl* at Dhū Ṭuwā and to enter Makkah from Kadā' (with *fatḥah* on the *kāf* and with a *madd*-long vowel) which is situated at the top of Makkah, and leave by Kudayy (with *ḍammah* (u) on the *kāf*, *fatḥah* (a) on the *dāl*, and *shaddah*-doubling on the *yā'* as a diminutive) at the lower part of Makkah, then to enter the mosque by the door of Banū Shaybah, come to 'the black corner' and commence with the *ṭawāf* of arrival.

3. The ṭawāf

They are three in number: the *ṭawāf al-qudūm* – the *ṭawāf* of arrival, *ṭawāf al-ifāḍah* – the *ṭawāf* of leaving en masse after 'Arafah, and the *ṭawāf al-wadā'* – the farewell *ṭawāf*.

Its farḍ obligations are seven in number

1. The conditions stipulated in the *ṣalāt* – with respect to ritual purity and covering ofone's *'awrah*, i.e. one's private parts and the area around them, except that it is permitted to speak.

2. That the seven circumambulations of the *ṭawāf* be done consecutively without interruption.

3. The proper manner of execution, contrary to Abū Ḥanīfah, that is that one has the House to one's left and one begins at the Black Stone.

4. That the whole of his body is outside of the House, such that he

does not walk on the Shādharwān, i.e. the remains of the foundational stone at the base of and around the Ka'bah, or on the Stone.

5. That he makes the *ṭawāf* within the mosque.

6. That he completes seven circumambulations – if he does only six then it does not suffice.

7. Two *rak'ahs* after it, and there is a difference of opinion as to whether they constitute an obligation or a *sunnah*.

AS FOR THE SUNNAHS

THERE ARE FOUR

1. That one makes the *ṭawāf* walking and it is *makrūh* to do it mounted, while it has also been said that it does not suffice.

2. That he touch the Black Stone with his mouth but if unable to kiss it then he strokes it with the palm of his hand or with whatever stick he has with him, and there are two narrations as to whether he kisses the thing that he has touched it with; and he strokes the Yamānī Corner with his hand at the end of each circumambulation.

3. *Du'ā*, and they are not restricted in kind or number.

4. The jog-trot for men, but not women, during the first three circumambulations – for the *ṭawāf* of arrival, while there is a difference of opinion as to whether it is prescribed for the *ifāḍah* and farewell *ṭawāfs*.

4. THE SA'Y BETWEEN ṢAFĀ AND MARWAH

ITS FARḌ ELEMENTS BEING FOUR IN NUMBER

1. That it be done consecutively without interruption;

2. That the proper order be adhered to such that one begins at Ṣafā by standing there, then making *du'ā*, then one walks to Marwah and one stands there and makes *du'ā*;

3. That one completes seven courses such that one stands at Ṣafā four times and at Marwah four times, ending with the latter;

4. That one precedes it with *ṭawāf.*

Its sunnahs are five in number

Making the *ṭawāf* immediately after completing the ritual purification for it; walking and not being mounted; *du'ā*; walking quickly in the case of men, not women, at Baṭn al-Masīl, that is what is situated between the two green hills.

Point to be noted

One raises one's hands to Allah, may He be blessed and exalted, on seven occasions: making the *takbīratu-l-iḥrām* at the beginning of the *ṣalāt*, on sighting the Ka'bah for the first time, at Ṣafā, at Marwah, at 'Arafah, at the joining of the two *ṣalāt*s and at the two *jamrah*s.

5. The 'standing', i.e. being present, at Minā and 'Arafah

One goes out to Minā on the 8th Dhu-l-Ḥijjah – which is the Day of Tarwiyah when one provides oneself with water, and one makes *ẓuhr* and *'aṣr* there and one spends the night there and then goes to 'Arafah after sunrise; then one joins *ẓuhr* and *'aṣr* together with the *imām* and stands where the people are standing and it is preferable to be mounted, that is in the place of 'standing'; and one avoids the Baṭn 'Uranah; and one accompanies the standing with *dhikr* and *du'ā* at all times until the sunset.

Various important points

1. Three *khuṭbah*s are delivered during the hajj:

First, on the 7th Dhu-l-Ḥijjah in the Ḥarām Mosque and there is a single *khuṭbah* and there is no sitting for it;

Second, at 'Arafah on the Day of 'Arafah after the sun has passed its zenith and before the *ṣalāt,* and it consists of two *khuṭbah*s and one sits between the two, and the mu'adhdhin commences with the *adhān* while the *imām* is making the *khuṭbah* or after he has finished it;

Third, on the 11th Dhu-l-Ḥijjah.

2. The *jumu'ah ṣalāt* is not performed on the Day of Tarwiyah at Minā, nor at 'Arafah on the Day of 'Arafah, nor the Day of Sacrifice or the Days of Tashrīq, i.e. the following three days of the 'cutting and drying of sacrificial meat'.

3. One does not go on from 'Arafah until after sunset; if one leaves before sunset then one must return at night – otherwise his hajj is invalidated, and whoever goes after sunset but before the *imām* then he has erred but does not have to make any compensatory act.

6. Muzdalifah

When the sun sets on the Day of 'Arafah, the *imām* together with the people set out as a vigorous body for Muzdalifah, which is situated between Minā and 'Arafah, and they proceed by the route of al-Ma'zimān. Then they join and shorten *maghrib* and *'ishā'* at Muzdalifah after the red twilight has disappeared, and they spend that night there.

Whoever performs the *ṣalāt* before Muzdalifah without any excuse should repeat it on arriving there; and they should not descend at any watering place for supper or to rest.

When the dawn breaks they perform the *ṣubḥ ṣalāt* during the darkness of the night immediately preceding daybreak. Then they move on to the Mash'ar al-Ḥarām, i.e. between the two mountains at the end of Muzdalifah, and they stand imploring and making *du'ā* until the lightening of the sky; then they move off from them in a vigorous body before sunrise to Minā and they break into a kind of running in Wādī Muḥassir.

7. Stoning the jamrahs

On the morning of the Day of Sacrifice at Minā then the stoning of the *jamrah al-ʿaqabah* is done, i.e. the last *jamrah*, when the sun has risen to the height of a lance – facing the *jamrah* with the House to one's left and Minā to one's right: one throws seven pebbles and utters *Allāhu akbar* for each pebble and pauses between each throwing for the amount one would spend in prostration in the *ṣalāt*.

One makes the stoning of the other *jamrah*s during the Days of Minā, i.e. the second, third and fourth days of the *ʿĪd*; then after the sun has passed its zenith on each of these days, one makes a *ghusl* and stones three *jamrah*s, throwing seven pebbles for each *jamrah* and beginning with the first *jamrah* which is beside the mosque of Minā, then the one following it and finishing with the final *jamrah*, the total number of pebbles being seventy, each pebble being like sling-shot; and one makes the stoning of the first two *jamrah*s from above them and the final *jamrah* from below, and one makes *duʿā* after the first and second *jamrah*, and one leaves after the final *jamrah* without making *duʿā*.

8. Shaving one's head

And this is more excellent than cutting some of one's hair: one begins at the front of the head, then one shaves the right side and then the left and then the back of the head. Women cut their hair and do not shave – cutting the amount equal to a finger-tip; and if a man cuts it, then he clips his hair close to the roots.

And he makes *duʿā* during the shaving – on the Day of Sacrifice and after the stoning of the last *jamrah* and the sacrifice. if he had brought a *hady*, i.e. a sacrificial animal, with him. Then he comes to Makkah and makes the *ifāḍah ṭawāf* which is a *farḍ* obligation.

9. Slaughtering

One slaughters after the *jamrah,* but if one does it before it or one shaves before slaughtering then one is not liable for anything; and if one shaves before the *jamrah,* then he pays the *fidyah.* And it is permitted to slaughter the *hady* before sunrise, contrary to the sacrificial animals.

10. The farewell ṭawāf

It is recommended, contrary to them regarding its being obligatory: whoever forgets it, should return to do it as long as he is still close by; and the people of Makkah are not instructed to do it, nor anyone who is resident there and who is not one of its people – as a 'farewell' is a matter of departing from somewhere – so if the person from Makkah wants to travel, then he makes the farewell *ṭawāf,* and whoever makes the farewell *ṭawāf* and remains resident after this for a day or part of a day then he renews it; and if someone from amongst those who come and go to Makkah, like sellers of firewood, leave it, then they do not do the farewell *ṭawāf*; and if a woman begins her menstruation after the *ifāḍah ṭawāf* then she leaves before the farewell *ṭawāf.*

5. The types of hajj

They are three in number: *ifrād, qirān* and *tamattu'*, and the most excellent of them in the madhhab is the *ifrād,* whereas it is *qirān* according to Abū Ḥanīfah and *tamattu'* according to ash-Shāfi'ī and Ibn Ḥanbal.

The ifrād

It consists of entering the *iḥrām* for just the hajj and then not doing *'umrah* until after completing the hajj.

The qirān

It is to make the *iḥrām* for the hajj and *'umrah* together, or one makes the intention for the *'umrah* first, then immediately follows it with the hajj such that one does the *ṭawāf* and makes the *sa'y* for the hajj and *'umrah* thus including the *'umrah* in the hajj, and one remains in the state of *iḥrām* until one has completed his hajj as above; and he must bring a sacrificial animal with him if he is from outside of Makkah, contrary to the Ẓāhirīs, and if from Makkah, then he does not have to sacrifice.

The tamattu'

It is to make the *'umrah* in the months of hajj in the case of someone who makes the hajj that year – so he has the ease (*tamattu'*) of the omission of the travel to the hajj if he does not return to his country, contrary to the person who does not make the hajj that year.

The person making the *tamattu'* has to bring with him a sacrificial animal that he can afford – and slaughter it at Minā if he brings it to 'Arafah, and if he does not bring it with him then he slaughters at Marwah; and if he does not find any sacrificial animals to take with him he fasts three days on the hajj from the time of his entering the *iḥrām* to the Day of 'Arafah, and if he does not do this then he fasts the Days of Tashrīq and seven more when he returns to his country. The sacrificial animal of *tamattu'* is obligatory for those from outside of Makkah not for the residents of Makkah and Dhū Ṭuwā.

A point of importance

There are four schools of thought in the interpretation of *tamattu'*:

1. That described above and this is what the majority hold to;
2. That is that it is the same as the *qirān* in that one has the ease

(*tamattu'*) of the omission of certain actions [like the prohibitions entailed by the *iḥrām*];

3. That it is the annulling of the hajj in the *'umrah* in order to have the ease of the omission of the actions of hajj and it is *makrūh*, contrary to the Ẓāhirīs;

4. That it is on account of being prevented by the enemy, this being how Ibn az-Zubayr interpreted the *āyah*.

6. The prohibited things of hajj

These are the things prohibited for the person in *iḥrām*, and they are numerous, but may be encompassed in four basic rules:

1. One must not wear any sewn clothing

Such as a *jubbah*, i.e. robe open at the front with long sleeves; upper shirt; trousers; or *khuffs* and shoes which are sewn – but rather ones without any stitching, and if one cannot find any and is unable to afford what they cost then he should wear *khuffs* after cutting them below the ankles, although Ibn Ḥanbal has said that he should not cut them. And he must not wear any sewn girdle or belt and should wear something that is not sewn next to his body not over his robe, and one must not hang any vessel comprising a sewn element from one's belt or girdle, nor a knife with a sewn sheath, nor should he carry the funds of someone else, nor gird a sword except if necessary, nor should he carry a vessel comprising a sewn element, but rather a container for his provision which is not sewn and which is fastened at the top and bottom, nor should he wear any article of clothing dyed with saffron or yellow dye of the *wars* or turmeric plant, or with any beautiful dye, and it is permitted for him to wear black or green although white is the best.

SUBSIDIARY MATTER

It is permitted to wear on one's back something sewn without wrapping oneself up in it or putting it on as a garment, and that which is not sewn is prohibited if it affords ease, like for example an animal skin.

2. AFFORDING EASE OR COMFORT TO ONE'S BODY AND CLEANING IT

Included here is not covering one's head and one does not shave it until the Day of Sacrifice, nor does one comb or brush it, nor does one braid or plait it. And one does not cover one's face. It is permitted to shade oneself in the shadow of a building or tent if one stops or alights, while there is a difference of opinion as to whether it is permitted to shade oneself with the litter of the camel when mounted, or with a cloth attached to a tree if one stops or alights.

One does not clip one's nails or pluck the hair of the armpits nor does one shave around the pubic area or clip one's hair or the hair of anyone else. One does not do anything to change the dishevelled, unkempt or matted state of one's hair or remove any dirt, nor does one discard anything from one's body like broken nails, plucked hairs or the like. Nor does one kill lice or fleas or remove or discard them from one's body. Nor does one remove or discard ticks from one's riding beast nor does one scratch roughly anywhere on one's body which is hidden from view lest there be a lice there which then falls down.

Nor does one wash one's head – other than making the *ghusl* for *janābah*. One does not enter the bath-room or *ḥammām* in order to wash, although it is permitted in order to cool down. One does not apply perfume or perfumed oil, nor does one apply kohl unless necessary, and if so, then with kohl without perfume, and one does not eat food containing an odoriferous substance unless it has been heated. One should stay around perfume or seek to make its smell last.

3. Hunting

The *muḥrim* does not kill any land prey whose meat may be eaten, nor any animal whose meat may not be eaten irrespective of whether it walks or flies in the *Ḥarām* or outside of it, nor does he instruct anyone else to hunt, nor show or indicate to anyone where the prey is – and if he does instruct someone or indicate to anyone, then he has done something wrong but he does not have to pay any *kaffārah*.

One does not eat the meat of a hunt undertaken for him or on his behalf, contrary to Abū Ḥanīfah, and any prey caught in the *ḥill* – outside of the *Ḥarām* – is permitted for the *muḥrim* to eat, contrary to one group, while any prey slaughtered by the *muḥrim*, that is killed deliberately or by mistake, then it is deemed on a par with carrion and is not permitted for him or anyone else to eat it, in agreement with Abū Ḥanīfah, while one group have said that it is *ḥalāl* for someone who is not in the state of *iḥrām*

It is permitted for him to slaughter livestock and birds which do not fly in the air such as chickens, and it is also said harmful animals like the lion, wolf, snake, mouse or rat, scorpion, rapacious dog, that is, within the madhhab, any wild animal of which one is afraid, while according to Abū Ḥanīfah it refers to any dog in the usual understanding of this word, crows and ravens and in particular kites, but he does not kill antelopes or gazelles, or pigs or monkeys unless he fears they will attack him, and it is forbidden for him to kill anything which is not harmful – from gnats or mosquitos to anything bigger than it, while it is permitted him to fish in the sea in all circumstances.

4. Women

It is not permitted for the *muḥrim* man to have intimate contact with a woman, be it intercourse, kissing, touching or marriage; nor does he make an offer of marriage for himself or on behalf of another, and any marriage is annulled irrespective of whether before it has been effected or afterwards, contrary to Abū Ḥanīfah with respect to the marriage contract and the engagement.

And it is permitted him to take back a wife whom he has divorced with a revocable divorce, as long as she is still in her *'iddah*, i.e. waiting period; and it is permitted him to buy slave girls – without having sexual intercourse with them.

The ruling regarding women in all of this is the same as men except in three matters: it is permitted her to cover herself, that is with something sewn, to wear *khuffs* and to cover her head – for her *iḥrām* is with respect to her face and her hands, but the *iḥrām* of the man is with respect to his face and head, for if he covers his head he has done wrong and must pay the *fidyah*.

CLARIFICATION

The *muḥrim* is prohibited from all these things until he shaves his head at Minā after which everything except hunting, women and perfume is permitted him, and when he has made the *ifāḍah ṭawāf* then all of these things are permitted him and he leaves the state of *iḥrām* completely.

7. THE FIDYAH, NUSUK I.E. SACRIFICE TO MAKE GOOD A MISTAKE, AND HADY – THE SACRIFICIAL ANIMAL TAKEN ON THE HAJJ

THIS CONSISTS OF TWO SECTIONS

1. THE FIDYAH

This refers to the *kaffārah* paid by the *muḥrim* for something he does that is prohibited – other than hunting and sexual intercourse.

Anyone who wears something sewn, or covers his head or cuts his hair or does other than this deliberately or by mistake or out of ignorance must pay the *fidyah* – either by fasting three days or feeding six destitute persons with two *mudd*s for each person – using the *mudd* of the Prophet ﷺ; or he sacrifices a sheep and gives it away in *ṣadaqah*, this being called a *nusuk*, this being one of the aspects of the *fidyah* – and this is optional both in the case of someone of means or someone in straightened circumstances, in whatever place he wishes.

As for hunting, the penalty is a *hady* beast corresponding to the hunted prey – the camel, cow, sheep or goat is sacrificed in Minā if he had it with him at 'Arafah, otherwise in Makkah, and he gives it away as *ṣadaqah*; or he feeds the destitute, giving away an amount in food equal to the worth of the hunted prey which he killed, that is a *mudd* for each destitute person using the *mudd* of the Prophet ﷺ; or he fasts a number of days equal to the number of *mudd*s of food and he has the choice in this, when two just persons from amongst the *fuqahā'* – whom he has given jurisdiction regarding the penalty against him – have made a decision in this, such that they assess the prey in terms of the *hady*, or food or fasting

The *hady* varies in accordance with the different kinds of prey: for the wild donkey or wild cow a cow is the penalty, for an ostrich a well fed camel or ox, for a gazelle a sheep and for anything smaller than this, the ruling prescribes food or fasting in accordance with the judgment of the two just persons, except in the case of a pigeon in the *Ḥarām* for which the penalty is a sheep.

Clarification

Payment of the penalty is obligatory for killing prey irrespective of whether deliberately or accidentally, according to the four, and one only distinguishes between the deliberate and the mistaken with respect to wrong action: the Ẓāhirīs have said that there is no penalty except if deliberate, in agreement with Ibn 'Abbās, Abū Thawr and Ibn al-Mundhir.

As for sexual intercourse, this invalidates the hajj irrespective of whether semen is emitted or not, and likewise whether emission is through intercourse or otherwise – except in the case of a wet dream; and that is if it occurs before the standing at 'Arafah.

If after it and before the stoning of the last *jamrah*, then there are two narrations, one invalidating and one that it is sound; if intercourse is had after the last *jamrah* but before the *ifāḍah ṭawāf* then the person's hajj is sound, but he has to make the sacrifice of the *hady* and the *'umrah*; and if the hajj is invalid, then he carries on to its end and makes it the following year, irrespective of whether it is a *farḍ* or voluntary hajj, and he makes a *hady* sacrifice.

2. The nusuk and the hady

Blood sacrifices on hajj are of two types: the *nusuk* and the *hady*.

The *nusuk* is the blood spilled as a *kaffārah* in compensation for any prohibited thing the *muḥrim* has done – except for hunting and sexual intercourse as explained above.

The *hady* is sacrificed for anything other than this and is of three types: the obligatory, that done in fulfilment of a vow for the benefit of destitute persons or without any particular stipulation, and the voluntary. The obligatory in turn is of five kinds:

1. The penalty for hunting as explained above;
2. For what he has omitted of obligatory *sunnahs* like stoning the *jamrahs*, staying overnight in Minā and Muzdalifah and other matters;
3. The *kaffārah* for sexual intercourse;

4. The *hady* for the *tamattu'* and *qirān*;
5. The *hady* for the missed out things.

There are various matters connected with the *hady*.

1. The nature of the hady

It is a livestock animal and the best is a camel, then a cow, then a sheep, then a goat and the ruling in their regard with respect to age and being free of defects is the same as that of animals for slaughter.

2. Taqlīd is recommended

i.e., to place a plaited rope or piece of leather around the neck of the *hady*, hang a pair of sandals to it or a single sandal;

make the *ish'ār*, i.e. mark it distinctively as a *hady* by slitting open the left side of the hump – the right side according to ash-Shāfi'ī – so that blood flows and to say then:

بِسْمِ اللهِ وَاللهُ أَكْبَرُ

Bismillāhi wa-llāhu akbar

"In the name of Allah, and Allah is greater";

and to make *tajlīl*, i.e. deck it by fastening the best quality of covering cloths one can afford by means of cords, and the slitting of the hump is made through it, and it is driven like this to the place of sacrifice where the covering is removed from it and it is sacrificed standing on the Day of Sacrifice; and one gives the cord and leading-rope away as *ṣadaqah* and the plaited rope, piece of leather and sandals are left at the place of the blood.

All this is with respect to camels; as for cows *taqlīd* and *ish'ār* are made but not *tajlīl*; as for sheep and goats no *taqlīd*, *ish'ār* or *tajlīl* are made, although ash-Shāfi'ī has said that *taqlīd* is made.

3. The owner of the hadys may eat of all of them except in four cases

When it is compensation for hunting; for shaving one's head during *iḥrām* in the case of injury or some other complaint; a vow made for the destitute; or if the voluntary *hady* is injured or perishes before reaching the assigned place – for if he eats from these four he must substitute an animal, although it has also been said that he substitutes what he has eaten of their flesh, in agreement with the two; and anything other than this then he has the option between eating of it or giving it away in *ṣadaqah,* while ash-Shāfi'ī has prohibited him from eating of any obligatory *hady*. In the case where the owner is prohibited from eating of it then it is for the destitute in particular, while other than this is permitted the owner and people of means; and it is permitted him to ride it if he needs to.

4. If someone is not able to supply the tamattu' hady, the qirān hady and the hady which is obligatory for doing something before or after its proper time

Then he fasts ten days, three of them on hajj the last of them being the Day of 'Arafah; and whoever is ignorant of this or forgets, then he fast three days of Minā and seven after this – if he wishes he may do this on his way back and if he wishes he may delay this until he has returned home to his country; and it is obligatory to do the three consecutively and the seven consecutively.

8. Things which prevent hajj

These are eight in number

1. Paternity

Parents may prohibit the child from the voluntary hajj or for him to hurry to do the *farḍ* hajj as quickly as possible, according to one of two judgments.

2. Slavehood

Such that the master prohibits his slave from doing the hajj; and he leaves the state of *iḥrām* if he prohibits him, like the person who is forcibly prevented; but he is not to prohibit him if he has already entered the state of *iḥrām* with his permission.

3. A married woman

The husband is not to prohibit the spouse who is capable of hajj – according to the judgment that says that a person is to go as soon as he or she is able; however according to the judgment that one may delay, then there are two judgments. And if she enters the state of *iḥrām* for the *farḍ* hajj then he is not to have her break her *iḥrām* and return to the normal state of *ḥill* unless this entails some harm, loss or prejudice to him.

4. Lack of legal competence

An incompetent or a fool is only to make the hajj with the permission of his legal guardian or caretaker.

5. Imprisonment

For injuring or killing someone, or for debt: such a person is as the sick person.

6. Claim from a debtor whose payment is due

The creditor may prevent a person of means who has entered the state of *iḥrām* from leaving for hajj. However, the latter should not leave this state and return to the normal state of *ḥill,* but should rather pay the debt; and if in straightened circumstance or the debt is deferred then he is not to prevent him.

7. When forcibly prevented by the enemy after having entered iḥrām

Any such person is allowed to leave the state of *iḥrām* according to the consensus; and a person prevented by the enemy or strife and unrest on hajj or *'umrah* is to keep watch as long as he hopes it might come to an end, but if he gives up hope then he should come out of *iḥrām* in the place he finds himself in, wherever it may be in the *Ḥarām* or outside of it and he does not have to sacrifice a *hady* animal, although if he has brought one along with him then he should sacrifice it, while ash-Shāfi'ī and Ashhab have said that he does have to sacrifice a *hady*, and he shaves his head or clips some of his hair but he does not have to make it up or do an *'umrah* – unless he has not made the hajj or *'umrah* before, in which case he has to make the hajj of Islam; and Abū Ḥanīfah has said he has to make it up the following year.

The person who is prevented by necessity may be in one of five situations, three of which permit him to leave the state of *iḥrām*, that is the cause occurs suddenly after or before his entering *iḥrām* but he is unaware of it, or is aware of it but considers that it is not such as to stop him;

and he is prohibited from leaving his state of *iḥrām* in the fourth situation, that is his path is blocked but he is able to arrive by another way;

and it is valid in a fifth case if the condition for leaving *iḥrām* is present, that is if he is uncertain as to whether they will block his path or not.

8. Illness

Whoever is struck by illness after entering *iḥrām* must stay in the state of *iḥrām* until he gets better, even if this lasts a long time, contrary to

Abū Ḥanīfah according to whom he is like someone forcibly prevented by the enemy. When he gets well he makes the *'umrah* and leaves the state of *iḥrām* by way of the *'umrah* and does not have to perform any remaining action of the rites, but the following year he makes up his hajj irrespective of whether it is a *farḍ* or voluntary one and brings a *hady* sacrifice according to his means. If he does not find a *hady* then he fasts the fast of someone performing the *tamattu'* hajj – three days during the hajj and seven when he returns. Abū Ḥanīfah has said that he must have a *hady* sacrifice. And if the illness persists such that the months of the hajj of the following year arrive and he is in the state of *iḥrām* then he remains in his *iḥrām* state until he has made up his hajj and he does not have to make the *'umrah,* but it is recommended for him to make the *hady* sacrifice.

The judgment regarding the person detained after entering *iḥrām*, someone who loses his way, someone who miscalculates the number of days and the person ignorant of the days of hajj – such that he misses it – is the same judgment as that of the sick person with respect to all we have mentioned.

Complementary aspects

Whoever misses the hajj after entering *iḥrām* must complete it on the basis of what he has done of the *'umrah* and make up the hajj the following year and make the *hady* sacrifice. And Abū Ḥanīfah has said that he does not have to make the *hady* sacrifice. One misses it because of three things:

1. Missing doing all of its actions;
2. Missing the standing at 'Arafah on the Day of 'Arafah or the night of the Day of Sacrifice; and if he makes the rites other than standing he does not reckon them as valid but he if he makes the standing at

'Arafah even for a short time during the night then he has made the hajj in a valid manner;

3. Whoever stays at 'Arafah until dawn on the Day of Sacrifice, whether he had stood there or not.

9. The 'Umrah

This is a *sunnah* whose importance is stressed to be performed once in a lifetime, while Ibn Ḥabīb, Abū Ḥanīfah and ash-Shāfi'ī have deemed it obligatory, and its judgment with regard to capacity, its performance by proxy or by someone hired to do it is the same as the judgment of hajj.

Its performance is permitted throughout the year except during the days of hajj in the case of someone preoccupied with the actions of the hajj, and the preferred time is during Ramadan. Abū Ḥanīfah has said that it is *makrūh* for the person performing hajj and for others for six consecutive days: 'Arafah, the Day of Sacrifice and the Days of Tashrīq. It is *makrūh* to repeat it during a single year, while Muṭarrif and ash-Shāfi'ī have deemed this recommended.

The form of *'umrah* is that one enters the state of *iḥrām*, then makes the *ṭawāf*, then the *sa'y*, then one shaves the head or cuts off some of one's hair – at which point one leaves the state of *'umrah* and becomes *ḥill*; and the *hady* sacrifice is recommended.

10. Visiting the tomb of the Prophet ﷺ

And mention of the Ḥarām and the sacrosanct places

It is fitting in the case of the person performing the hajj that he proceed to Madīnah, then enter the Mosque of the Prophet ﷺ, then make the *ṣalāt* in it and invoke peace on the Prophet ﷺ and on his Companions, Abū Bakr and 'Umar ؓ, and he seeks his intercession with Allah and makes *ṣalāt* between his tomb and the minbar and he makes his farewell to the Prophet ﷺ when he leaves Madīnah.

Madīnah is more excellent than Makkah, contrary to ash-Shāfi'ī, and both of them are inviolable *Ḥarāms*, in which whatever is prohibited in the state of *iḥrām* – by way of hunting or anything else which causes its invalidity – is also prohibited, contrary to Abū Ḥanīfah with respect to hunting in Madīnah. Whoever does hunt, must pay compensation just as the *muḥrim* is liable for hunting in Makkah, not as in Madīnah [for a resident].

Nor must one cut down any tree in the *Ḥarām*, irrespective of whether dead wood or not; if he does, then he must seek forgiveness of Allah, but he does not have to pay anything in compensation, while ash-Shāfi'ī has said that he is liable for a cow as compensation for a large tree and a sheep for a small one; but there is no harm in cutting down date palms, trees and vegetable bushes burnt by fire in the *Ḥarām*, contrary to ash-Shāfi'ī and Ibn Ḥanbal, while he has excluded Senna and Idhkār a sweet smelling rush.

And among the places that one should make for to partake of their Barakah is the tomb of Ismā'īl ﷺ and his mother Hājar and they are both in the Ḥijr i.e. the space included between the north wall of the Ka'bah and the low circular wall to the north of it, and the tomb of Adam ﷺ in the mountain of Abū Qays, and the cave mentioned in the Qur'ān which is in the Abū Thawr mountain, and the cave in mount Hirā' where the revelation to the Messenger ﷺ first began, and visiting the tombs of the Companions, the Tābi'īn, i.e. the Followers – the generation who came after the Companions, and the Imams of Makkah and Madīnah.

Conclusion

The '*specific/well-known days*' [Al-Ḥajj: 28] refer to the three Days of Sacrifice and the '*designated or numbered days*' [Al-Baqarah: 201] refer to the days of Minā, namely the Days of Tashrīq, that is the three days after the Days of Sacrifice – so the Day of Sacrifice is specific/well-known but not designated or numbered whereas the second and third days are specific and designated/numbered while the fourth is designated/numbered but not specific/well-known; although Abū Ḥanīfah has said that the 'specific/well-known days' refer to the ten days of Dhu l-Ḥijjah, the last being the Day of Sacrifice.

7 – *Jihād*

1. Preliminary Aspects

1. Its ruling

It is a *farḍ kifāyah* according to the majority, while Ibn al-Musayyab said that it is a *farḍ 'ayn*, Ṣaḥnūn said that it became voluntary after the Fatḥ [the Opening of Makkah to Islam], and ad-Dāwūdī that it is *farḍ 'ayn* for those living adjacent to the *kuffār*.

Subsidiary matters

If the outlying reaches of the territory are protected and any gaps have been stopped, then the *farḍ* obligation for *jihād* is annulled and the *nāfilah* remains, but it then becomes incumbent for three reasons:

1. The command of the Imam-Leader – such that whoever is stipulated by the Imam must go out;

2. When the enemy suddenly attacks a part of the territory of the Muslims, then it becomes incumbent on them to defend it and if they are unable to do so, then it becomes obligatory on those close by, and if their combined efforts are not up to the task, then it becomes obligatory on the rest of the Muslims until they repulse the enemy;

3. In order to rescue Muslim prisoners from the hands of the *kuffār*.

2. The six conditions for its obligation

Namely, Islam, puberty, sanity, freedom, male and having physical and financial capacity. However, if the enemy afflicts the Muslims severely, then it also becomes obligatory on slaves and women.

3. The two things preventing a person from making jihād

1. A debt which is due – but not one which is not yet due; however if the debtor whose debt is due is in straightened circumstances he may travel without permission of the person to whom the debt is owed.

2. Paternity – such that parents may forbid it unless it has been made specifically incumbent upon him. It may not be forbidden by the grandfather or grandmother, contrary to ash-Shāfi'ī. And the *kāfir* father is like a Muslim father regarding his forbidding a son from journeying or exposing himself to danger – except in the case of *jihād*, on account of the suspicion that he might be preventing him lest the Muslims be strengthened, although it has also been said that such a father may prevent him in all circumstances.

4. Its six farḍ obligations

The intention, obedience to the Imam, not taking booty before its division by the amir (*ghulūl*), fulfilling the obligation of safety if accorded, holding one's ground on the advance of the army, avoiding corruption, viciousness or immorality; and there is no harm in *jihād* with unjust, oppressive or tyrannical leaders.

2. The fighting

This is composed of seven matters

1. Those who are fought

They are classed in three ways: *kuffār*, rebels and armed robbers or highway men – and the ruling with regard to these two latter groups will follow in the chapter on *ḥudūd*.

As for the first group, this comprises all kinds of *kuffār*, although it has been narrated from Mālik that one should abstain from fighting the Abyssinians and the Turks.

Women and children are not to be killed, according to the agreed judgment, unless they are fighting – and what is taken into account in determining whether they are children is the growth of the beard, although it has also been said whether they are capable of seminal emission or not.

Monks are not killed, nor the inhabitants of monasteries, nor very old men, contrary to ash-Shāfi'ī, unless one fears harm from them or that they will scheme against you.

The insane or demented are not to be killed, nor the blind or the chronically sick, although there is a difference of opinion if these two latter are capable of scheming. There is also a difference of opinion regarding hired labourers and agricultural workers.

And a Muslim is not to kill his father who is *kāfir* unless forced to do so because he fears for his own life.

2. The call to Islam before fighting

This is in specific regard to those whom the call to Islam has not yet reached: they are invited to embrace Islam in the first instance and if they respond, then one desists from fighting them; if they refuse, then the *jizyah* is proposed to them; if they refuse to pay, then they are fought.

As for those who have heard the call, they are not invited again and one seeks to attack them while they are unawares, although one group have said that one must make the invitation to Islam in all circumstances, while another group say that it is recommended.

3. Those one may have recourse to for assistance

They are the free Muslims who are of age; and it is permitted to use slaves with permission of their masters and those approaching adulthood who are strong, while it is not permitted to use *mushrikūn*, contrary to the two; and Ibn Ḥabīb has said this refers to their use in military detachments and the advancing army, but in the case of the destruction of buildings or razing of forts, then there is no harm in this. He has also said there is no harm in using those with whom one has made peace treaties against those one is fighting.

4. What one may take with one when going out to fight

One may not take one's family to the land of the enemy, nor may one travel with the Qur'ān to the land of the enemy lest it fall in their hands, and even if the army is huge, one does not travel with it lest one drops it or forgets it, contrary to Abū Ḥanīfah.

5. Aspects of the fighting

There is no harm in razing their settlements, their fortresses and submerging them in water, cutting them off from water, reducing them to ruins, bombarding them using mangonel catapults, while with respect to the use of fire there is a difference of opinion; and there is no harm in cutting down their trees, irrespective of whether they are fruit trees or not.

If they have Muslim prisoners with them, then their settlements are not set on fire or submerged in water, and there is a difference of opinion regarding the mangonels and the cutting off of their water supply.

If there are women and children with them, then there are four opinions – that mangonels are permitted but not burning.

If they shield themselves with women and children, then we leave them unless by leaving them one fears for the Muslims, in which case one fights them even if they protect themselves in this way.

And it is permitted to kill their animals, contrary to ash-Shāfi'ī and Ibn Wahb, while it is narrated from Mālik that one has the option of either killing them or hamstringing them. And there is agreement as to the killing of a horse beneath its rider, while there is a difference of opinion regarding date palms.

It is not permitted to carry the heads of the *kuffār* from one place to another or to carry them to the leaders.

6. Fleeing

It is not permitted to turn back from the fighting ranks if there is a risk of a rout or defeat; if there is no threat, then it is permitted to withdrawing to rejoin the fight or withdrawing to support another group (See: Sūrat al-Anfāl 8:16), and 'withdrawing to rejoin the fight' means appearing to retreat while in fact scheming – by the tactics of war – and intending to rejoin the fight. Withdrawing to support another group that is present is permitted, while there is a difference of opinion regarding joining a group that is absent or withdrawing to a town.

Accepting defeat is not permitted unless the *kuffār* increase their force to twice that of the Muslims, and what is taken into account is the number according to the well-known view, although it has also been said that it is the strength that is taken into account, while it has also been said that if the number of Muslims reaches twelve thousand, then accepting defeat is not permitted even if the number of *kuffār* is more than twice that of the Muslims. If the Muslims know that they will be killed, then retreat is preferable and if they are also aware that they will have no effect in harming the *kuffār*, then flight becomes obligatory. And Abu l-Ma'ālī [al-Juwaynī] has said that there is no difference of opinion about this.

If a town is besieged and the Muslims become weakened, then Rabī'ah said that going out to fight is preferable than dying of hunger, and there is a difference of opinion whether in the case of a ship which is bombarded with fire a man should throw himself into the sea to drown or not; if however he is fought, he is not to drown himself but rather should stand and fight until he dies.

7. Mubārazah – a man fighting with another of the enemy in single combat in sight of the two opposing armies

It is not permitted if for reputation and fame. If however the intention is pure, then it is only allowed with the permission of the Imam if he is just; and fighting in single combat against the enemy army is approved of although it has also been said that it is *makrūh* because it would be exposing oneself to certain death.

3. The Booty

This comprises seven matters: men, their women and children from amongst the *kuffār*, their wealth, land, foodstuffs and drink.

Their men

The Imam has five options in their respect: putting them to death, granting them freedom, ransoming them, exacting the *jizyah* or enslaving them. He does what is of the most benefit in this respect. And it is permitted to ransom them for Muslim prisoners, according to the agreed judgment, while there is a difference of opinion regarding ransoming them for money, while Abū Ḥanīfah has said that neither granting them their freedom nor ransoming them is permitted, and one group has said that they are to be put to death in all circumstances.

Women and children

One has the option of granting them their freedom, ransoming them and enslaving them.

If a woman and her small child have been taken prisoner they are not to be separated when sold or when being divided as booty, while it is permitted to separate the child from its father, contrary to Abū Ḥanīfah; and one may separate him from his grandmother – and what is being referred to here is a small child who has not yet lost its milk teeth, while it has also been narrated that it refers to a boy who has not yet had a seminal emission, in agreement with Abū Ḥanīfah.

If a woman is pregnant by a Muslim she is enslaved but not the child unless she was pregnant with him while the father was in the state of *kufr* and she was then taken prisoner after the father embraced Islam, in which case the result of the pregnancy is *fay'* booty.

If a married couple are made prisoner together, or one of them, the marriage is annulled and her new master may have sexual intercourse with her, although it has also been said that their marriage is recognised, and it has also been said it is annulled if she is made prisoner before him.

If amongst the booty there is someone who is subsequently set free – from the possession of someone with a right to booty who has been allotted this person – then this owner is compensated for his portion of the booty which he has lost.

Wealth

It is of four kinds

1. That which belongs to Allah exclusively, this being the *jizyah*, the *kharāj*, the *'ushr* of the *dhimmī*s and those with whom peace has been concluded, and that which has been acquired without fighting, this

all being *fay'* booty, and the Imam disposes of it in a manner which he deems of benefit and it is not subject to the *khums* tax, contrary to ash-Shāfi'ī.

2. That belonging to the person who took it, there being no *khums* on it – that is, what is taken by someone who was in the war zone but not mounted on horse or camel, like for example the prisoner who flees from them with wealth; and whatever the enemy throws away when they fear drowning, other than gold or silver for this is subject to the rules of *zakāt*.

3. That of which a fifth – *khums* – is for Allah and the rest for those who took it, this being *ghanīmah* booty and buried treasure, and what we mean by *ghanīmah* is what is taken in fighting, and anything taken by stealing or snatched is treated as being in this category.

4. That about which there is a difference of opinion – as to whether it is subject to *khums* or not, that is, what is taken as *ghanīmah* booty by slaves when there is no free person with them, or women and children when there is no man with them, and that which has been abandoned by its owners without the arrival of the army, this being *fay'* booty and nothing of it belongs to the army, although it has also been said that it is subject to the *khums*.

Three subsidiary matters

1. Regarding the *salb*, this being like all the other *ghanīmah* booty and does not belong in particular to the person who killed the fighter, contrary to ash-Shāfi'ī and Ibn Ḥanbal; and the Imam may give it to him from the *khums* if he sees benefit in this, but it is not permitted to announce this before the fighting lest the intention of those fighting be adversely affected.

2. Embezzling booty (*ghulūl*) is *ḥarām* i.e. taking it before the division

of the spoils by the amir, according to the consensus, and if someone who has embezzled something comes to repent before the division takes place, then he is not punished and he is to return what he has embezzled to the booty; if he repents after the army has left, he is punished and what he has embezzled is given away as *ṣadaqah*.

There is a difference of opinion as to whether *ghanīmah* booty becomes the possession of someone by his taking it, in agreement with ash-Shāfiʿī, or by means of the division, in agreement with Abū Ḥanīfah – in which case whoever has intercourse with a slave girl from the booty before the division is subject to the *ḥadd* punishment and if he steals something from it, then his hand is cut off, contrary to Ibn al-Mājishūn with respect to both cases; and Ṣaḥnūn has said that if he steals three dirhams more than he is due from his portion, then his hand is cut off, otherwise it is not.

3. If the Muslims take livestock and animals from the *kuffār* as *ghanīmah* booty and fear that the enemy may take them from their hands, then it is permitted to wound and hamstring them, while ash-Shāfiʿī has said that it is not permitted and that they should be left alone.

AGRICULTURAL LANDS

If they are conquered by force, then they are of three kinds:

Far from our control, in which case they are damaged, burnt or destroyed;

Under our control but uninhabited in which case the Imam allots them to those who have enterprise and show intrepidity in these places, but the army has no right to any of them;

Lands which are close and desirable in which case the well-known judgment is that they are *waqf* lands and that the *kharāj* tax issuing from them is used for the benefit of the Muslims – to assure provisions for the fighters and workers, to build bridges, mosques and walls and for other purposes, although it has also been said that they are divided up like the rest of the wealth of the *ghanīmah* booty, in agreement with ash-Shāfiʿī, and it has also been said that the Imam has the option as to its disposal, in agreement with Abū Ḥanīfah.

If these lands are opened up for the Muslims as a result of reconciliation or a peace settlement, then they are subject to the demands and conditions of this settlement.

Foodstuffs and drink

It is permitted to make use of them without their having been first divided up as long as they are in the arena of war, and included here are storable foodstuffs, fruit, meat, fodder – as much as needed by the person, irrespective of whether he is in need or not in need; and if there is a superfluity of it after the person has entered the territory of Islam and the army has disbanded, and if the amount is large, then it is given away in *ṣadaqah*, while if the amount is small, then it may be made use of.

And it is permitted to slaughter livestock to eat and to take the hides for shoes and *khuffs*, although it has also been said that it is not permitted to slaughter them. There is no need for the permission of the Imam in this respect.

If the Imam has gathered together any superfluity of this stuff and the people find themselves in need, then they may eat of it without his permission.

Weapons may be taken to fight with but then they are returned; and likewise animals may be ridden to one's home but then they are returned to the *ghanīmah* booty; likewise clothes may be worn but they are then returned to the *ghanīmah* booty, and Ibn Wahb has said that neither weapons, clothing or animals may be made use of.

4. Division of the ghanīmah booty, the khums and fay'

Comprising seven matters

1. That the Amir sets apart the army for special distinction

He shares among them four-fifths of the *ghanīmah* booty while they are in the Abode of War, although Abū Ḥanīfah has said that it is not divided amongst them until it reaches the Abode of Islam; and the Amir has the option of dividing up individual items of the booty or their value, and he does this according to what he deems to be of the most benefit.

2. Those who receive a portion

As for the Muslim who is free, male and of age, then he receives a share according to the agreed judgment.

As for the *kāfir*, if he has not taken part in the fighting, he is not accorded a share, while if he has, then there are three judgments, and in the third one a distinction is made as to whether the Muslims were in need of his help, in which case he is accorded a share, otherwise he is not.

And the slave is treated like the *kāfir*, and a young lad who is underage is accorded a share if capable of fighting, although it has also been said that he is not accorded a share, in agreement with the two; and a woman who has not fought is not accorded a share, but if she has fought, then there are two judgments as to whether she has a right to a share.

The trader and the hired worker are given a portion if they have fought according to the well-known judgment.

The lame person, the leper and the person whose left arm is missing are given a portion, but not a blind, disabled or infirm person, or someone with both hands missing.

3. One has a right to the ghanīmah booty by virtue of having been present at the fighting

This is even if the *ghanīmah* is taken after the fighting, according to the best-known judgment, although it has also been said by being present and as long as the booty is taken while present, and it is also said by virtue of one's entering into the land of the enemy.

Thus according to the well-known judgment, whoever dies in the fighting or is sent by the Amir for the purpose of benefitting the Muslims or his horse dies or he sells it, then his portion is assured; but whoever lingers behind on the way abandoning the military expedition (*ghazwah*), then he has no share; and if he loses the army and it takes *ghanīmah* booty, then there are three judgments: a share is accorded him, he is denied a share, and a judgment – this being the well-known judgment – based on discriminating whether his getting lost was before entry into enemy territory, in which case he has no share, or after entering it, in which case his share is assured. And likewise, in the case of ships, if some are driven back by the wind.

If an army arrives at a river and one group crosses it and take *ghanīmah* booty, while the other is left behind, then the latter have no right to a share of it.

And if the army splits up into two groups and each group for its part takes *ghanīmah* booty, then they are partners as long as each would have afforded help to the other if needed.

If a military detachment from the army goes out to raid and takes *ghanīmah* booty in a place nearby such that the army would have been able to afford assistance, then the army has a share if they take booty, while if they go a long way off, then they do not. If the army takes *ghanīmah* after it, then the share of the detachment is assured if it went out with permission of the Imam, and Abū Ḥanīfah has said that if help comes to them after the war is over and booty has been taken, then they share in the booty.

4. Foot soldiers have one portion and someone mounted has three shares

One for himself and two for his horse; while Abū Ḥanīfah has said that the horse has one portion; and the portion is alike for a horse that is owned, one assigned as a *waqf*, one hired, lent or usurped and its portion is all for its rider in every such case, and in the case of usurpation he must pay compensation for the hire of a similar beast.

Whoever has several horses is granted a portion for one of them and according to the agreed judgment there is no portion for more than two and, according to the well-known judgment, not for a second, contrary to Ibn Ḥanbal. The portion of the Amir is like any other person.

There is no portion for a mule, or a donkey, a camel, an elephant, or an emaciated horse which is of no benefit, contrary to one which is merely hurt in the foot or ill, as long as the illness is light.

5. The khums (the Imam's fifth of the booty)

According to the madhhab, the *khums* is according to the judgment of the Imam who takes enough to fulfil his needs, even if this means all of it, and he disposes of the rest for matters of benefit; and ash-Shāfi'ī has said that the booty is divided in five portions: a portion for the Prophet ﷺ which is disposed of by the Imam for matters of benefit, a portion for his descendants who are not permitted to take *ṣadaqah*, irrespective of whether they are rich or poor, a portion for orphans, a portion for the destitute and a portion for travellers. And Abū Ḥanīfah has said that it is divided in three portions: one for the orphans, one for the destitute and one for travellers – his portion ﷺ together with that of his descendants having been annulled upon his death. One group however has said that there are six portions, adding a portion for Allah which is used to maintain the Ka'bah.

6. Raḍkh – small presents, naql – assignments and transfers of property, and salb – spoil and plunder

As for *naql*, this refers to what is given of the *khums* to those who are of benefit to the Muslims; the *raḍkh* is what he gives of the *khums* to those who have no portion, like women, slaves, children – although according to the well-known judgment they are not given of the *raḍkh*; as for the *salb*, this has been mentioned above.

7. The fay' booty

The way the *fay'* and *khums* are dealt with by the Imams of just and equitable behaviour is that they are used initially to secure dangerous highways, passes and entrance roads on the borders of the territory, for the maintenance of the implements of war, for gifts for the fighters, and if anything is left over then for the judiciary and those working for it, for the building of mosques and bridges, and then it is distributed to the poor; and if there is still any leftover, then the Imam has the option of giving it to the rich or holding it as a *waqf* for any times of disaster that might befall Islam.

There is a difference of opinion as to whether preference is shown those who are respected and have precedence and who are rich – or whether they are treated like any others.

5. Muslims' wealth in the possession of the kuffār

This may be divided in four categories

1. That which they have when they accept Islam

It belongs to them;

2. That which they came with to the territories of the Muslims with safe passage

This also belongs to them, although he has said in the *Mudawwanah* 'I would not like to buy this from them', while Ibn al-Mawwāz has said that it is permitted to buy this. If however its owner comes, then he may acquire it by paying its price and the purchase of a Muslim slave from them is better than leaving him to them – this having been said by Ibn Rushd – and likewise his personal belongings.

3. That which a Muslim who had entered with safe passage purchased from them

In this case there is nothing for its owner unless he gives the price for it, but if they gave it as a gift to the person who entered their territory, then its owner has a greater right to it – without having to pay the price of it unless he requited the donor for it with something as a gift; but if he freed a slave or had a child by a slave girl, then this is deemed to be concluded as a matter – without any possibility of any further legal recourse to it, contrary to Ashhab.

4. That which has been acquired as booty by the Muslims

It belongs to the person from amongst the Muslims who had owned it, and it is not permitted to divide it up if the owner becomes aware of this; thus if he becomes aware of it before the division, then he takes it without paying any price for it, but if he is unaware of it and it is subject to the division, then he has more right to it on payment of the price, in agreement with Ibn Ḥanbal, while ash-Shāfi'ī has said without payment of its price. Abū Ḥanīfah has said: If they overcame us and seized it, then its owner has more right to it before the division without payment in return, while after it in return for payment; and if they took it without overwhelming us, then it belongs to its owner in all cases, while one group has said that its owner is not to take it after the division or before it.

Secondary matters

If a *kāfir* becomes Muslim and he has a free Muslim with him, then he is taken from him without payment and he is freed.

If the enemy takes a free Muslim woman prisoner and then she is taken by the Muslims then is free; and if she gives birth to children with them and they are taken [by the Muslims] when small then they have the same status as her, while there is a difference of opinion if they are grown up; and if she had been a slave girl of a man, then she and her children belong to her master.

If they take a *dhimmī* as booty, and we then take him as *ghanīmah* booty, he is returned to his state as a *dhimmī*.

If they take a slave as *ghanīmah* or a *mudabbar* or *mukātib* or a slave to be freed after a certain time or an *Umm walad*, then they belong to their master as any other wealth.

If a prisoner comes over to us having left his wealth behind with them and this is then taken as *ghanīmah* booty by the Muslims, he has more right to it before the division without payment, while after division on payment of the price.

If a *kāfir* fighter becomes Muslim and the Muslims raid his country, then his wife is *fay'* booty and likewise his children according to the well-known judgment, while it has also been said they are considered his, and his wealth is *fay'* booty, while it has also been said that it is his; and it has also been said that it belongs to him before the division without payment and after it in return for payment.

6. Concerning Muslim prisoners

This comprises four matters

1. The ruling on ransom

It is obligatory to save them from the hands of the *kuffār* by fighting, but if the Muslims are incapable of this, then it is obligatory on them to pay a ransom of wealth.

So it is obligatory on the wealthy prisoner to pay the ransom for himself , and on the Imam to pay the ransom for the poor from the *Bayt al-Māl*, and whatever is lacking, then it becomes an imposition on the whole wealth of the Muslims even if it is exhausted in doing so; and the Imam coerces the owners of non-Muslim, non-Arabs to ransom the Muslims with them and makes a payment for them.

2. Claiming restitution from someone for ransom

Whoever ransoms a prisoner at this latter's instruction, then he may claim from this latter for the ransom according to the agreed judgment, and if he ransoms him without his instructions and without his being aware of it, then he may also claim from him, contrary to ash-Shāfi'ī; and it has also been said that he may claim from him if he is of means and from the *Bayt al-Māl* if he is of restricted means. The ransom money has priority over debt.

If one spouse from a married couple ransoms the other, then he or she has no claim over the other unless the one spouse has ransomed the other on his or her instruction; and likewise relations, fathers, mothers, grand-fathers or -mothers, children, paternal or maternal uncles and aunts, brothers and sisters and their children.

If the enemy demands horses or weapons in the ransom, these are handed over to them, contrary to wine or pigs, although Ṣaḥnūn has permitted the ransom price consisting of these two, while Ibn al-Qāsim has prohibited whatever entails the risk of harm to the Muslims. Whoever ransoms a prisoner with wine and the like, then this does not entail any claim for restitution in kind nor for the price of the wine, and whoever ransoms prisoners for a thousand, then claim or restitution may be made against the person of means and the poor person alike unless the enemy was aware that the person was of means and was greedy for a larger sum.

3. A DIFFERENCE OF OPINION BETWEEN THE ONE WHO PAYS THE RANSOM AND THE PERSON RANSOMED

If they differ, then the word of the person ransomed is accepted regarding his denial of the original sum or reason for the ransom and its amount, and if the person claims what does not appear to be true, then the one who has been ransomed is strengthened in his denial of the reason, while it has also been said that the word of the person who paid the ransom is accepted if the person ransomed agrees with him as to the original sum and reason for the ransom; and if he says 'I was capable of devising a stratagem and leaving without paying anything' then he is not pursued if he appears to be telling the truth and the person paid his ransom without his knowledge; and if he said 'I was ransomed without this ransom of yours' and it becomes clear he is telling the truth, then the extra paid for him is null and void with respect to any obligation he might have in its respect; and if he was aware and does not deny it, then he is pursued for payment in all circumstances.

4. Pawning or pledging another person

It is not permitted to put up a free Muslim as a pawn or pledge in place of a Muslim prisoner. However it is permitted to a *kāfir* to pledge another *kāfir* from amongst his relations or from someone other than his relations, and if he stipulates that the person pawned be a slave – if he does not advance money – then he is granted this condition; and if he pawns his son or someone else but does not pay the ransom – then if there is an excuse, such that he has died, he has been detained or some other reason, then the person pawned is not to be enslaved; if there is no excuse, then an adult man or woman is enslaved but not a girl or boy who is not of age; and forfeit of the person pawned is permitted in this instance, contrary to the other instances of persons pawned as pledges or security.

Secondary matters

If the prisoner has been accorded safety for his person, his wealth or been assured an amnesty for any requital outstanding regarding his having killed someone, then he must pay the ransom, but if he has not been given this assurance, then he may flee and take whatever he can lay his hands on – whether it be persons or wealth – and to kill whoever of the *kuffār* he has got the better of; and no *khums* is taken on what he flees with. And if – with the prisoner – there is his wife or his slave girl, then it is permitted to have sexual intercourse with them if he is sure that they have had no intercourse with the *kuffār* although this is *makrūh* when any children might remain in the Zone of War; and the *ḥadd* punishment for fornication is to be applied to him if he fornicates with a free woman or owned slave woman, contrary to Ibn al-Mājishūn.

7. Assurance of Protection – Safe Passage

The granting of security is of three kinds, two being of a general nature, and these are contracted in particular by the Sultan, and they are *ṣulḥ* – reconciliation or settlement and *dhimmah* – guarantee of life and property and they shall both be discussed below. The third kind is particular to a single *kāfir* or to a number of them who have been confined together.

It is valid on the part of any Muslim with discrimination and this includes women, according to the four, and slaves, according to the three, and the child who is incapable of understanding the import of this assurance of protection, according to the madhhab – such that the Imam and anyone else must honour it as long as it does not entail any harm, irrespective of whether it is of benefit or not, irrespective of whether it is by word or by written agreement, in whatever language and by whatever indication or understood gesture.

If a *kāfir* thought that a Muslim wanted to grant assurance of protection but the Muslim did not want it, then he is not to be killed, and if he stipulated assurance of protection for his family and wealth, then he must honour this.

Whoever enters as an ambassador or intermediary is in no need of assurance of protection for that intention itself assures him protection.

A champion fighter who goes out in single combat must honour the conditions agreed upon with his *kāfir* counterpart before the fight.

If a Muslim prisoner grants assurance of protection to someone in the same situation, then he is bound by this unless he was coerced; and if he swears to them when coerced, then his oath is not binding.

If we lay siege to the inhabitants of a fortress and they show their submission to a man, then this is valid if he is of sound intellect, has integrity and is of insight with regard to the means whereby one may reach a settlement during fighting, but if the matter is decided by a woman, a lad who is not of age, a slave or a corrupt person, then the decision is subject to the decision of the Imam.

If a fighter from the enemy comes over to us with the assurance of protection and leaves wealth with us, then it belongs to him or his inheritors after him.

If an able-bodied *kāfir* is taken on the highway and he claims something which would mean that one spares him and it cannot be ascertained as to whether he is telling the truth or lying, then he must be returned to his place of safety even if his word is not accepted.

CLARIFICATION

The difference between assurance of protection, which is binding, and guile and subterfuge, which is permitted in war, is that the *kāfir* feels peace of mind and ease by the act of assuring protection to him, while guile and subterfuge is the manipulation of obscure, hidden aspects of the war – such that the enemy imagines that one is shunning confrontation or withdrawing from it – until an opportunity opens up for the Muslim. And in such manipulation is included dissemblance, camouflage or feints in army movements, sudden attacks at night, scattering to split them up, setting up ambushes, seeking to lure them away during the fighting to a position of greater advantage – and in any of such manoeuvres the person must not make it appear that he is one of them or that he follows their *dīn* or that he has come to give them counsel such that if he finds a moment of heedlessness he may cause harm to them – for this would be treachery and is not permitted.

8. Reconciliation or settlement with the enemy

On the basis of truce negotiations or making peace, this consisting of two matters

1. The conditions making it permitted

They are four in number:

1. That it be needed, for if without benefit, then it is not permitted, even if the enemy pay money; and if it is for some benefit, like a general incapacity to fight or an incapacity at a specific moment, then it is permitted for compensation or without compensation – depending on what is advantageous for the Muslims;

2. That the Imam takes charge of the matter;

3. That it be free of any invalid conditions, like abandoning a Muslim in their hands or handing money over to them when fear does not exist – and it is permitted if it does;

4. That it does not carry on beyond the time necessary for such a settlement based on *ijtihād* – the judgment of [the Imam], while Abū 'Imrān has said that it is recommended that it does not extend beyond four months, except in the case of incapacity.

2. Its ruling

That is that it is binding and its valid conditions must be fulfilled, but it is not permitted that one stipulate that anyone from among them who comes as a Muslim – man or woman – should be returned to them, while al-Māzarī has said that it is permitted to return men but not women, while there is a difference of opinion as to the return of their monks if they become Muslim.

If we suspect treachery on their part, then it is permitted to default on the agreement before its term.

9. The taking of jizyah from dhimmīs

This comprises three matters

1. The one who may conclude the arrangement and the person with whom it is concluded

Only the Imam may conclude *dhimmah* – the covenant of protection. It is only concluded with the *kāfir* who is free, of age, male and capable of paying the *jizyah* – it being permitted to have him acknowledge this commitment to pay, with the person who is not mad, or deprived of intellect nor secluded in a monastery having taken on the life of a monk. As for women, slaves and children, they pertain legally to their menfolk and the *jizyah* is not incumbent on them, nor is it incumbent on the poor person or the one unable to earn his living; but when the child becomes of age, then it is taken from him. And Ibn al-Mājishūn has said that there is only *dhimmah* – the covenant of protection – with the People of the Book, while ash-Shāfi'ī has said with the people of the Book and the Magians, but not the other *kuffār*.

2. That which is obligatory for them in our regard

This consisting of twelve issues

1. The payment of the *jizyah* personally by their own hand and in a state of submission, payment consisting of four dinars annually per capita for those who deal in gold, and forty dirhams in the case of those who deal in silver, and this amount does not increase or decrease in accordance with the financial strength or weakness of a person, while ash-Shāfi'ī has said the *jizyah* is a dinar per head, while if they have made a settlement based on more than this, then this is permitted; and Abū Ḥanīfah and Ibn Ḥanbal have said that it is twelve dirhams for the poor person, twenty four for the person of average means, and forty eight for the rich person; and if the *dhimmī* becomes Muslim

then the *jizyah* is annulled for him even if only a single day remains of the year in question.

2. The hosting of Muslims for three days if they pass by them.

3. A tenth-tax of what they trade in outside of their territory in which they live – the *jizyah* being of three types: the tithe or tenth which has just been mentioned; the *'anawiyyah jizyah* – that of submission after use of force – which has been mentioned above prior to this; and the *ṣulḥiyyah jizyah*, that is resulting from conciliation and settlement – which has no limits as to the sum or the persons from whom it may be taken – other than the terms of the settlement.

4. That they do not build any church or leave it standing as such in a territory established by the Muslims or which has been conquered by force; however, if opened up to the Muslims by settlement and they stipulated that such should remain standing, then this is permitted, while there are two judgments as to the stipulation that they will be built.

5. That they do not ride horses or mules of any worth, contrary to donkeys.

6. That they are prevented from using the main streets and open highways and are confined to use of the most narrow ways.

7. That they have a sign by which they are recognized, like a belt, and they are punished if they do not wear it.

8. That they do not cheat the Muslims nor give shelter to any spies.

9. That they do not prevent the Muslims from entering their churches night or day.

10. That they acknowledge the status of the Muslims, they do not hit Muslims, nor insult them nor employ them as servants.

11. That they conceal or muffle their bells and do not propagate any part of their religious ceremonies publicly.

12. That they do not insult any of the Prophets, on whom be peace, nor do they promulgate what they believe.

3. What is incumbent on us with respect to them

That we honour their acknowledgement of their status in our territory except the Arabian Peninsula, that is the Hijaz and Yemen, and that we desist from harming them, protect them by guaranteeing their lives and wealth, that we do not interfere with their churches or raise objections to their wine or pigs as long as they do not promote them publicly, but if they do openly show wine, then we pour it away in front of them; and if they do not let it be shown and a Muslim pours it away, then he is liable for it, although it has also been said that he is not. Anyone who openly shows his pigs is disciplined.

If they leave without any injustice having been done to them or force used against them, then they are enslaved, but if they leave on account of some injustice or violence then they are not, although Ashhab has said that they are not enslaved in any circumstances.

10. Racing and Shooting

Racing with horses is permitted, and it is also said that it is desirable. If it takes place without reward, then it is permitted in all circumstances with respect to horses and other animals, as well as boats and birds – with a view to having the messages they carry arrive quickly; and it is permitted to compete on foot, to use slings, to hurl stones and wrestling.

If done for a *rihān* , a prize, then this has three forms:

1. The governor or someone else puts up money which is then taken by the winner, and this is permitted, according to the agreed judgment;

2. Each of two contestants pools an amount and whoever of the two wins takes the money of his fellow contestant and that which he himself has put up – there being no one else but these two: this is prohibited according to the agreed judgment, while if there is a third person, the *muḥallil*, i.e. the person who makes it permitted, and they hand over their money to him if he is the winner – and he has not had to put up anything if he is not the winner – then Ibn al-Musayyab and ash-Shāfiʿī have permitted this, while Mālik has forbidden it;

3. That the money is put up by one of the two contestants, in which case it is permitted if it does not return to him and is taken by someone other than him who raced or by someone who attends.

And archery is like racing with regard to what is permitted or prohibited. And for shooting, javelin throwing or archery one erects a target and for racing a distance marker.

8 – Oaths and Vows
Containing five chapters

1. Types of oath

This consists of seven matters

1. The ruling regarding an oath

This contains three sections:

1. An oath 'by Allah' – swearing 'by Allah', and this is permitted;

2. One not said by Allah, and this is *makrūh* and it has also been said that it is *ḥarām*;

3. An oath by the likes of [the *jahiliyyah* 'gods'] al-Lāt or al-'Uzzā: if one believes in expressing such an oath one is venerating them, then the person is *kāfir*, otherwise it is *ḥarām*.

2. What oaths are necessarily binding

This is also divided into three sections

1. What is necessarily binding – and it is annulled by the exception – 'if Allah wills' – enunciated with the oath and by payment of *kaffārah*: it is a swearing by Allah and his names, like ar-Raḥīm, al-'Azīz, and by His attributes like His Power, His Hearing, His Sight, His Speech, His Oneness, His Existence from Before Endless Time, His Going On after Created Time, His Majestic Power and Strength, His Majesty, His Contract, His Covenant, His Custody, His Guarantee

and His Charge, and swearing by His name and by His Truth and Reality, and included here are swearing by the Qur'ān and the *Muṣḥaf*, i.e. the copy of the Qur'ān, according to the well-known position (*mashhūr*).

2. What is not binding, and an exception is not necessary, nor is *kaffārah*, and it refers to the oath made by other than the names of Allah, like swearing by the Ka'bah, the *qiblah* or the Prophet, or like someone saying 'by your life span', 'by your life', 'by your living' or 'by what is due to you'; as for someone saying 'if he is such, then he is a Jew' or '… he is a Christian', or 'free of Allah' or 'he is a *kāfir*' so some similar saying, in which case he is not liable for *kaffārah* in such instances if he breaks his oath, contrary to Abū Ḥanīfah, but he should seek forgiveness of Allah.

3. What is binding but which is not annulled by the exception or the *kaffārah*, namely when one swears that one shall cause something specific to happen or by a specific vow, in which case it is binding on him to carry out what he has sworn by, like divorce or setting free a slave, and the person is disciplined until he carries these two things out; and like swearing to walk to Makkah or giving *ṣadaqah* and other things.

3. The form of the oath

This may be divided into three:

1. By mention solely of the name by which the person swears, like one's saying '*Allāhi*! I did not do it';

2. By an addition to the wording of the oath – of '*wa*', '*ta*' or '*bi*', like one's saying *w-Allāhi*, *t-Allāhi* or *bi-llāhi* i.e. 'by Allah' – or by 'the oath of Allah' or 'I swear by Allah' or 'by the Life of Allah' – for there is no difference of opinion that these two kinds of oaths are effected;

3. The addition of the future verb, like one's saying 'I shall swear' or

'I shall make an oath' or 'I shall testify'; or the past, like one's saying 'I have sworn' or 'I have made an oath'; or of a noun like one's saying 'my oath' or 'my swearing' – for these are deemed oaths if accompanied by 'Allah' or His attributes irrespective of whether expressed explicitly or as an intention. But if other than this is intended or is devoid of an intention then it is not an oath and no ruling applies. And ash-Shāfi'ī has said that they are not deemed oaths in any circumstances if they are not accompanied by the explicit expression of the names of Allah, may He exalted, while Abū Ḥanīfah says the opposite to this. And whoever says to someone else 'by Allah, do such-and-such!' then nothing is binding on either of them.

4. What is sworn about

If about something past then it is not binding and there is no *kaffārah* to be paid, like one's saying 'by Allah it was like that' irrespective of whether he swore about the truth that he was aware of or deliberately about a falsehood, thereby entailing a wrong action, or about a doubtful matter, or about something which he believes to be the case but which then becomes clear to him that it is not so – and this is with respect to an oath by Allah.

As for binding matters, like divorce and the like, then if he swears to this occurring in the past, deliberately lying then this is binding, and if he swears by something he would have done like his saying 'my wife is divorced if you had come to me yesterday, I would have done such-and-such' [i.e. If you had come yesterday, I would have, for example, invited you to eat with us – and divorced my wife], then if it is something which he would have been able to do [i.e. the inviting], then he will have fulfilled [his oath - to divorce], otherwise he will have broken [his oath].

If what is sworn on is on the future, then it is binding – and it is of two types, affirmative or negative. As for the affirmative: like one's saying 'Surely I shall definitely do it,' or 'If I shall not have done it... [then such and such is binding on me']; as for the negative: like one's saying 'I shall certainly not do it', or 'if I were to do it... [then such and such is not binding on me]'.

5. That for which kaffārah is paid and that for which it is not

Swearing is of three kinds

Laghw, i.e. inadvertent statements;

Ghamūs, i.e. a knowingly false oath;

'Aqd, i.e. that which is concluded and thus binding.

As for *laghw*, there is no *kaffārah* to be paid according to the agreed judgment, and it refers to swearing on something which he believes to be just as he has sworn, then it becomes clear to him that this is not the case, in agreement with Abū Ḥanīfah, while it has been said that it is the saying 'No, by Allah, yes by Allah' which one happens to utter but without intent, in agreement with ash-Shāfi'ī and Ismā'īl al-Qāḍī. And Ṭāwūs has said it refers to a man making an oath when he is angry and Ibn 'Abbās has said it refers to his swearing to do an act of disobedience.

As for the *ghamūs*, no *kaffārah* is payable contrary to ash-Shāfi'ī, although the person swearing is committing a wrong action – and it refers to telling a lie deliberately about a matter in the past.

As for the *'aqd* this entails the *kaffārah*, and is that which is conditional upon the future, be it affirmative or negative.

6. Whoever makes an oath by deeming what is ḥalāl to be ḥarām with respect to foodstuffs, drinks, clothes or something else

This is like one's saying 'If I were to do that then bread would be *ḥarām* for me', then this is not binding on him in any way unless it is with regard to his wife, in which case it would be divorce, while with respect to the male or female slave it would mean setting them free, if he intended setting them free, while if he meant a deeming *ḥarām* but not setting free then nothing is binding on him, and Abū Ḥanīfah has said in this respect that all of this entails the *kaffārah* of an oath.

7. As for if one swears 'by the oaths which are binding on me' and then breaks one's oath

Nothing is reported from Mālik or his followers in this regard, while Ibn al-'Arabī has reported five judgments from those holding to the madhhab:

1. That the matter in this respect is dependent upon the person's intention, such that if he intended something then what he intended is binding on him, while if he did not intend anything one single divorce is binding on him;
2. The same ruling and it is recommended that he divorce three times thereby completing the action;
3. One final divorce is binding on him;
4. Three expressions of divorce are binding on him;
5. Three *kaffārahs* of the type for violating an oath are binding on him such that he is to feed thirty destitute persons, unless he intends something, in which case it is binding – and this is the preferred judgment of aṭ-Ṭarṭūshī.

One of the later *fuqahā'* has said that divorce, setting free, walking to Makkah, giving *ṣadaqah* of a third of one's wealth and fasting two consecutive months are binding. Aṭ-Ṭarṭūshī said that only the oath by Allah is included in these instances, not what they have mentioned with regard to divorce, setting free and other matters, unless he intends this or it is customary practice in the country in question such that people swear there by such an oath.

If then it is determined in this manner, this oath is firmly established in our country as meaning and intending divorce uttered three times, i.e. irrevocable divorce, but not fasting or manumission or anything else, then it is obligatory to interpret it according to this fixed customary practice because it is what the one swearing the oath meant rather than something else. One does not reduce the number of divorces below three. If one pays the *kaffārah* for the oath by Allah then this is meritorious, interpreting the oath as a *sharī'ah* divorce, unless the oaths are to be understood as having a general import by virtue of his intention in which case whatever is comprised in his intention is binding on him with respect to fasting, manumission or other than this.

2. What fulfilling or breaking an oath entails

This consisting of two sections

1. Fulfilling or breaking an oath

Fulfilling an oath means the conformity with what one has sworn to do. Breaking an oath means to contradict what one has sworn to do – with respect to negation or affirmation

Anyone who swears to forgo something or to its non-existence then he is fulfilling the oath until the action occurs at his hand such that he breaks the oath. Whoever makes an oath to undertake an action or swears to its existence then he is breaking the oath until the action occurs in which case he is fulfilling it.

And the breaking of an oath, according to the madhhab, begins or comes into being for the minimum of reasons while the fulfilling of an oath only exists by virtue of the most complete reasons, so that whoever makes an oath to eat a loaf does not fulfil his oath until he eats the whole of it. If he makes an oath not to eat it then he would have broken his oath by eating a part of it.

Whoever makes an oath not to do something and then does it has broken his oath irrespective of whether he did it deliberately, absent-mindedly or out of ignorance – unless he forgets and does it out of forgetfulness, for as-Sayyūrī and Ibn al-'Arabī prefer the judgment that he has not broken his oath, in agreement with ash-Shāfi'ī. Thus if he does it out of ignorance, as for example he makes an oath not to greet Zayd with the *as-salāmu 'alaykum* and then greets him during darkness not having recognized him, he has broken his oath, contrary to ash-Shāfi'ī. However if he was compelled to do the action he shall not have broken his oath, like for example if he swears not to enter a house but he is made to enter it by force, while if he is able to leave but he does not leave then he shall have broken his oath.

If he swears to do something then is unable to do it then there are three aspects to the matter:

1. That he is prevented from doing so because of the non-existence of an opportune fit occasion, like for example someone who makes an oath to hit his slave, who then dies [before he can hit him], or to kill a pigeon which then flies away, then he has not broken his oath, as long as he is not negligent or remiss.

2. That he is prevented legally, like for example someone who makes an oath to have sexual intercourse with his wife but then finds she is menstruating – if he does not have intercourse with her then there is a difference of opinion as to whether he has broken his oath or not,

whereas if he does have intercourse with her then it is said that he has committed a wrong action but has fulfilled his oath, while it is also said that he should not fulfil it as he intended to have legitimate intercourse with her.

3. That he is prevented for another reason, like for example the thief or usurper, for they must break their oaths, according to Ibn al-Qāsim contrary to Ashhab.

2. What an oath necessarily entails

This comprises four matters

1. The intention, if it is such that it lends itself to expression, irrespective of whether it corresponds to it, is additional to it or is deficient, and it is made in the heart without moving the tongue on condition that the oath is effected by it; if however he emends it after the oath then it is of no use. And what is taken into account in this is the intention of the person taking the oath except in the case of claims where the intention of the person asks someone to take the oath is taken into account, according to the well-known position (*mashhūr*).

2. The reason which has led to the oath, this being the circumstances – by which the intention is indicated if concealed.

3. Customary practice, by which I mean what is customarily intended by people with respect to oaths.

4. What is required by the expression – linguistically and legally.

As for the order of these matters there are four judgments, and the well-known position (*mashhūr*) is that these matters are in the order we have mentioned – so one examines the intention: if absent, then one examines the circumstances; if this latter is absent then one examines the customary practice; if this latter is absent then one examines what is required by the expression although it is also said that one examines the intention, then what is required by the expression and the circumstances and customary practice are not taken into account; and it is also said that one examines the intention then the circumstances then what is required by the expression while the customary practice is not taken into account; and ash-Shāfi'ī has said one takes into account the form and manner of the expression but not the intention or the circumstances.

Ibn Rushd has said that this difference of opinion exists in the case where customary practice and what is intended by it is surmised – but if known, then there is no difference of opinion that it is taken into account, as for example when someone says: 'by Allah I shall most certainly show so-and-so the stars at midday' it being clear that he means something other than the literal expression, in which case one understands it accordingly. And there are twenty subdivisions on the basis of this principle, all of them attributable to what we have mentioned:

1. Whoever swears not to enter a house then goes up on to the roof has broken his oath, contrary to ash-Shāfi'ī.

2. Whoever swears not to enter the house of so-and-so, but then enters a house rented by him has broken his oath – as long as he did not have the intention of [a house to which so-and-so had] ownership, contrary to ash-Shāfi'ī.

3. If a man gives another food, clothing or something else and swears that he will not drink of his water, then he has broken his oath if he drinks his water, eats his food, wears his clothing or avails himself of something else of his, contrary to the two, for he only breaks his oath according to the two if he drinks of the water; and likewise, if he gifts him a sheep and gives it to him swearing that he will not eat of its meat or drink of its milk, then if he makes use of its price, he has broken his oath.

4. Whoever swears not to sell or buy anything, not to divorce his wife or set his slave free, but instructs someone else to do this, has broken his oath unless his intention was to undertake any of this himself, contrary to ash-Shāfi'ī.

5. If he swears not to enter the house of so-and-so and then ownership of the house is transferred to another, then he does not break his oath by entering it, but if he says 'this house' then he has broken his oath; and if he swears not to enter 'a house' then he has broken his oath if he enters a hamam but not if he enters a mosque; and if he enters when dead, there are two judgments. And if he swears that he shall not live in it and both the hamam and mosque are in the house and he has a wall placed between them, then Ibn Qāsim said that he has not broken his oath, while Mālik had misgivings. And if he swears that he shall not enter the house of so-and-so and it is demolished and becomes a street or pathway and he enters it, then he has not broken his oath contrary to Abū Ḥanīfah.

6. Whoever swears that he shall not eat food bought by so-and-so, but this latter buys some – while the other is with him – and he eats of it without intending to, then he has broken his oath, contrary to the two.

7. Whoever swears that he will not eat fruit (*fākihah*) has broken his oath if he eats grapes, apples, pomegranates or other than these, even green beans, while Abū Ḥanīfah said that he has broken his oath with all of these except eating grapes and pomegranates; and if he swears not to eat tamar i.e. dried dates, has broken his oath if he eats *ruṭab*, i.e. fresh dates, contrary to Abū Ḥanīfah.

8. Whoever swears not to eat a condiment but eats cooked or grilled meat has broken his oath, as he has even if he consumes oil or vinegar – depending on what is considered customarily to be a condiment,

and Abū Ḥanīfah has said that *idām*, i.e. condiment, only refers to whatever is prepared with oil, vinegar or honey.

9. Whoever swears not to eat bread, then there is a difference of opinion as to whether he has broken his oath by eating something made of wheat such as *harīsah* i.e. a meal made of pounded wheat, or *iṭriyah*, i.e. vermicelli, or cake, Ibn Bashīr saying that cake is closer in meaning and more likely to entail a breaking of one's oath – except if the oath has been made specific or general by means of the intention or by the context such that the difference of opinion is removed.

And whoever swears not to eat heads [of animals] and he eats the heads of fish or birds has broken his oath if he had not specified some of the things by means of the intention or by the context, while Abū Ḥanīfah has said that he has only broken his oath by eating sheep or goats' heads or those of cows, while ash-Shāfiʿī has added camels and birds.

Likewise if he swears not to eat eggs he has broken his oath, according to Ibn al-Qāsim, even in the case of fish eggs, but he has only broken it, according to Ashhab, in the case of chicken eggs and any other eggs customarily eaten.

Anyone who swears not to eat meat has broken his oath by eating any meat and any fish, and has also broken his oath by eating fat, but not vice versa.

10. If a person says 'by Allah I will fulfil your right tomorrow' and fulfils it today, he has not broken his oath, contrary to ash-Shāfiʿī.

11. If he says 'I shall do such-and-such in due time' then according to Mālik this is a year, while according to Abū Ḥanīfah it is six months, and according to ash-Shāfiʿī any time in the future.

12. If someone swears to beat his slave with a hundred lashes, and joins [a hundred whips] together such that he beats him once, has not fulfilled his oath, contrary to the two.

13. Whoever swears that he will not live in a particular house while he is actually living in it, or that he will not wear some particular clothes while he is actually wearing them, or that he will not ride a particular riding beast while he is actually mounted on it, then he must cease doing the action in question as soon as possible – but if he delays when able to cease the action, he has broken his oath; and in *al-Wāḍiḥah* he states that he has not broken his oath.

14. Whoever swears that he will not speak to someone, but writes to the person or sends a messenger to him, then it is said that he has broken his oath in both cases, while it is also said that he has not broken it, and it is also said that he has broken it by writing but not by sending a messenger; and if we assume he has written and the letter arrives but he does not read it, then there are two judgments as to whether he has broken his oath; and likewise if he swears not to speak to someone and he does so but the person does not hear him.

If he swears that he will speak to him, then the oath is not fulfilled by means of a letter or a messenger.

If he swears that he will not speak to him and he greets him with the *as-salāmu 'alaykum* outside of the *ṣalāt*, he has broken his oath; and if it is during the *ṣalāt*, he has not broken it if he is one of the persons behind the *imām* or if the person intended by the person who has made the oath is the *imām*.

15. Whoever swears that his wife shall not go out except with his permission and he gives her permission but she does not know this or has not heard and she goes out, then he has not broken his oath, contrary to ash-Shāfi'ī.

16. Whoever swears he will not eat but he drinks *sawīq*, i.e. a wheat and barley soup, or drinks milk, has broken his oath if he intended

to constrain himself by leaving food, but if he intended to leave off eating but not drinking, then he has not broken his oath.

17. Whoever swears that he will only leave his creditor when the latter's claim has been fulfilled, then he has not fulfilled his oath by means of a pledge, or affirmation of liability or transfer by delegating the matter, but if his intention is a guarantee of the person's claim then he has fulfilled his oath by means of each of the aforementioned.

18. Whoever swears that he shall avoid such-and-such a person then he shall have fulfilled his oath by avoiding him for three days because this is the limit of what is legally, permitted with respect to avoiding someone, although it has also been said that he shall only have fulfilled it by avoiding him for a month for this is customarily often the term with respect to oaths – so if he swears to avoid him for some days or months or years then he is required to fulfil the minimum intended by the plural form, i.e. three days, months or years.

19. If he swears to do something then there are two judgments as to whether one understands the minimum action implied by the expression employed, or the maximum, this being the well-known position (*mashhūr*) – there is a difference of opinion with regard to someone who swears he will eat a loaf of bread and then eats some of it: according to the well-known position (*mashhūr*) he has broken his oath; and if he swears that he will eat it then he has not fulfilled his oath unless he eats all of it.

And likewise if he swears that he will have sexual intercourse then he has broken his oath if only the head of the penis penetrates according to the well-known position (*mashhūr*), while for others he has not broken his oath without emission of sperm.

And if he swears he shall not eat bread and oil and he eats one of them, then there is a difference of opinion in this regard – and all this applies in the absence of an intention.

20. Whoever swears to do something then non-fulfilment of the oath also applies to anything within the same spectrum of meaning, like for example someone who swears with respect to wheat and then eats bread, or with respect to milk and eats cheese or cream, or with respect to grapes and then eats currants, although it has also been said that he does not break his oath.

NOTE

The rulings we have mentioned in the above sub divisions apply in the absence of intention and specific context; if the person swearing forms an intention and the context is clear then one is to understand the oath in the light of these latter.

3. KAFFĀRAH AND EXCEPTIONS

THIS CONSISTS OF TWO SECTIONS

1. KAFFĀRAH

This comprises three things the choice of which is optional: the feeding or clothing of ten destitute persons or the freeing of a slave; and the fourth is placed after these, namely fasting three days.

AS FOR FEEDING

It is one *mudd* using the *mudd* of the Prophet ﷺ for each destitute person if in Madīnah, while if in another place then Ibn al-Qāsim has said that the *mudd* of any location is acceptable; and others have said one is to give the average amount which would satiate, while yet others have said it is two Baghdadi *riṭl*s and some seasoning condiment or sauce – reckoning this to be the average of what satiates in any given city; and the average with regard to what satiates in our country is a *riṭl* and a half, using one of our *riṭl*s, while Abū Ḥanīfah has said that one gives half a *ṣā'* of wheat or two *ṣā'*s of barley or currants and has said that if he gives that for lunch and supper then this suffices.

But it is not acceptable for a person to feed one destitute person for ten days, contrary to Abū Ḥanīfah. 'Destitute' is conditional upon the person being a Muslim and free, contrary to Abū Ḥanīfah.

As for clothing

The minimum in this respect for a man is a garment that covers his whole body, and for a woman, that in which she is permitted to make the *ṣalāt*, i.e. a garment covering her body and a head covering. And according to the two, it is acceptable by means of the minimum known by the name *qamīṣ* i.e. long upper garment, or *izār*, i.e. long waist cloth, or *sarāwīl*, i.e. long, ample trousers or *'amāmah*, i.e. turban.

As for the slave

This is conditional upon his or her being a *mūmin*, contrary to Abū Ḥanīfah, free of defects, contrary to the Ẓāhirīs, not owned jointly by a partnership, nor subject to a contract guaranteeing the slave's future freedom. These conditions likewise apply with respect to the slave used in the *kaffārah* for breaking the fast in Ramadan and for the *ẓihār kaffārah*.

As for the defects of a slave

They are of three kinds

Those which render them unacceptable in *kaffārah*, that is whatever renders them incapable of gain or profit, or render them incomplete as in the case of chronic illness when there is no hope of cure, and blindness, dumbness, madness, or extreme senility;

Those which do not make them unacceptable, namely that which does not disfigure or mar them such as slight lameness, the severing of a finger-tip;

And that about which there is a difference of opinion, namely that which does not disfigure nor prevent from gain or profit, like deafness, being one-eyed or a noticeable limp.

As for fasting

It is not conditional upon it being consecutive days, contrary to Abū Ḥanīfah, although it is recommended.

Five secondary matters

1. If a slave makes *kaffārah* by fasting then this is acceptable, but by means of manumission it is not acceptable, while there are two judgments regarding feeding and clothing the destitute.

2. Breaking one's oath is not *ḥarām* although it is preferable that one does not break one's oath unless this is of benefit.

3. It is permitted to make the *kaffārah* before breaking the oath, in agreement with ash-Shāfi'ī, while it has also been said that it is not permitted, in agreement with Abū Ḥanīfah.

4. If the *kaffārah* is made by joining two types of permitted *kaffārah,* like feeding five persons and clothing five persons, then there is a difference of opinion as to whether this is acceptable or not.

5. With respect to repetition: if the person making the oath swears by a number of names of Allah, like saying 'by Allah', 'by the All-hearing and the All-knowing' and the like, then the *kaffārah* is not to be repeated a corresponding number of times, although one group have said that it is to be repeated.

And breaking one's oath is not repeated by a repetition of the action unless the expression used necessitates a repetition like one's saying 'whenever', 'when' and the like, or one intends repetition.

And there is no difference of opinion that whoever swears with respect to various things with one single oath is only required to make a single *kaffārah,* but if he swears with respect to a single thing using many oaths then he is required to make *kaffārah* for each oath – so if he swears to a single thing several times like his saying 'by Allah, by Allah, by Allah', then for each oath there is *kaffārah* to be made unless he intended emphasis only, while one group has said a single *kaffārah.*

2. Making an exception

This has an effect on the oath according to the agreed judgment and it is of two kinds: the first kind, 'by the will of Allah' which annuls completely the ruling governing oaths and only has effect with respect to oaths made 'by Allah', but not with respect to divorce, manumission and other matters, contrary to the two. Second, by means of 'except' and similar words, and it annuls part of what is covered by the oath and is of effect in all oaths. And three conditions are stipulated in the two kinds above:

1. That the expression of it be in words, for it is not enough to merely make the intention, but only making an exception by means of 'by the will of Allah', while there is a difference of opinion with regard to 'except' and the like, if the oath is such that makes this necessary and there is no additional clarification about this. And if he expresses it silently then this is acceptable unless he is required to swear by someone else or he swears with respect to a claim or right of someone or a condition.

2. That it be connected directly with the oath, without any interruption or delay, except in cases such as coughing, sneezing,

yawning or the like, while ash-Shāfi'ī has said that there is no harm in a short moment of silence in order to remember something, to breath in or out or pause for breath or when one's voice goes. And one group have said that the exception is valid as long as he has not got up from his place of sitting, while Ibn Abbās has said that it is valid for him when he remembers it even if after some time.

3. That he intends the actual matter and circumstance of the oath, for if he intends mere confirmation of the oath – by reassuring himself by means of the exception, or a handing over the matter to Allah or a restraining of oneself out of politeness or by way of meriting or obtaining a blessing, then it is of no use to him. And it is stipulated that his intention be accompanied by some letters of expression, while Ibn Mawwāz has stipulated that he intend the exception before completing the letters expressed in the oath, even if this is a single letter.

Two secondary matters

1. The expression of exception when one says 'by the will of Allah' is on a par with the 'will of someone else' when one says for example 'unless so-and-so wants' or 'unless it appears to me that…' and the like.

2. If he says 'unless Allah decides or decrees…' or '…[unless] Allah wants something else' or other such expressions then there is a difference of opinion as to whether this constitutes an exception or not.

4. The basic elements that constitute making a vow

These are three in number: the person making the vow, the thing vowed and the form of the vow.

As for the person making the vow

It may be any *mukallaf*, i.e. sane person of age; and a vow is not binding on a child, a mad person or a *kāfir*.

AS FOR THE THING VOWED

It is of two kinds, what is unspecific and what is specific. The unspecific refers to that whose kind is not clarified, like one's saying 'I have to make a vow for Allah' in which case there is the *kaffārah* for an oath and its ruling is as an oath made by Allah, in the case of an exception or *laghw*, i.e. something uttered 'about which one is mistaken'; and one group have said that there is due the *kaffārah* made for *ẓihār*, while yet another group have said two *rak'ah*s of *ṣalāt* are to be made, or a fast of one day.

In the specific there are four divisions:

1. If the action in question is a *qurbah*, i.e. an act undertaken to come closer to Allah, then it must be fulfilled irrespective of whether it is obligatory or recommended.

2. If it is an act of disobedience, then it is forbidden to fulfil it, but the person who makes the vow is not liable for anything, although Abū Ḥanīfah has said that he is liable for *kaffārah* of the oath, as for example in the case of fornication and drinking wine, and likewise for performing the *ṣalāt* at a time when it is prohibited, or fasting the days when it is prohibited to fast.

3. If *makrūh*, then it is *makrūh* to fulfil it.

4. If licit, then it is licit to fulfil or not to fulfil it and the person who does not fulfil it is not liable for anything, although Ibn Ḥanbal has said that he is liable for the *kaffārah* of an oath.

THE FORM OF THE VOW

This may be of two kinds: unrestricted or restricted.

As for the unrestricted, this refers to that made in gratitude to Allah for His blessing, or that without a cause, like for example one's saying 'I must fast for Allah such-and-such a fast' or 'I must perform such-

and-such a *ṣalāt*' – and such a vow is recommended and must be fulfilled irrespective of whether one mentions the word 'vow' or not, unless one intends to inform [someone else about it], in which case he is not liable for anything.

As for the restricted, this refers to that which is dependent upon a condition, as for example one's saying 'if so-and-so comes' or 'if Allah cures the sick person in my care' or 'if Allah sees to my need' then I must do such-and-such – and this is licit, while it is also said that it is *makrūh*, and its fulfilment is binding irrespective of whether the condition is an act of *qurbah*, an act of disobedience, a *makrūh* or a licit act.

However fulfilment is not required if it is only accepted of the person by means of an intention.

And there is no vow with respect to anything which is not owned, unless accompanied by a condition of ownership.

And the various circumstances in which a vow may be made – such as when disputing or when angry or in other circumstances – are not to be taken into account.

5. The rulings governing vows

This consists of eight matters

1. The vow to fast

If one makes the vow to fast or swears to do it and one does not fulfil this, then one has to make up the number of days which one intended; if one did not specify the number of days then one single day is enough

If one makes a vow to fast a day which one names and this turns out to be the day of the *'Īd*, or of illness or menstruation, then one does not have to make it up, although it has also been said that one does have to make it up.

If one vows to fast continuously then this is binding on the person, although he is not liable for anything on the days of the *'Īd*, of menstruation and in Ramadan, and he may break the fast when ill, travelling and he does not have to make them up, as this is not possible for him.

If he vows to fast a whole year then he breaks the fast on the days of the *'Īd*, the days of Tashrīq and fasts Ramadan for Ramadan and does not have to make up unless he has made the intention to make up; and it is also said that he does have to make up unless he has made the intention not to make up.

If he makes a vow to fast on the day that so-and-so arrives and he arrives at night then he fasts from the morning of that night, and if he arrives during the day then he fasts another day instead, while it is also said that he is not liable at all; and it is not acceptable that he make the intention to fast during the night before the person arrives.

2. Ṣalāt

If one makes a vow to perform *ṣalāt* then whatever he intends is binding on him; otherwise it is enough that he make two *rak'ah*s; and if he intends less than one *rak'ah* then two *rak'ah*s are binding on him, and likewise if one has made the intention to fast part of a day then a a day is binding, just as if he intended half a divorce then it is binding to complete it.

3. Ṣadaqah

If one makes a vow to give away all of one's wealth in *ṣadaqah* or one makes an oath to do so and then one does not fulfil this, then it is enough for the person to give a third; and if one makes a vow to give less than the whole, like a half or two thirds or a specific thing like one's house and he does not possess anything other than this, or a specific number of things then whatever he intended is binding even if it is most of his wealth or all of it, although it has also been said that a third frees him of further liability; and if he does not specify then whatever he gives away in *ṣadaqah* is enough, be it a small or large amount.

Abū Ḥanīfah has said with respect to someone who has vowed to give away all of his wealth that the whole is binding on him, whereas ash-Shāfi'ī has said if the reason was a vow then he must fulfil it while if the reason was a dispute or out of anger then he must pay the *kaffārah* of an oath, while Ibn Ḥabīb has said that if he is of means then he pays a third of his wealth and if a third would harm him then he pays the amount he would pay in *zakāt* on his wealth; if poor, then he pays the *kaffārah* of the oath. Ṣaḥnūn has said he pays whatever does not harm him irrespective of whether he specified or did not.

Moreover if he says 'for the face of Allah' then what he gives is given as *ṣadaqah* not anything else, while if he says 'in the way of Allah' then what he gives is given for military expeditions and *jihād* in particular, and if he says it about his slave then what he gives is given for the purpose of manumission.

4. Walking to Makkah

Whoever says 'I must walk to Makkah' or '...go...' or '...proceed...' and mentions the hajj or *'umrah,* then this is binding on him, and he performs the *'umrah* up to the last *sa'y* and the hajj up to the *ifāḍah ṭawāf*; but if he does not mention the hajj or *'umrah* and does not intend these, then Ibn al-Qāsim has said that he is not liable for anything while Ashhab deemed the hajj and *'umrah* obligatory for him; Ṣaḥnūn said that Ibn al-Qāsim reverted to this judgment.

If he says 'I must walk', then it is binding upon him to make the hajj and *'umrah* by walking, irrespective of whether he mentions the hajj or *'umrah*; and if he specifies one of them then this specific one is binding on him; and if he wants to change from the hajj to an *'umrah*, this is not permitted him while there are two judgments regarding changing from an *'umrah* to the hajj.

If he walks the whole way without interruption then this is acceptable of him, according to the agreed judgement, but if he interrupts it and completes it over two years, then there is a difference of opinion.

If he rides for a short distance on account of his incapacity to walk then this is accepted of him but he has to sacrifice an animal, while if the distance is long then he must walk another time from the place where he began to ride and he must slaughter a *hady* animal – unless he is old and decrepit or chronically ill and there is no hope of fulfilling this, in which case he does not have to return to the place, while one group have said he must slaughter a *hady* animal.

If he vows to walk to the Ḥarām Mosque, or to Zamzam, the Stone or the Station then hajj or *'umrah* is binding on him, but not in the case of Minā, 'Arafah or places outside of the zone of Makkah, while Ibn Ḥabīb said it is binding on him if he mentions the *Ḥaram* or anything in it but not if he names anything outside of the *Ḥaram* other than 'Arafah. And it is recommended that whoever vows to walk barefooted but then wears shoes should slaughter a *hady*.

5. Whoever vows to slaughter a camel

Then a cow will not do instead when one is able to supply a camel; if unable then there is a difference of opinion as to whether it would be acceptable, that it is acceptable is the madhhab, i.e. the judgment, of the *Mudawwanah*; and likewise the difference of opinion as to whether seven goats or sheep are acceptable if he is unable to supply a cow.

If he makes the intention to slaughter a *hady* he must do what he intended, but if he does not intend anything he must slaughter a camel in Makkah; and if he does not find one then he slaughters a cow and if he does not find the latter then a sheep is acceptable.

6. Whoever vows to make the ṣalāt in Madīnah or the Bayt al-Maqdis in Jerusalem

Then he is obliged to do it, contrary to Abū Ḥanīfah. Similarly, he is obligated if he mentions either of the two mosques but without mentioning the *ṣalāt*, or if he mentions Madīnah or the Bayt al-Maqdis and intended the *ṣalāt* in them. If he did not intend the *ṣalāt* in them he is not obligated to do anything.

If he vows to walk to any other mosque and it is close, then he should go to it and make the *ṣalāt*, and if far, then he should make the *ṣalāt* in the place he finds himself in and he is not liable for anything as it is an act of disobedience.

7. Whoever vows to slaughter his child at the Station of Ibrāhīm ﷺ

Then he slaughters a camel as a sacrifice instead of what he intended, whereas Abū Ḥanīfah said that he slaughters a sheep while one group said that he slaughters a hundred camels and ash-Shāfi'ī said that he is not liable for anything as it is an act of disobedience.

8. Whoever vows to take up post in a ribāṭ or to make jihād on the borders

Then this is binding on him.

Clarification

In the case of a vow, one examines the intention, then customary practice, then what is understood by the linguistic expression used, and making an exception by means of 'by the will of Allah' is of no avail.

9 – Food, drink, hunting and slaughtering

Consisting of five chapters

1. Food – when one has the choice

All foods are of two kinds, animal or inanimate – i.e. plant or otherwise. All of what is inaminate is *ḥalāl* except what is *najāsah*, i.e. ritually impure, or what has been mixed with *najāsah*, intoxicating substances and noxious substances like poison; and clay is *makrūh* while it is also said that it is *ḥarām*, and ash-Shāfi'ī deemed mucus of the nose and semen *ḥarām*.

As for animals, there are those which are *ḥarām* for a specific reason like carrion, i.e. that which has not been ritually slaughtered, and animals which have been strangle, or are subject to the same judgment i.e. animals which have been killed by a blow, animals which have fallen to their death, and animals which have been gored, and these shall be dealt with in the chapter on slaughter; and there are those which are *ḥarām* in themselves: aṭ-Ṭarṭūshī said that within the madhhab, according to one of two narrations, that is the narration of the Iraqis, all animals may be eaten – from elephants to ants and worms and anything between these, except for humans and pigs for these two are *ḥarām* according to the consensus, although from among these some are licit in all circumstances and others are *makrūh*. A discussion of animals may be divided into seven matters:

1. Sea creatures

These are classified as five kinds:

1. Fish are *ḥalāl* according to the consensus, although Abū Ḥanīfah does not permit the eating of what is floating, but rather permits what has died for a reason like fishing or angling for them or when their leaving water or for some other cause.

2. That which resembles something *ḥalāl* on land.

3. What has no resemblance to anything on land, and both are *ḥalāl* according to the two Imāms contrary to Abū Ḥanīfah who only deemed fish licit.

4. That which has a resemblance to something *ḥarām* like dolphins or sharks: these may be eaten although it has also been said that they are *makrūh*, and it has also been said that they are *ḥarām*, in agreement with the two.

5. That which lives a long time on land: such may be eaten, like frogs, contrary to them.

2. Wild animals, like lions, wolves, cheetahs or panthers, bears, tigers, dogs

These are *makrūh*, while it is also said that they are all *ḥarām*, in agreement with them, although ash-Shāfiʿī deemed lizards, hyenas and foxes – from amongst the wild animals – *ḥalāl*, while it is also said that the common amongst them are *ḥarām* but the uncommon are not, like the fox and the cat, and there is no difference of opinion as to the permissibility of eating lizards, while Abū Ḥanīfah deemed them *makrūh*.

3. Birds and other flying creatures

These are licit, whether with talons or not, while it is also said that those with talons and claws are *ḥarām*, such as falcons, hawks, eagles and vultures, in agreement with them.

Swifts and swallows are *makrūh*, while it is also said that they are permitted, and ash-Shāfi'ī deemed them *ḥarām*, together with all animals which are forbidden to be killed, like ants and bees together with those ordered to be killed in the *ḥarām* such as crows, kites, snakes, mice and rats, and scorpions.

As for locusts, these may be eaten if they die for a specific reason, like removing part of their body, grilling them or immersing them in hot water, but they are not to be eaten if they did not die for a specific reason, contrary to the two and Muṭarrif.

4. Animals with hooves

Horses are *makrūh*, although it has also been said that they are *ḥalāl,* in agreement with ash-Shāfi'ī, while it is also said that they are *ḥarām*. Donkeys are particularly *makrūh*, and it has also been said that they are *ḥarām,* in agreement with them; and mules are deemed likewise. Al-Lakhmī said that horses are less *makrūh* than donkeys, and that mules are between the two. As for wild donkeys they are *ḥalāl*, but there are two judgments if tamed and used to ride or carry things.

5. Those creatures about which there is disagreement as to whether they have been metamorphosed (mamsūkh) [from men and women]

Like elephants, bears and monkeys, and as for hedgehogs, it is said they are *ḥalāl* but also that they are *ḥarām*.

6. Animals which are deemed filthy like flies and crawling insects

In *al-Jawāhir* he said: "Those holding a contrary opinion to that of the madhhab have narrated that they may be eaten," while Ibn Bashīr said that the madhhab is contrary to this; and ash-Shāfi'ī has said they are *ḥarām* because they are filthy.

As for snails, those boiled or fried may be eaten but not those which die of themselves.

7. Blood

Al-Lakhmī has said the blood of whatever may not be eaten is *ḥarām*, be the amount a little or a lot, as well as the blood of anything before it is ritually slaughtered – and any blood spilt after the ritual slaughter is also *ḥarām*. And if a sheep is used before being cut up and before any blood shows, when for example it is roasted whole, then there is agreement that it is permitted, while there is a difference of opinion if it is cut up and blood becomes visible as to whether it is *ḥalāl* or *ḥarām*.

As for any other creatures other than these mentioned above they are *ḥalāl,* according to the agreed judgment unless they have eaten something *najas*, like for example chickens allowed to roam in areas of *najāsah*, in which case there is a difference of opinion.

2. When there is no option

It is quite evident that carrion is licit when an exceptional need arises. Then one examines the degree of need and the kind of sustenance that would become licit in this case and the amount in question.

As for need

This refers to the situation in which one fears death, but it is not stipulated that one wait patiently until one is close to death.

The kind of sustenance that would become licit

This could be anything which would ward off hunger or thirst, like carrion from any animal except that of the son of Adam, and blood, pig, food or water which are *najas,* except wine as this is only *ḥalāl* to clear something on which someone is choking, although there is a difference of opinion here. It does not become licit, neither in the case of hunger or thirst as it does not remove them, although it has also been said that it is licit. It is not licit for using as medicine, according to the well-known judgment (*mashhūr*), although it has also been said that it is permitted, in agreement with ash-Shāfi'ī.

The amount permitted

It is that he eats his fill, and if he fears that he shall want in the future, then he may take some as provisio,n but if he no longer is in need he must discard it, while ash-Shāfi'ī has said that he should not eat his fill or take any as provision, but rather just eat enough to allay his hunger and ward off approaching death.

Secondary matters

The person in need must not eat dead human flesh, contrary to ash-Shāfi'ī.

If he finds carrion and a pig then he should give preference to the carrion.

If he does eat pig, then it is recommended he slaughter it.

And if he finds carrion and food belonging to someone else, then he should eat the food as long as he is sure of not being treated as a thief – and he becomes liable for its restitution, although it has also been said that he does not become liable. He should restrict himself to eating his fill but not take any as provision.

And he should request that its owner sell or give him food if the owner is not in need, and if he refuses then one should take it without his permission and he may fight him for it even if this leads to his death, as is the ruling of a brigand.

There is licence for a person who travels engaged in an act of disobedience to eat carrion, according to the well-known judgment, contrary to the absence of any licence to shorten the *ṣalāt* or break the fast in his case, while it is also said that there is no licence in the case of someone who persists in his act of disobedience.

3. DRINKS

WINE

It is *ḥarām* whether the amount is a little or a lot, according to the consensus, I mean grape juice which is intoxicating, but if it does not intoxicate, then it is *ḥalāl* according to the consensus.

OTHER INTOXICATING DRINKS

Those made from currants, dates, honey, wheat, barley or anything else are the same as wine, according to the two Imams and Ibn Ḥanbal, while one group has said that what is *ḥarām* in their case is a large amount that causes intoxication not a small amount, and Abū Ḥanīfah said that what is made from anything other than the date palm or the vine is not *ḥarām* irrespective of whether it is intoxicating or not, and that what is made from dates and currants is *ḥarām* if intoxicating but not if it is a small amount.

TEN SUBSIDIARY MATTERS

1. What is taken into account in the case of grape juice is whether it can intoxicate, but one does not take into account whether it has been heated or not, while it is also said that if heated until only a third remains then there is no harm in it as its capacity to intoxicate has been removed.

2. Steeping dates or raisins is permitted except in a gourd or container treated with tar, which is *makrūh,* while it is also said that it is *makrūh* to steep them in fired pottery and wooden vessels, although Abū Ḥanīfah has permitted it in all containers.

3. It is *makrūh* to steep a mixture of two things or drink of them, like dates and currants, even if they are not intoxicating, and one group have deemed a mixture of two things *ḥarām* while another has deemed them licit as long as they do not intoxicate.

4. It is not permitted for a Muslim to own wine or anything intoxicating and anyone with whom it is found then it must be poured away in spite of him. There is a difference of opinion as to the containers, it being said that they are all to be broken and smashed up, while it is also said that the ones ruined by the wine are to be broken and smashed except for the ones used when the smell of the wine no longer exists, while it is also said that skins are not to be used but earthenware pots may be used if water is boiled in them twice and they are washed.

5. It is not permitted for anyone to hire himself out, or his slave or animal, or his house for the business of wine, contrary to Abū Ḥanīfah.

6. It is not permitted for a Muslim to buy wine from a Muslim or a *kāfir*, nor to sell grapes to someone who makes wine from them; if the wine which has been sold is discovered then the containers are to be broken and the sale annulled. If the buyer has not yet paid the price, then he is no longer liable to pay, but if he has then the price is returned to him, and it is said that he is to give it away in *ṣadaqah*. If a *kāfir* becomes Muslim and he has some wine then he pours it away, and if he becomes Muslim and he has the price paid for some wine with him, then there is no harm in this.

7. If the wine turns from what it was to vinegar, then it becomes *ḥalāl* and ritually pure, according to the agreed judgment. As for making it turn to vinegar by treating it, there are three judgments: that it is prohibited, in agreement with the two, that it is permissible but

makrūh, and a judgment which discriminates between someone who takes it as wine, in which case it is not permitted to turn it to vinegar, and the person whose grape juice ferments without him wanting it to become wine, in which case it is permitted to turn it into vinegar. As to the permissibility of consuming it based on the judgment as to its prohibition – there are three judgments.

8. In the *Mudawwanah* Mālik, when asked about wine in which fish were placed in order to preserve them, replied: 'I do not consider this proper', and he deemed it *makrūh,* while Ibn Ḥabīb has said that it is *ḥarām*; and if it intoxicates, then it is *ḥarām,* by the agreement of the *fuqahā'*.

9. Al-Qarāfi has said, "As for soporifics which remove the capacity for rational thinking, there is no *ḥadd* punishment for someone who imbibes them, and a small amount is permitted, according to the consensus, and they do not render anything *najas,* irrespective of whether there is a small or large amount, as they are not intoxicating – for it is what is intoxicating which enraptures and transports."

10. It is permitted to drink human milk if in a container, like any other kind of milk, while Abū Ḥanīfah deemed it *ḥarām*; and he prohibited its sale as it is of human derivation.

4. HUNTING AND AN EXAMINATION OF ITS RULING AND CONDITIONS

As for its ruling, it may be divided into five sections: licit for the purpose of securing sustenance, recommended when provided something extra for one's family, obligatory when in order to sustain oneself in state of necessity, *makrūh* when for sport – while Ibn 'Abd al-Ḥakam has deemed this licit – and *ḥarām* when done in jest on account of the absence of intention and because of the prohibition of causing suffering to animals without any benefit. As for its conditions they are sixteen in number with respect to the person hunting or fishing and five with respect to the instrument used to hunt or fish and five with respect to the prey – and we will devote a section to each.

1. The conditions with respect to hunter

1. That it be someone whose sacrifice is valid – i.e. in accordance with what is mentioned in the chapter on rulings regarding slaughter, such that the prey hunted by the Muslim is permitted, according to the agreed judgment, but that of the Zoroastrian, i.e. the Magian fire-worshippers is not, while there are three judgments regarding what is hunted by People of the Book, namely permissibility, prohibition and its being *makrūh*; and if the father of the person in question is Zoroastrian and his mother one of the People of the Book or vice versa then Mālik takes into account the father while ash-Shāfiʿī the mother and Abū Ḥanīfah takes into consideration either one of them whose slaughtering is permitted.

2. That he not be in *iḥrām* – this, with respect to hunting on land.

3. That he see the prey with his own eyes.

4. That he makes the intention to hunt.

5. That he names Allah ta'ala when releasing the dogs or throwing the missile or shooting the arrow just as the person who slaughters an animal would name Allah when slaughtering; and if he omits to invoke His name, then the ruling is the same as that governing slaughtering, and this shall be discussed later.

6. That he goes after the prey after releasing the dogs or throwing or shooting, and if he returns and then later comes upon it and it has not been pierced and killed by a deep fatal wound, then he slaughters it; and if he ascertains that it has been pierced and killed by a fatal

wound, it is not to be eaten unless he ascertains that what caused its death was the instrument he used for hunting.

2. The instrument

It is of two kinds: a weapon or an animal.

Weapons

It is conditional upon their being sharp, like a lance, arrow or sword but anything else, like teeth/tusks, nails/hooves/claws or bones may not be used to slaughter. Whoever throws and strikes with a sword or anything else and cuts the prey in half may eat the whole of it. It is not permitted, according to the majority, to hunt by using a heavy object like a stone, or a headless, featherless arrow-shaft, thin at both ends thick in the middle, that often strikes sideways – unless it has a sharp edge and one knows for sure that it has struck with this sharp edge not sideways with its middle part.

Animals used to hunt

According to the majority it is permitted to hunt with dogs, hawks falcons, eagles and all animals which may be taught, even vultures, this being the judgment of Ibn Sha'bān, contrary to he who prohibits hunting with black dogs, that is Ibn Ḥanbal, or he who prohibits using anything other than dogs.

If the prey is killed by the animal or bird used to hunt, then it may be eaten – for this is its ritual slaughter; if it does not kill it, then it is ritually slaughtered. As for the mongoose, one may not eat what it kills as it is not receptive to training.

Four conditions are stipulated with regard to animals and birds used to hunt

1. That they be trained, and what is intended by this is that they

undergo a transformation from their original nature such that they become at the disposition of the hunter, like an instrument, not being a hunter of its own volition; and it is also said training is such that if it is held back or called to feed, then it restrains itself and responds, and if incited to hunt, it complies; and it is also said that one adds to these two that if called then it obeys, and according to Abū Ḥanīfah if it abstains three times from eating the prey.

2. That the hunter sends it off after the prey from his hand after sighting it with his own eyes; if however it went off of its own accord the prey is not to be eaten, contrary to Abū Ḥanīfah.

If it had gone off by his releasing it but not directly from his hand, then it is said that it may be eaten, while it is also said that it may not and it has been said that it may be eaten if close by.

If he tries to restrain it after it has gone off of its own accord, and it returns to him, and then he urges it to chase, it may be eaten, but if it does not return to him, it is not eaten.

If he sends if off after a specific prey and it hunts something else, it is not to be eaten, contrary to the two.

If he thinks it is a wild ox and he cast at it and kills it, then it turns out to be a cow, for example, then there are two verdicts.

If he sends off the trained animal or shoots or throws a missile but does not intend to catch something specific but rather intends whatever the trained animal or bird catches or what is killed by the thing thrown or shot when in a confined space like a cave or the like, then this is permitted, according to the well-known position (*mashhūr*) contrary to Ashhab; but if the place is not specific like an open plain or thicket or jungle, then it is not permitted, contrary to Aṣbagh.

And there is no difference of opinion within the madhhab that it is not licit for a person to shoot or send off the trained animal or bird after any object of prey which is right before him. If he sees that the trained animal or bird has become agitated but the hunter himself cannot see anything and he releases it, then Mālik has permitted this on one occasion while deeming it *makrūh* on another, saying that the prey caught might be other than the one which had first aroused it.

3. That it does not leave off holding the prey, and if it leaves it completely then it is not to be eaten, and likewise if it becomes preoccupied with another prey or with eating something; but if it stops in the areas in which it has sought the prey then the prey may be eaten – and this is all stipulated if the trained bird or animal kills the prey, but if it does not kill it, then the prey caught is to be slaughtered.

4. That no other animal whose wounding or slaughtering would not result in a permitted slaughtering – like an untrained beast or bird – has taken part in wounding or slaughtering the prey; but if one is certain that the trained bird or animal has been responsible for the wounding or slaughtering alone then the prey may be eaten; but if one is certain of the opposite of this or one has doubts as to this, then it is not to be eaten; and if one only thinks it is more likely that the trained beast was the one that has killed the prey, then there is a difference of opinion. If the hunter finds it alive without any fatal wound and slaughters it, then it may be eaten in all circumstances.

3. Conditions regarding the prey

1. It is stipulated that it be permitted to eat and so, if it is *ḥarām* to eat, then the hunting of it or the slaughtering of it do not affect the status of this ruling.

2. That it cannot be apprehended on account of its basic nature, as in the case of wild animals and birds – so if it is domesticated, like the camel, cow, sheep or goat and then becomes wild, it is not to be eaten

after having been hunted, contrary to them, and contrary to Ibn al-'Arabī in the case of runaway animals, and to Ibn Ḥabīb with respect to cows in particular.

If one gains control over an animal that has become wild, such as when it is caught in a snare, then it is to be slaughtered but it is not to be eaten by any wound sustained from this way of hunting.

If an animal which was originally wild becomes domesticated then runs away, it may be eaten when hunted.

3. That it dies from the wound not from being hit by the trained animal or bird, or from fright, in agreement with the two, while Ashhab permits it to be eaten.

4. That he have no doubt as to whether he or someone else has killed the prey, and no doubt that the instrument used has killed it, for if he entertains any doubts then it is not to be eaten, and if he cannot locate the prey but finds it the following day dead from a fatal wound, then he is not to eat it, according to the well-known position (*mashhūr*), although it has also been said that he may eat it, and it has also been said that it is *makrūh*.

If he shoots it or lets loose an animal after it and if falls in water or dies by falling from a mountain, then it is not to be eaten as it may be that the death was by drowning or falling, unless his arrow had pierced it before that, in which case there is no harm if it drowned or fell from a height.

5. That it is to be slaughtered if the instrument used to hunt has not caused the fatal wound; and if he catches it alive and is in a position to slaughter it but he does not slaughter it and it dies or is killed by the trained bird or animal, then he is not to eat it; and if the trained bird or animal kills it before he gains control over it, he may eat it, in agreement with ash-Shāfi'ī but contrary to Abū Ḥanīfah.

It is not stipulated that the trained bird or animal should not eat any of it, according to the well-known position (*mashhūr*), contrary to ash-Shāfi'ī, Ibn Ḥanbal, Ibn Ḥazm and al-Mundhir al-Ballūṭī.

Nine subsidiary matters

1. If the instrument or trained animal or bird has severed a limb of the prey then it is not permitted to eat this limb as it is deemed ritually impure – given that it has been severed from a living creature, but it is permitted to eat the rest of it – except for the head, if severed, for this may be eaten; and if what has been severed amounts to a half or more then it is permitted to eat the whole of it.

2. Mālik has said in the *'Utbiyyah* and the *Mawwāziyyah* that if the animal is shot at with a poisoned arrow, then it is not to be eaten out of fear for those who then eat it, and it may well be that this helped to kill the prey. Ibn Rushd has said if it does not inflict a fatal wound and one is not able to slaughter it in time, then it is not to be eaten according to the agreed judgement; and if one is able to slaughter it in time then Mālik and Ibn Ḥabīb have prohibited it, while Saḥnūn has permitted it, saying 'this is the more manifest judgment'; and if the arrow kills on account of the poison, then Ibn Ḥabīb has prohibited it while al-Bājī has said that if the poison is one of the poisons that are safe [for humans] and one that one does not have to be on one's guard about consuming, then it is permitted based on the principle of Ibn al-Qāsim.

3. Hunting merely on the basis of a sighting – and not a catching of the prey – is not allowed: so if one sights the prey and the other hunts it, it belongs to the one who hunted it; and if one hunts it and it then runs off and another hunts it, then there is a difference of opinion as to whether the prey belongs to the former or the latter – except where

the animal becomes wild after having been hunted by the first in which case it belongs to the second contrary to the two.

4. If a dog or falcon are illegally taken and used to hunt with then there is a difference of opinion as to whether any prey caught belongs to the person who usurped them or to the owner of the trained animal or bird; but if a weapon or horse is taken illegally the prey caught belongs to the person who took them illegally; and if a slave is taken illegally and is used to hunt, any prey he catches belongs to his master.

5. The place where the fangs of a dog have entered may be eaten as they are ritually pure, according to the madhhab, while ash-Shāfiʿī has said it is to be washed seven times or the place affected by its saliva is cut out.

6. Whoever pursues a prey and it enters the house of someone, then if he had to do this it belongs to him, but if he did not have to do it then it belongs to the owner of the house.

7. It is not prohibited for anyone to set up a pigeon house or beehive in a place where there are already such things belonging to another person, unless he knows that it would harm the person who came before him, for example that he locates it near his and intends to catch what does not belong to him – in which case it is prohibited; so if he sets them up and catches a pigeon or bees belonging to the other then he is to return them if he is able to do so, but if he is not able to return them then it is said that anything produced or generated or born of these belongs to the first person, while it is also said that it belongs to the person with whom the pigeons or bees ended up.

8. Everything we have mentioned with regard to the conditions for hunting are stipulated if the prey is wounded by the trained bird or animal or the weapon or dies as a result of a fatal wound; if, however,

it is found alive and the wound has not been fatal, then it is to be slaughtered – and the conditions stipulated for this are the same as those for slaughtering and sacrifice.

9. These conditions apply for hunting on land; as for fishing at sea then this is permitted without any conditions whatsoever, irrespective of whether the person doing the fishing is a Muslim or *kāfir* and irrespective of whatever means are employed.

5. Slaughtering

Ritual slaughter for food or sacrifice by cutting the throat, and slaughter by stabbing a camel in the pit of the throat are all killing an animal in one's power; while putting an animal to death by hunting refers to killing an animal which is not in one's power.

Examination of the person performing the slaughter, that which is slaughtered, the instrument of slaughter and the manner of slaughter.

This chapter has four sections.

1. Those who slaughter

They are of three classes of persons:

There is agreement as to the permissibility of slaughtering by one class, namely persons who are Muslim, of age, sane, male and who perform the *ṣalāt*.

There is agreement concerning another class whose slaughtering is deemed *ḥarām*, namely *mushrik*s – i.e. those who attribute partners to Allah – who worship idols.

There is a difference of opinion regarding another class of person, these being ten in number: the People of the Book, Magian-Zoroastrians, Sabeans, women, children, the insane, the intoxicated, those who have abandoned the *ṣalāt*, usurpers and thieves.

As for the People of the Book from amongst the Jews and Christians, both their men and womenfolk, what they slaughter is permitted in general, according to the agreed judgment, while there is a difference of opinion with regard to secondary matters, that is:

If the Person of the Book is an Arab what he slaughters is permitted, according to the majority contrary to ash-Shāfi'ī according to one of his judgments;

If the person is a renegade then what he slaughters may not be eaten, according to the majority contrary to Abū Isḥāq;

If he has slaughtered on behalf of a Muslim then there are two judgments within the madhhab;

There is no difference of opinion as to permissibility if he slaughters for himself unless he slaughters for their holiday festivals or their churches, in which case this is *makrūh* while Ashhab has permitted this and ash-Shāfi'ī has deemed it *ḥarām*;

If the animal slaughtered is forbidden to them then there are four judgments: prohibited according to Ibn al-Qāsim, licit according to Ibn 'Abd al-Ḥakam, *makrūh* according to Ashhab and a judgment which distinguishes between something which we know is *ḥarām* for them, like animals with claws or talons – in which case they are not permitted, or animals which are singled out individually for prohibition like rare or uncommon animals in which case they are permitted.

As for the fat of what they have slaughtered there are judgments of prohibition, and permissibility – according to the two, as well as that of being *makrūh*.

If the person of the Book is absent from the slaughtered animal and we know that they deem non-ritually slaughtered animals *ḥalāl* like the Christians of Andalusia or we suspect this then it is not to be eaten as long as the people of the Book are absent.

It is not fitting that a person go with intent to buy of animals slaughtered by the Jews and it is prohibited the Muslims to buy it from them and it is prohibited the Jews to buy and sell from them, and whoever buys from them then he is an evil man but his act of buying it not invalidated.

Ibn Sha'bān said, 'I deem *makrūh* the dried jerked meat and cheese of Rūm, i.e. Byzantium or Europe, because of what it contains of rennet of non-ritually slaughtered animals.' Al-Qarāfi said 'and its being *makrūh* is understood as meaning a prohibition because of the proven fact that they eat non-ritually slaughtered meat and that they strangle animals and beat them until they die.' Aṭ-Ṭarṭūshī has made a compilation on the prohibition of their cheese and that it renders the seller, the buyer and the scales *najas*, i.e. ritually impure.

As for Magians and Zoroastrians, what they slaughter is not permitted according to the majority contrary to a group.

As for the Sabeans, what they slaughter is not permitted in the madhhab, contrary to one group – and their *dīn* is to be located between the Magians and the Christians, and it has also been said that they believe in the influence of the stars.

As for children, if they do not comprehend the sacrifice and are not physically capable of carrying it out then it is not valid for them to slaughter, but if they do comprehend what it is and are capable of it then their slaughter is permitted according to the well-known position (*mashhūr*), although it has also been said that it is not to be eaten, and this prohibition is understood as its being *makrūh*.

As for women, their sacrifice is permissible according to the well-known position (*mashhūr*).

As for the insane or intoxicated person their slaughtering is not permitted, contrary to ash-Shāfi'ī.

As for the person who has abandoned the *ṣalāt* his slaughtering is permitted, contrary to Ibn Ḥabīb.

As for the person who steals the animal which he slaughters or the person who usurps its ownership their slaughtering is permitted, according to the majority but contrary to the Ẓāhirīs.

A SUMMARY WITHIN THE MADHHAB

Ibn Rushd has said that the slaughtered animals and slaughtering of six persons are not permitted in the madhhab: minors who do not comprehend, the insane when in a state of insanity, the intoxicated person who has lost his senses, the Magian-Zoroastrian, the renegade from Islam and the *zindīq* i.e. someone who manifests Islam and is secretly a *kāfir*;

And six who are *makrūh*: minors who do not have discrimination, women, hermaphrodites, eunuch, the uncircumcised and the corrupt;

And there are six about whose slaughtering there is a difference of opinion: the person who has abandoned the *ṣalāt*, the intoxicated person who both makes mistakes and gets some things right, the person who has newly embraced Islam about whom people differ as to whether aspects of *kufr* remain in him, the Arab Christian and the Christian who slaughters on the instructions of a Muslim and the untaught, inexperienced non-Arab who assents to Islam before puberty.

2. THE ANIMAL SLAUGHTERED

THIS COMPRISES FOUR MATTERS

1. That which needs to be slaughtered for it to be *ḥalāl*.

Living creatures are of two kinds, land and sea creatures.

As for land creatures which are warm blooded and whose blood spurts out when slaughtered, these must be slaughtered, according to the agreed judgment, and all of them admit of being slaughtered except for pigs, which if slaughtered are then treated as non-ritually slaughtered meat on account of the severity of the degree of their *ḥarām* nature – contrary to all the other animals whose meat is deemed *ḥarām*; for there is a difference of opinion as to whether they may be used after having been slaughtered given the ritual purity of their meat, their bones and their skins – this being the well-known position (*mashhūr*) in agreement with Abū Ḥanīfah – or they may not be used; and ash-Shāfi'ī has said that one may use the skin and bones but not the meat.

As for land creatures which are not warm blooded, these too need to be slaughtered, although it has also been said that they do not need to be.

As for sea creatures, if they do not spend a long time on land then they do not need to be slaughtered, like fish; and likewise, according to the well-known position (*mashhūr*), if they do spend a long time on land, contrary to Ibn Nāfi'.

2. Regarding the slaughter of sick animals: the animal to be slaughtered must clearly be alive; as for the sick animal which is not on the point of death, it may be slaughtered and eaten, according to the agreed judgment, and likewise an animal on the point of death, according to the majority and the well-known position (*mashhūr*) except if there is doubt as to whether one has slaughtered it when alive or not, in which case it is not eaten; if one considers it more likely that one has slaughtered it when still alive then there is a difference of opinion.

If no part of the animal to be slaughtered is moving, be it healthy or sick, and it is not on the point of death then it may be eaten; but if close to death it is not to be eaten unless there is proof as to its being alive – and the indications of life are five in number: flow of blood not just the exuding of a little from the animal, and the kicking of the fore- or rear-legs, the blinking of the eye, moving of the tail and exhalation, and if it moves but no blood flows then it may be eaten but if blood flows and it does not move it is not eaten, as movement is a stronger indication of life than the flow of blood. As for light convulsion or twitching this is not an indication as meat twitches after skinning.

And there is a difference of opinion as to the time of taking into consideration any sign of life, namely three judgments – after slaughter, during it and before it.

3. Regarding the five mentioned in the Qur'ān, that is animals which have been strangled with a cord or the like, those killed by a blow of a stick or the like, those which have fallen to their death from a mountain or some other place, those which have been gored and those which wild beasts have eaten – these being classed in four ways: if they died before being slaughtered then they are not to be eaten according to the consensus, but if they are still alive then they may be slaughtered and eaten according to the consensus, and if that which leads to its death is effected then it may not be eaten, according to the agreed judgment within the madhhab according to Ibn Rushd, although others have recorded two judgments, and 'Alī ibn Abī Tālib and Ibn Abbās ﷺ have permitted it; and if there is not expectation of its survival but that which leads to its death has not yet been effected, or one is uncertain as to their state then there are three judgments: it is slaughtered and may be eaten, according to Ibn al Qāsim in agreement with the two, or it is not slaughtered and may not be eaten, or one makes a distinction between being uncertain, in which case one may slaughter and eat, and one having no expectation of its survival in which case one does not slaughter and does not eat it.

And the reason for the differences are whether His words, exalted is He *'except those you are able to slaughter properly'* (5:3) are an exception connected to what precedes or a distinct exception: thus those who deem it connected say that one may carry out the slaughter with respect to such animals, while those who deem it distinct say that one may not carry out the slaughter with respect to them as what is referred to by *'except those you are able to slaughter properly'* are animals other than these. And Ibn Bukayr has said that the meaning of the *āyat* is whatever dies through strangling or one of the other causes mentioned then it is *ḥarām* like meat which has not been ritually slaughtered or blood.

Clarification

The causes leading to death about which there is agreement are five in number: severing of the arteries, swelling of the brain, swelling of the intestines, or severing of the upper gut at the point where food and drink passes not the lower part at the point of the excrement, and the severing of the spinal cord, that is the marrow in the bone of the neck and spinal column.

There is a difference of opinion in the case of a crushed neck when the spinal cord is not severed or the bursting of the arteries without their being severed.

If you slaughter an animal and find its stomach to be cleft then the correct judgment is that it is permitted to eat it – given that the animal was alive despite this.

4. Regarding the slaughter of foetuses, this comprising four possible circumstances:

First, that the mother-animal expels it already dead before it itself is slaughtered, in which case it is not eaten according to the consensus.

Second, that it expels it alive before it itself is slaughtered in which case it is only to be eaten if it is slaughtered when confirmed to be alive.

Third, that it expels it when already dead after itself having been slaughtered in which case it is *ḥalāl* and its slaughtering is deemed to have taken place at the slaughtering of the mother animal, contrary to Abū Ḥanīfah, and this is conditional upon its being fully formed and its hair having grown, contrary to ash-Shāfi'ī.

Fourth, that it expels it when alive after the mother animal itself has been slaughtered in which case if one has time to slaughter it then one does so, but if one does not then it is said that it is subject to the judgment of ritually non-slaughtered meat, while it has also been said that its slaughter is deemed to have taken place with the slaughter of its mother.

Subordinate matter regarding eggs

If boiled and one finds a dead chick in it, then it is not to be eaten, and if one takes out an egg from a dead chicken, then it is also not eaten, while Ibn Nāfi' has said that it may be eaten if [the shell] has become firm, just as if when thrown into something ritually impure [then it may be washed and eaten].

3. The instrument used to slaughter

It should be sharp such that it may effect the killing and cause blood to flow, irrespective of whether of iron, bone, wood, bamboo, or stone with a sharp edge, baked clay or glass, although it is *makrūh* to use anything other than iron when not necessary, but the animal may be eaten.

As for teeth and tusks or fingernails and claws there are three judgments:

1. That slaughtering is not permitted with them irrespective of whether still joined to the person or animal in question or separate, in agreement with ash-Shāfi'ī;

2. That it is permitted both joined or separated and;

3. That it is permitted when separated, in accordance with Ibn Ḥabīb and Abū Ḥanīfah while ash-Shāfiʿī has prohibited bone and Mālik and Ibn Ḥanbal have permitted it.

Ibn al-Qasār has stipulated with respect to what is used to slaughter that it severs the arteries and the throat in one go and that if they are only severed in two, then it is not permitted to make the slaughter with it even if it is iron and Ibn Ḥabīb has said there is no good in a serrated scythe or hooked blade.

4. The manner of slaughter

This comprises three matters:

1. Regarding the various kinds of slaughter – by hunting in the case of animals not under one's control, slaughter by cutting the throat in the case of birds, sheep and goats, and piercing the upper part of breast in the case of the camel, and one has the option between these two latter methods in the case of cows, and causing the death of locusts by cutting them or some other action.

If one slaughters by cutting the throat of what ought to be slaughtered by stabbing the upper part of the breast or one slaughters by stabbing the upper part of the breast of what ought to be slaughtered by cutting the throat when there is no compelling reason, then the animal is not to be eaten, although it has also been said that it may be eaten, in agreement with the two, and it has also been said that this is *makrūh*, and it has been further said that if one slaughters an animal by slitting the throat when it should be slaughtered by stabbing its upper breast then it may be eaten, but not vice versa.

2. There are six *farḍ* aspects to slaughtering by cutting the throat:

First, the intention, that is the resolution to carry out the slaughter – Ibn Rushd has reported that there is a consensus as to its obligation, contrary to ash-Shāfiʿī according to what is related by Abū Ḥāmid.

Second, that the act be accomplished promptly without interruption – so if he person raises his hand before completion of the slaughtering then returns it, Ibn Ḥabīb has said that it may be eaten if he does this without delay but if a considerable time elapses then it may not be eaten, but Ṣaḥnūn has said that it may not be eaten, even if he does this without delay; and some have interpreted this by saying that if he raises his hand to examine what he has done then it may be eaten, but if he raises it and sees that he has already finished the animal off then it may not be eaten; and yet another has said if done the other way round then it is the most correct; and al-Lakhmī and Abu-l-Qāsim accord preference to the judgment that it is permitted to eat it.

3. 4. & 5. The severing of the two arteries, the throat and the oesophagus – although Mālik does not recognise the oesophagus.

The throat is the channel for breathing and usually the severing of the two arteries is not arrived at unless this latter is severed as it is located before these two.

The oesophagus is the pipe or gullet used to channel food and drink and it is behind it and joined to the bone of the nape of the neck.

It has been narrated from Mālik that it is stipulated that the four be severed, and that if one of the three is not severed then the animal is not to be eaten, whereas ash-Shāfiʿī stipulated the severing of the throat and oesophagus, while Abū Ḥanīfah stipulated the severing of three of the four without prescribing precisely which ones.

Four secondary points

1. The epiglottis, i.e. the flap of cartilage at the root of the tongue that is depressed during swallowing to cover the opening of the windpipe, between the Adam's apple and the head, must remain as

the throat is located beneath it, i.e. between the epiglottis and the upper part of the breast where the throat is slit – if it is not severed and one passes over it to the trunk of the animal and nothing of its circular form is left in the head then the animal is not to be eaten according to the well-known position (*mashhūr*), although it has also been said that it may be eaten, and this is the judgment preferred by Abu-l-Qāsim ibn Rabīʿ; if a part of it is severed then – on the basis of the judgment of prohibition – it may be eaten if the circular form extends to the head, otherwise it may not.

2. An animal slaughtered by cutting from the occiput, i.e. the back of the head, is not to be eaten, nor if slaughtered from the back of the neck even if one severs the parts which one is obliged to sever during the slaughtering, contrary to the two.

3. If one severs part of the arteries and throat then Ṣaḥnūn has said that this is not permitted, while Ibn al-Qāsim has said that if a half or two thirds is severed it is permitted, but that if only a little is severed then it is not permitted.

4. If one continues to cut until the head or spinal cord is severed then it may be eaten, although *makrūh*, while Muṭarrif has said that it may be eaten if this was done out of forgetfulness or ignorance and that it is not to be eaten if done deliberately.

3. The sunnahs of slaughtering

These are five in number

1. Saying [in Arabic] 'in the name of Allah', while it is also said that it is a *farḍ* obligation when one remembers it but that one may be allowed to omit it in the case of forgetfulness – and this judgment is strengthened by the agreement within the madhhab that is narrated by Ibn Bashīr, namely that the slaughtered animal of whoever omits

it deliberately and out of disdain for its importance is not to be eaten, but if omitted out of forgetfulness, then it may be eaten, and whoever omits it deliberately but not out of contempt, then the well-known position (*mashhūr*) is that it is still not to be eaten, contrary to Ashhab, while ash-Shāfiʿī has permitted it to be eaten in all cases when the saying [in Arabic of] 'in the name of Allah' is omitted, it being recommended according to him. And what is said is *bismillāh* and if *Allāhu akbar* is added to this then this is good.

2. To turn the animal to be slaughtered towards the *qiblah*, but if one does not turn it towards the *qiblah* out of heedlessness or for a valid excuse, then it may be eaten while if deliberately not done then there are two judgments, the well-known position (*mashhūr*) being that it is permitted.

3. That one gently places the animal to be slaughtered on its left side and one grasps hold of the skin of its throat at the lower part of wool or hair and one stretches it until the skin becomes visible, then one passes the knife over the throat beneath the Adam's apple until it stops at the bone. And if the person is left handed, then it is permitted to place the animal on its right side, although it is *makrūh* for a left handed person to slaughter. A camel is slaughtered by stabbing the upper part of its breast while it is standing with its shank bound to its arm.

4. That he sharpens the blade and does it such that the animal cannot see him.

5. That he treats the animal gently and does not throw it down onto the ground or put his foot on its neck or drag it by its foot or skin or go beyond what is necessary when slaughtering such that he cuts the spinal cord, and he is not to cut off any part of the animal until it dies.

10. ʿĪd sacrifices, ʿAqīqah and circumcision

This comprises five chapters

1. Animals which are sacrificed for ʿĪd al-Aḍḥā

It comprises three sections

1. Its ruling

It is a *sunnah mu'akkadah*, a particularly important *sunnah*, in agreement with ash-Shāfiʿī, while it has also been said that it is obligatory, in agreement with Abū Ḥanīfah.

Five secondary matters

1. Anyone with the following characteristics is commanded to do it: being a Muslim, free, that he is not on hajj at Minā – for its *sunnah* is the *hady* – that he is able to perform it, and that he not be overburdened by it even if he is able, and Ibn Ḥabīb has said that if the poor person finds someone who can lend him the money then he should borrow this and buy it.

2. Just as the resident is instructed to make a slaughter or sacrifice so too is the person travelling, contrary to Abū Ḥanīfah, and it is permitted to those on a military expedition (*ghazwah*) to slaughter of the sheep or goats of Rūm, as they may eat of them and they do not deposit them with the booty.

3. Just as the person of age is instructed to do this so the guardian of a minor is instructed to slaughter for him, even if he is born on the Day of Sacrifice or on the last, i.e. third day, and likewise someone who becomes Muslim during these three days, and the trustee may take it from the wealth of the orphan.

4. The most complete manner for the person who is able, is for him to sacrifice a sacrificial animal for each person with him, and if a person wishes to sacrifice one animal for all those with him, then this is permitted within the madhhab on condition that they be related to him and receiving their living expenses from him, irrespective of whether these living expenses are legally incumbent on him or not; but if they are not related and he spends voluntarily on them or employs them, then it is not permitted for him to include in his slaughtering; and the trustee or guardian is not permitted to include the orphan in his care in his sacrifice; and it is permitted according to the two for seven persons to share in a camel or a cow, but not a sheep.

2. The time of sacrifice

The *imām* sacrifices at the *muṣallā* after the *'Īd ṣalāt* so that the people can see him, and then they sacrifice after him, and it is not acceptable for anyone to sacrifice before the *ṣalāt* or before the *imām* has sacrificed, while it is acceptable according to Abū Ḥanīfah before the *imām* has sacrificed and after the *ṣalāt,* while according to ash-Shāfi'ī it is acceptable after a period of time has elapsed sufficient for the *ṣalāt* irrespective of whether the *imām* has in fact performed it or made the sacrifice or not.

Five secondary matters

1. If the inhabitants of a village do not have an *imām* then they should seek out the closest of *imāms* to them, and if they accidentally

precede them, it is accepted of them, although it has also been said that it is not acceptable, whereas ash-Shāfiʿī said that they should take note of the period of time needed for the *ṣalāt* and *khuṭbah* to elapse, while Abū Ḥanīfah said that if they sacrifice after *fajr* then it is accepted of them.

2. If the *imām* does not perform his sacrifice openly, it is not accepted of those who sacrifice before him, while it is also said that it is.

3. The time for the sacrifice extends to sunset of the third day of the *ʿĪd,* while ash-Shāfiʿī has said to the fourth day of the *ʿĪd,* and one group has said the day of the *ʿĪd* only.

Whoever sacrifices on the second and third days should find out the time when the *imām* made the sacrifice on the first day – but if they sacrifice before it then it is acceptable if after the break of dawn.

4. Whoever sacrifices during the night or before the break of dawn then this is not accepted of him, according to the well-known position (*mashhūr*) but contrary to ash-Shāfiʿī, although it has also been said that it is accepted of him.

5. The best is to sacrifice before the sun has passed its zenith, and if he misses doing this on the Day of Sacrifice then there is a difference of opinion as to whether it is best to sacrifice during the rest of the day or delay it until the morning of the second day, and, if he misses doing this on the second day, whether it is best to delay it to the morning of the third day, but if he misses doing it on the third day then he is to sacrifice after the sun has passed its zenith as there is no further time to wait.

3. The person who slaughters

It is preferable that the person performs the sacrifice of his animal himself, but if this is not possible then he delegates a Muslim who performs the *ṣalāt* to make it – making the intention himself; however if the person he delegates makes the intention for the owner of the animal, then this is permitted, and if he makes the intention for himself this is permitted, contrary to Ashhab; as for delegating one of the People of the Book there are two judgments, and based on the opinion that it is permitted, then the Person of the Book does not make the intention.

Two subordinate matters

1. If the sacrificial animal is slaughtered without permission of its owner, this is not permitted and the person who has slaughtered it is liable for its price and its owner is responsible for replacing it – unless the person who slaughtered is his son or someone from his family, in which case it is permitted, according to Ibn al-Qāsim but contrary to Ashhab.
2. The manner of slaughter and the characteristics of the person who slaughters are as we have mentioned above, and if someone who has abandoned the *ṣalāt* makes the sacrifice, it is recommended to have the sacrifice repeated.

2. The types of animal sacrifices

This comprises three matters

1. The type of animal

Only livestock is permitted, and if something is born from an animal deemed livestock and another animal then it is the mother animal which is taken into consideration.

The best livestock are goat and sheep, then cows, then camels because of their good meat, although ash-Shāfi'ī has deemed the contrary in the case of an abundance, like for example the *hady* animals; and sheep are better than goats; and male animals of any type are better than female, and female animals are better than males of succeeding animals (e.g. the female of sheep and goats are better than bulls), stallions are better than castrated animals, but Ibn Ḥabīb has said that fat geldings are better than weak stallions.

2. Its age

That is a *jadh'a* in the case of sheep – a beast of the age when it is about to shed its milk incisors – and a *thanī* in the case of other animals – a beast of the age for shedding the incisor milk teeth, normally those who have completed two years and above.

A *jadh'a* in the case of sheep and goats refers to those which are six months old, although it has also been said eight months, ten months, and a full year, in agreement with Abū Ḥanīfah.

A *thanī* in the case of sheep and goats is two years old, in agreement with ash-Shāfi'ī, although it has also been said that it refers to those that have entered their second year, in agreement with Abū Ḥanīfah.

A '*jadh'a* cow' is one which is two years old, while a *thanī* is one which has entered its third year, in agreement with the two, while it has also been said that it is one of four years.

And a *jadh'a* camel is one which is five years old, while a *thanī* is six years old.

3. The types

These are three in number: those which are recommended, those which are excluded as unacceptable, and those which are *makrūh*.

As for the recommended, it is a fat un-gelded ram, of white colour mixed with black (*amlaḥ*), horned, its eyes, mouth and feet black [in contrast to the rest of its body – i.e. the best and finest of its type]. *Amlaḥ* is predominantly fair in colour.

As for those which are not acceptable they are three in number, according to the agreed judgment: the sick animal which is manifestly sick; the emaciated whose condition cannot be remedied i.e. that without any fat, although it has also been said the animal without the white fat round the eyeball of a fat beast; the one-eyed animal – whose one-eyedness is obvious, even if the pupil remains, although there is no harm in the whiteness in the eye as long as it does not affect the sight.

There is a fourth that is not accepted according to the two Imāms, and according to others besides these two, contrary to Abū Ḥanīfah, namely the lame or limping beast.

There is a fifth type which is unacceptable according to the four, contrary to the Ẓāhirīs, that is the blind, and the beast whose leg is broken; and the mangy or decrepit are subject to the same ruling as the sick if the mange and decrepitude are advanced, and likewise madness if this madness is chronic.

As for those which are *makrūh*, they are:

Beasts with ear defects such as those born without ears (*sakkāʾ*); those with split ears (*sharqāʾ*); or perforated ears (*kharqāʾ*); and it has also been said those beasts whose ears have been cut or torn somewhat from below; those whose ears have been cut (*jadʿāʾ*), and those with more than a third cut off are unacceptable, while there is a difference of opinion with regard to exactly a third, while there is no harm in just a little; and those whose ears have been cut from in front (*muqābilah*) or behind (*mudābirah*); while it has also been said that all of these are unacceptable;

And those beasts whose teeth have fallen out: but if it is the front teeth then these are permitted, although if they have fallen out due to age there are two opinions; if slightly broken then such beasts are permitted, while there are two opinions regarding teeth which are much broken;

And defects of the horns: if it is an *'aḍbā'* i.e. a horn is broken, then there are three opinions: that they are acceptable, that they are not permitted, and that one must distinguish whether it bleeds or not, this being the well-known position (*mashhūr*), while it is also said that *'aḍbā'* refers to a beast with a deformed horn, and this is also *makrūh*, while there is no harm with beasts born without horns (*jammā'*).

A secondary matter

Whoever buys a sacrificial animal and then defects occurs to it such as to invalidate it as a sacrifice, then he should exchange it, and if it had a broken limb that he healed and it mended, then this is acceptable.

3. The rulings before and after the slaughter

As for those rulings before the slaughter

These are six matters

1. On its specification

A beast is specified for slaughter, according to the agreed judgment, and an intention is made beforehand. There is a difference of opinion regarding this latter within the madhhab and with regard to the purchase without an intention of the sacrificial animal according to Abū Ḥanīfah; and in the fulfilling of a vow if specified for this, according to the agreed judgment. Thus if the person says, "I make this a sacrificial beast" then he shall have specified it according to one of two judgments – and if it dies then on the basis of both judgments he shall not be liable for anything else, but if he sells it then he must buy another for the same price and he is not to leave any remainder of the price but rather it is better to exchange it for something better than it.

2. Whoever dies before slaughtering his sacrificial animal

Someone inherits it from him, and so Ibn al-Qāsim recommends that it should be slaughtered on behalf of [the deceased], while this is not the judgment of Ashhab.

3. Whoever has his sacrificial animal unlawfully taken from him

And if he is then reimbursed its price, he is to buy another for this price, and it has also been said that he may dispose of this as he wishes; and if the price reimbursed is not enough for the price of another sheep then he is to give the sum away in *ṣadaqah* or dispose of it as he wishes – in accordance with the above mentioned difference of opinion.

4. Offspring

If it gives birth before the slaughtering it is fitting to slaughter it along with the mother – but this is not obligatory, but it is not to be slaughtered instead of its mother as this is not acceptable it being below the required age; if it is born alive after the slaughtering then it is as its mother.

As for its milk, Ibn al-Qāsim has said that if the new born animal does not drink it, then it may be given away as *ṣadaqah*, in agreement with Abū Ḥanīfah while Ashhab has said that he may drink of it if it wants, in agreement with ash-Shāfiʿī. As for its wool after the slaughtering, it is as its meat, but it is not clipped before the slaughtering as it is the beauty pertaining to it, and Ibn al-Qāsim has said that it is not to be sold, contrary to Ashhab.

5. If various sacrificial animals get mixed up before the slaughter

Then each takes a sacrificial animal and slaughters it and it is accepted.

6. It is recommended for the person who wants to slaughter not to cut his hair or trim his nails

This is if Dhu-l-Ḥijjah begins, until he has made the slaughtering, while Abū Ḥanīfah does not deem this recommended, and Ibn Ḥanbal has deemed this obligatory.

As for the rulings after the slaughtering

These are four in number

1. The meat, skin, wool or hair or anything else from the slaughtered animal are not to be sold

But Abū Ḥanīfah has said that it is permitted to sell these in exchange for things but not for gold dinars or silver dirhams, while 'Atā' has permitted the sale of all of these.

These are not to be exchanged for other things, contrary to Ibn Ḥanbal.

And there are two judgments regarding the renting out of its ski.

One is not to pay the butcher his fee with meat or skin from it, nor give the tanner any of its skin in return for the tanning.

If he gifts it or gives it away as *ṣadaqah* then there are two judgments as to whether the person it is given to may sell it. And whoever does sell it then the sale is invalid, and if it has gone ahead then Ibn al-Qāsim has said that he is to give away the price as *ṣadaqah* and not to make use of it, while Ibn 'Abd al-Ḥakam has said that he may do as he wishes with it.

And if these are stolen or taken illegally then one is not to accept any reimbursement, and it is also said that it may be taken and given away as *ṣadaqah*.

2. If he dies after having slaughtered it

Then it is not to be included in whatever inheritance is left, and it is not to be subject to any debts the deceased incurred, but those who inherit from him may dispose of it as he might have disposed of it, and there are two judgments as to whether they may divide up the meat.

3. If it is mixed up with another carcass after the slaughtering

Yaḥyā ibn 'Umar has said that it is accepted and that the two owners are to give them away in *ṣadaqah* and not eat of them, while 'Abd al-Ḥaqq has said that it is not prohibited to eat them.

If the heads get mixed up with others while roasting, it is disapproved to eat them, for perhaps you will eat the goods of someone who will not eating your goods, but if the heads become mixed up with those of the roasting, then this is not of great importance as he is liable; and it has also been said that the person whose head has got mixed up is not to demand its price.

4. The best is that one eat of the slaughtered beast and give the rest away in **ṣadaqah**

However, if one only does one of these two, then it is acceptable although *makrūh*, while one group have deemed it obligatory to eat of it, and there is no specific amount stipulated with regard to what one eats or gives away, although Ibn al-Jallāb prefers that one eat less than one gives away, and Abū Ḥanīfah and Ibn Ḥanbal have said that one eats a third, gives away a third, and stores a third. And it is *makrūh* to feed a Jew or a Christian with it.

4. The ʿAqīqah

This comprises eight matters

1. Its ruling

It is a *sunnah*, while the Ẓāhirīs have deemed it obligatory and Abū Ḥanīfah has said that it is *mubāḥ*, i.e. licit but not recommended.

2. The type of beast

It is like the ruling for sacrificial animals, according to the well-known position (*mashhūr*), while it is also said that the *ʿaqīqah* is not fulfilled by means of a cow or a camel.

3. Its age & 4. The type of animal sacrificed for it

With regard to both, it is as the sacrificial animals mentioned above

5. The number

It is a sheep for a male infant and for a female, within the madhhab, while for ash-Shāfiʿī it is two for a male and one for a female, and Ibn Ḥabīb said it is fitting to be generous and give more food than just the sheep or goat of the *ʿaqīqah* and invite the people to it, while Ibn al-Qāsim has said 'I do not like that it be a banquet or feast with food distributed to the poor; one should restrict it to the people of one's household'. And if the new-born dies before it is seven days old, then there is no *ʿaqīqah* for it, and likewise if there is a stillbirth.

6. Its time

It is done on the seventh day after the birth if it was born before dawn, and the day of its birth is not reckoned if it is born after dawn, contrary to Ibn al-Mājishūn, although it is also said that the day is reckoned if born before the sun passes its zenith, but not after this. And if it dies on the first seventh day, then no *ʿaqīqah* is made for it in the following seven days, nor in the seven days after that, contrary to Ibn Wahb.

And the sacrificial animal is slaughtered up to the time the sun passes its zenith, but not during the night or the time before daybreak, nor in the evening, and whoever does slaughter before the proper time then it is not accepted of him, contrary to Ibn Ḥanbal. And one does not make the *'aqīqah* for an adult, contrary to one group.

7. Its meat and skin

It is the same as the sacrificial animals mentioned above: one may eat of its meat and give away of it in *ṣadaqah*, but it is not permitted to sell any of it. And it is permitted to break its bones, contrary to Ibn Ḥanbal.

8. It is recommended to shave the head of the new born on the seventh day and to name it

But it is *makrūh* to stain the head of the new born with its blood, and it is recommended to stain it with saffron, and it is recommended to give gold or silver away in *ṣadaqah* equal to the weight of its hair, in agreement with ash-Shāfi'ī, while it is also said that this is *makrūh.*

5. Circumcision

This comprising eight matters

1. Its ruling

The circumcision of a male is a *sunnah* of particular importance, according to Mālik and Abū Ḥanīfah, like the other 'aspects of the *fiṭrah*' – the natural acts of grooming – which are mentioned with it, but it is not obligatory according to the agreed judgment, although ash-Shāfi'ī has said that it is a *farḍ* obligation and this is apparently the case from the statement of Ṣaḥnūn, as it is a sign of Islam on account of His saying, exalted is He, *'Follow the religion of Ibrāhīm, a man of pure natural faith'* (Sūrat an-Naḥl 16: 123), and what has been narrated in the *ḥadīth* 'that Ibrāhīm ﷺ was circumcised 'at Qadūm/with a *qadūm*' when he was eighty years old', while it is also narrated 'when he was a hundred and twenty years old' and there is a difference of opinion as to the word *qadūm* in Arabic, whether it is written *qadūm* or *qaddūm,* and about its meaning, whether it refers to a place or the instrument (axe) used to cut.

2. There is a difference of opinion regarding whoever is born already circumcised

It is said that Allah has taken sufficient care of him, in which case he is not subjected to it, while it is also said that the razor is passed over him, and if there is anything to cut then it is cut.

3. If an adult fears that he may die as a result of circumcision

Ibn Abī al-Ḥakam has given him licence not to do it, while Ṣaḥnūn has rejected this.

4. It is reported from Mālik

'Whoever desists from being circumcised without any excuse, then it is not permitted that he be an *imām* for the *ṣalāt* or a witness'. And Ibn 'Abbās has said, 'his *ṣalāt* is not accepted and any sacrificial animal he slaughters is not to be eaten'.

5. The time for the circumcision

It is recommended that one waits until the child is old enough to be commanded to do the *ṣalāt,* that is from seven to ten years old, for this is the first encounter with the acts of worship, and it is *makrūh* to make the circumcision on the day of birth and the seventh day as this is the practice of the Jews.

6. Men circumcise boys and women girls

This is as it is not permitted for men to see this in women.

7. It is recommended to invite people to the circumcision-feast which is called I'dhār

However, this is not done in the case of the circumcision of women – in order to keep them hidden from view.

8. The foreskin which is the part which is removed during the circumcision is najas – ritually impure

This is as it has been cut from a living person, and so it is not permitted for the person who makes the *ṣalāt* to carry it on him, nor to enter a mosque with it or to be buried with it – some people however do this out of ignorance.

Detailed Table of Contents

Dedication v
Ibn Juzayy al-Kalbī xi
Translator's Preface xii

AUTHOR'S INTRODUCTION 1
An explanation of the terminology of the book 4
An explanation of the arrangement of the book 5

THE OPENING DISCOURSE CONCERNING WHAT IS NECESSARILY TRUE IN MATTERS OF *'AQĪDAH* 7
1. The existence of the Creator, His majesty is majestic and His favour is cherished 7
2. The Attributes of Allah, exalted is He and mighty is His affair and His authority is overwhelming! 8
'Life' 8
'Power' 9
'Will' 9
'Knowledge' 10
As for 'Hearing and Sight' 11
'Speech' 11
3. The beautiful names of Allah, exalted is He 12
4. The *Tawḥīd* of Allah, exalted is He 14
Supplement: the various groups holding to contradictory interpretations of *tawḥīd* 15
A Sufi indication 17
5. *Tanzīh* – freeing Allah, exalted is He, of any defect 17
Note 18
6. *Īmān* in the Angels of Allah, His Books and His Messengers 19
1. Those miracles whose soundness we may be absolutely sure of and so we may use as proof 21

2. Those transmissions about which we are absolutely sure on account of their multiple occurrences 21
3. Those narrated on this matter by single persons 21
7. *Īmān* in the Abode of the *Ākhirah* 22
1. *Īmān* in the *barzakh*, i.e. the interspace after death, and in the punishment in the grave 22
2. The questioning of the two angels 22
3. The raising up of creation from their graves 22
4. The reckoning up of actions 23
5. The settlement of accounts between the slaves 23
6. The weighing of one's actions in the scales 23
7. The giving of the record (of one's actions) either in the person's right or left hand 23
8. People's passing over the *Ṣirāṭ* 23
9. The Pool of the Prophet ﷺ 23
10. The intercession of the Prophet ﷺ for his ummah 24
11. The entry of people into the Fire 24
12. Entering the Garden 25
8. Imamate, 26
1. Affirmation of the imamate of the four *Khalīfahs* ﷺ 26
2. The conditions of imamate 27
9. Iman and Islam 28
1. What they mean 28
2. The legal rulings covering both 28
10. Holding fast to the Sunnah 29
1. Refraining from innovation 29
2. Rational examination and theoretical speculation as opposed to imitation and following others (*taqlīd*) 30

PART 1 33

1 – PURIFICATION 35
Introduction 35
1. Kinds of purification 35
2. Conditions for the obligation of purification 36
1. *Wuḍū'* 37
1. Kinds of *wuḍū'* 37
2. The *farḍ*, i.e. obligatory aspects of *wuḍū'* 38
3. The Sunnah aspects 42
4. Excellent and disliked aspects of *wuḍū'* 43

2. Things which invalidate *wuḍū'* 46
1. Things which invalidate *wuḍū'* in the madhhab 46
Three secondary matters 46
The causes of the physical changes which break someone's *wuḍū'* 47
2. The causes – recognised outside of the madhhab – which break one's *wuḍū'* 48
3. *Ghusl* i.e. the ritual washing of the whole body 49
1. Types of *ghusl* 49
2. The five *farḍ* aspects of the *ghusl* 50
3. The *sunnah*s 50
4. The aspects of excellence 50
5. The *makrūh*, i.e. disliked aspects 50
6. The form of the *ghusl* 51
4. Those matters which make the *ghusl* obligatory 52
Janābah 52
Additional remarks 53
Summary 56
5. Water 58
1. The five ways in which water is classified 58
2. What is left over [of drink] 60
3. Receptacles 62
6. *Najāsāt* – ritually impure things 63
1. Discriminating between *najāsāt* 63
Summary 66
2. Judgments pertaining to *najāsāt* 67
3. Nosebleeds 69
7. *Instinjā'* and associated matters 70
1. The courtesies of going to the lavatory 70
2. making *instinjā'* with water and *istijmār* with stones 71
8. *Tayammum* 73
1. The conditions for its permissibility 73
2. The *farḍ* aspects of *tayammum* 73
3. *Tayammum* stands in place of 74
4. *Tayammum* renders permissible that which is rendered permissible by purification using water 75
9. Wiping over *khuff*s and splints/ligatures/bandages 75
Splints 76
10. Menstruation, bleeding after childbirth, the period of purity and the *istiḥāḍah* 76
1. Its measure 76

2. Menstruation and bleeding after childbirth 78

2 – THE *ṢALĀT* 81
1. There are five kinds of *ṣalāt* 81
The *farḍ 'ayn ṣalāt*s 81
The *farḍ kifāyah* 81
The Sunnah 81
The acts of excellence (faḍā'il) 82
The *nāfilah* 82
Section 83
2. The times of the *ṣalāt* 83
1. The optimal (*ikhtiyārī*) time 83
2. The *ḍarūrī* times 85
Three secondary matters 88
3. The times when *ṣalāt* is prohibited 89
3. The *adhān* and the *iqāmah* 90
1. The ruling on the *adhān* 90
2. The way the *adhān* is called 91
3. The qualities and courtesies required of the *mu'adhdhin* 92
4. What the person who hears the *adhān* says 93
5. The *iqāmah* 93
4. Mosques and places for *ṣalāt* 94
1. Mosques 94
2. Places where the *ṣalāt* may be performed 95
5. The conditions and essential elements of the *ṣalāt* 96
farḍ aspects 96
The *sunnah*s 97
The prostration of negligence 97
The aspects of excellence 98
The things which invalidate 98
The things that are *makrūh* 100
Summary 101
6. Clothing to be worn for the *ṣalāt* 102
What is covered 102
The covering 104
A supplementary note 104
7. Facing the *Qiblah*, 106
1. Facing the *qiblah* 106
2. The three possible states of the person performing the *ṣalāt* 106
Three subsidiary matters 107

3. The *sutrah* i.e. anything set up as a screen in front of the person performing the *ṣalāt* 108
8. The intention and the *takbīratu-l-iḥrām* 109
1. The intention 109
Four subsidiary matters 109
2. The *takbīratu-l-iḥrām* 110
Two subsidiary matters 110
3. Raising one's hands 111
9. The Standing 111
1. The proper form of this standing 111
2. The *ṣalāt* of the sick person 112
Five secondary matters 112
10. The recitation 113
1. The Umm al-Qur'ān 113
2. The *sūrah* 114
Subsidiary matter 115
3. Concerning the recitation softly and aloud 115
11. The *Qunūt* Supplication 115
1. Its words 115
2. Four subsidiary matters 117
12. The bowing 118
13. The Prostration 120
1. Its form 120
2. It is permitted to cover the knees and feet with one's clothes, according to the consensus 121
3. The finer aspects or courtesies 121
4. What one says in it 121
1. 4 – The sitting 122
1. Its form 122
Subsidiary matter 123
2. Its ruling 123
1. 5 – The *tashahhud* 124
1. What is said 124
2. Its ruling 125
3. The sending of praise and blessings of Allah to the Prophet ﷺ 125
1. 6 – The *Salām* 125
A concluding remark 126
1. 7 – The role of the *imām* and the *jamā'ah* – the *ṣalāt* in a group 127
1. The attributes of an *imām* 127
Subsidiary matter 129

2. The *ṣalāt al-jamā'ah* i.e. the five daily *ṣalāt*s performed in a group 130
3. The form of following the *imām* 131
Subsidiary matters 132
4. The *imām*'s indicating someone should replace him during the *ṣalāt* 133
1. 8 – Completing the *ṣalāt* after coming late 133
Banā' 'building upon' 134
Qaḍā' 134
Ṣubḥ and the *jumu'ah* 134
Ẓuhr and *'Aṣr* 134
'Ishā' 135
Maghrib 135
Three subsidiary matters 135
1. 9 – *Qaḍā'* – Making up Missed *Ṣalāt*s 136
1. Making up missed *ṣalāt* 136
2. The order 136
3. Doubt 137
2.0 – Omissions, additions or mistakes in the *ṣalāt* 139
1. Prostrations 139
2. What makes prostrations necessary 142
As for the omission of *sunnah*s 149
2.1 – The Jumu'ah 152
1. The obligation of the *ṣalāt al-jumu'ah* 152
Six subsidiary matters 152
2. With respect to the conditions for its validity 154
3. The *jumu'ah* has two fundamental elements – the *ṣalāt* and the *khuṭbah* 155
4. There are special duties that pertain to the *jumu'ah* 156
2.2 – Joining two *ṣalāt*s together 157
2.3 – Fear 158
1. That which prevents one from completing the *ṣalāt* in its proper form 158
2. The fear which arises when one expects to be molested or harmed by the enemy if all of the Muslims become occupied with the *ṣalāt* 159
Secondary matters 160
2.4 – Travel 160
1. The ruling of shortening the *ṣalāt* 160
Two secondary matters 161
2. The conditions for shortening 161
2.5 – The two *'Īd*s 162

1. The ruling of the *ṣalāt* for the two *'Īd*s 162
2. Its form 163
3. The duties of the *'Īd* 164

26. *Istisqā'* – the *ṣalāt* for rain 164
1. The rulings for the rain *ṣalāt* 164
2. As for its form 165
3. The duties of the rain *ṣalāt* 165

27. Eclipses 166
1. The *ṣalāt* for eclipses 166
2. Its form 167

28. The *witr* 167
1. Its ruling 167
2. Its form 168

29. The remaining voluntary *ṣalāt*s 168
1. The two *rak'ah*s of *fajr* 168
2. The rest of the *nāfilah ṣalāt*s 169

30. The prostrations of the Qur'ān 170
1. Its rulings 170
2. The number of places of prostration in the Qur'ān 170

3 – THE *ṢALĀT* OVER THE DEAD 172

Introduction 172

1. The *ghusl* 172
1. The form of the *ghusl* 172
2. The person who makes the *ghusl* 173

2. Shrouding 174
1. The cost of the shroud 174
2. Its form 174

3. *Ṣalāt* over the dead person 175
1. Regarding the person over whom the *ṣalāt* is made 175
2. The persons who lead the *ṣalāt* 176
3. The nature of the *ṣalāt* 177
Four secondary matters 177

4. The carrying of the corpse and its burial 178
1. The carrying of the corpse 178
2. The burial 179

5. The form of the graves 180
1. The form of graves 180
2. Respect for graves 181
Conclusion 181

4 – *ZAKĀT* 182
1. Conditions for the obligation of *zakāt* 182
  1. Islam 182
  2. Freedom 183
  3. That the wealth be such that *zakāt* is obligatory on it 183
  4. *Nisāb* 184
  5. *Ḥawl* (the passage of a year) 184
  6. The absence of debt 184
2. The characteristics of *zakāt* 184
  1. Intention 184
  2. Its payment after it becomes obligatory by the elapsing of a lunar year over it, or the ripening of the crops or the arrival of the tax collector 185
  3. Payment to those who are entitled to receive it 185
3. *Zakāt* on gold and silver 186
  1. The *nisāb* 186
  2. If the dinars and dirhams are deficient 186
  3. If the dirhams and the dinars are adulterated 187
  4. The amount payable 187
  5. Those who come into possession of wealth 187
  6. *Zakāt* paid on jewellery 188
  7. Which jewellery is permitted. 189
4. Buried treasure and mined material 189
5. Trade 191
  As for *qirād* 192
6. The *zakāt* of debts [returned to the lender] 194
  1. The kinds of debt 194
  2. If one takes possession of that of one's debt which amounts to the *nisāb* 194
7. *Zakāt* on agricultural produce 195
  1. The produce on which *zakāt* is payable 195
  2. The *nisāb* 196
  3. How much is payable 196
  4. Which produce may be put together with which other produce in order to attain the *nisāb* 197
  5. The time of its obligation 197
8. *Zakāt* of livestock 198
  1. The *zakāt* on camels 198
  2. The *zakāt* on cows 199
  3. The *zakāt* on sheep and goats 199
  4. *Zakāt* is obligatory on livestock 199
  5. The case of two persons in a co-proprietorship 200

6. Increase in the livestock through the birth of young 201
7. Exchange 202
9. Division of the *zakāt* 202
The poor (*fuqarā'*) 202
The destitute (*masākīn*) 202
Those who collect it 203
Reconciling people's hearts 203
Freeing slaves 203
Those in debt 204
Spending in the way of Allah 204
Travellers 204
10. *Zakāt al-fiṭr* 206
1. Those who are commanded to give it 206
2. What is obligatory to pay 207
3. The time of its obligation 207
4. Those who may receive it 207

5 – FASTING AND I'TIKĀF 209
1. Regarding the conditions for fasting 209
Islam 209
Being of age 209
Being sane 210
As for becoming free of the blood of menstruation or childbirth 210
As for health and being resident 211
2. The various kinds of fasting 211
The *wājib* 211
Sunnah fasting 212
The *mustaḥabb* 212
The *Nāfilah* 212
And it is *ḥarām* 212
And it is *makrūh* 212
3. The characteristics of fasting 213
4. Sighting the crescent moon 213
1. If a person sights the crescent moon of Ramadan 214
2. If one witness bears testimony as to the sighting 214
3. If two just witnesses testify specifically in front of the Imam 214
4. If a large crowd sights it together in public 215
5. That the Imam informs that it has been reliably sighted in his view 215
6. That a just person informs that the Imam has

confirmed a reliable sighting or that there has been a general sighting 215
7. That the people of the land informed of a public sighting 215
8. That two just persons declare that they have made a sighting 215
9. That a just person declares having sighted it in a place where there is a no Imam to act on the matter 215
1. If the crescent moon is obscured by clouds 215
2. If the people of one particular land sight it 215
3. If the crescent moon is seen during the day 216
4. If the crescent moon is anticipated but does not appear 216

5. The Intention 216
1. The intention for all kinds of fasting is obligatory 216
2. One intention made at the beginning of Ramadan suffices 217
3. If a captive in the land of the enemy is confused as to the months 217

6. Desisting from eating, drinking and sexual intercourse 218
1. Food and drink 218
2. Sexual intercourse and that subsumed with it 219
3. Vomiting and cupping 221
4. The time for refraining from food 221

7. The things which permit one to break the fast 222
As for travel 222
As for the ill person 223
Old age 225
The pregnant woman 225
The breastfeeding mother 225
Someone who is overcome by hunger and thirst 225
Someone who is obliged to break the fast against his will 226

8. The requirements attached to breaking the fast 226
1. Making up 226
2. The *kaffārah*s 226
3. As for the *fidyah* compensation 229
4. As for desisting from food, drink and sexual intercourse for the rest of the day 230
5. As for the punishment 230
6. As for interrupting the continuous and successive nature of the months to be fasted 231
7. As for interrupting one's intention 231

9. *I'tikāf* 231
Its judgment 231

Its location 232
Its time 232
Its conditions 233
The things which invalidate it 233
10. The Night of the Decree 233
1. That it is specific but not known, indeed hidden 234
2. That it is specific and known 234
3. That it is not specific nor known 234

6 – HAJJ 235
1. The Introductory Aspects 235
1. Its judgment 235
2. Its conditions 235
3. Delegating someone to perform one's hajj 237
2. The various elements which make up the hajj 238
The obligatory *sunnah*s which are not fundamental elements and which may be put right by sacrifice 238
The aspects of excellence 238
3. The *mawāqīt* 239
The time 239
The locations 240
Section 240
4. The actions of hajj 241
1. The *iḥrām* 241
2. Entry into Makkah 243
3. The *ṭawāf* 243
4. The *sa'y* between Ṣafā and Marwah 244
5. The 'standing', i.e. being present, at Minā and 'Arafah 245
6. Muzdalifah 246
7. Stoning the *jamrahs* 247
8. Shaving one's head 247
9. Slaughtering 248
10. The farewell *ṭawāf* 248
5. The types of hajj 248
The *ifrād* 248
The *qirān* 249
The *tamattu'* 249
6. The prohibited things of hajj 250
1. One must not wear any sewn clothing 250
2. Affording ease or comfort to one's body and cleaning it 251
3. Hunting 252

4. Women 252
7. The *fidyah*, *nusuk* i.e. sacrifice to make good a mistake, and *hady* – the sacrificial animal taken on the hajj 253
1. The *fidyah* 253
Clarification 254
2. The *nusuk* and the *hady* 255
8. Things which prevent hajj 257
1. Paternity 257
2. Slavehood 258
3. A married woman 258
4. Lack of legal competence 258
5. Imprisonment 258
6. Claim from a debtor whose payment is due 258
7. When forcibly prevented by the enemy after having entered *iḥrām* 259
8. Illness 259
Complementary aspects 260
9. The *'Umrah* 261
10. Visiting the tomb of the Prophet ﷺ 261
Conclusion 263

7 – *JIHĀD* 264
1. Preliminary Aspects 264
1. Its ruling 264
2. The six conditions for its obligation 264
3. The two things preventing a person from making *jihād* 265
4. Its six *farḍ* obligations 265
2. The fighting 265
1. Those who are fought 265
2. The call to Islam before fighting 266
3. Those one may have recourse to for assistance 267
4. What one may take with one when going out to fight 267
5. Aspects of the fighting 267
6. Fleeing 268
7. *Mubārazah* – a man fighting with another of the enemy in single combat in sight of the two opposing armies 269
3. The Booty 269
Their men 269
Women and children 270
Wealth 270
Agricultural lands 272

Foodstuffs and drink 273

4. Division of the *ghanīmah* booty, the *khums* and *fay'* 274
1. That the Amir sets apart the army for special distinction 274
2. Those who receive a portion 274
3. One has a right to the *ghanīmah* booty by virtue of having been present at the fighting 275
4. Foot soldiers have one portion and someone mounted has three shares 276
5. The *khums* (the Imam's fifth of the booty) 276
6. *Raḍkh* – small presents, *naql* – assignments and transfers of property, and *salb* – spoil and plunder 277
7. The *fay'* booty 277

5. Muslims' wealth in the possession of the *kuffār* 278
1. That which they have when they accept Islam 278
2. That which they came with to the territories of the Muslims with safe passage 278
3. That which a Muslim who had entered with safe passage purchased from them 278
4. That which has been acquired as booty by the Muslims 278

6. Concerning Muslim prisoners 280
1. The ruling on ransom 280
2. Claiming restitution from someone for ransom 280
3. A difference of opinion between the one who pays the ransom and the person ransomed 281
4. Pawning or pledging another person 282

7. Assurance of Protection – Safe Passage 283

8. Reconciliation or settlement with the enemy 285
1. The conditions making it permitted 285
2. Its ruling 285

9. The taking of *jizyah* from *dhimmī*s 286
1. The one who may conclude the arrangement and the person with whom it is concluded 286
2. That which is obligatory for them in our regard 286
3. What is incumbent on us with respect to them 288

10. Racing and Shooting 288

8 – OATHS AND VOWS 290

1. Types of oath 290
1. The ruling regarding an oath 290
2. What oaths are necessarily binding 290
3. The form of the oath 291

4. What is sworn about 292
5. That for which *kaffārah* is paid and that for which it is not 293
6. Whoever makes an oath by deeming what is *ḥalāl* to be *ḥarām* with respect to foodstuffs, drinks, clothes or something else 294
7. As for if one swears 'by the oaths which are binding on me' and then breaks one's oath 294

2. What fulfilling or breaking an oath entails 295
1. Fulfilling or breaking an oath 295
2. What an oath necessarily entails 297

3. *Kaffārah* and exceptions 303
1. *Kaffārah* 303
2. Making an exception 306

4. The basic elements that constitute making a vow 307
As for the person making the vow 307
As for the thing vowed 308
The form of the vow 308

5. The rulings governing vows 309
1. The vow to fast 309
2. *Ṣalāt* 310
3. *Ṣadaqah* 310
4. Walking to Makkah 311
5. Whoever vows to slaughter a camel 312
6. Whoever vows to make the *ṣalāt* in Madīnah or the Bayt al-Maqdis in Jerusalem 313
7. Whoever vows to slaughter his child at the Station of Ibrāhīm ﷺ 313
8. Whoever vows to take up post in a *ribāṭ* or to make *jihād* on the borders 313

9 – FOOD, DRINK, HUNTING AND SLAUGHTERING 315

1. Food – when one has the choice 315
1. Sea creatures 316
2. Wild animals, like lions, wolves, cheetahs or panthers, bears, tigers, dogs 316
3. Birds and other flying creatures 316
4. Animals with hooves 317
5. Those creatures about which there is disagreement as to whether they have been metamorphosed (mamsūkh) [from men and women] 317
6. Animals which are deemed filthy like flies and crawling insects 317

7. Blood 318
2. When there is no option 318
As for need 318
The kind of sustenance that would become licit 318
The amount permitted 319
3. Drinks 320
Wine 320
Other intoxicating drinks 320
4. Hunting and an examination of its ruling and conditions 322
1. The conditions with respect to hunter 323
2. The instrument 324
3. Conditions regarding the prey 326
5. Slaughtering 330
1. Those who slaughter 330
2. The animal slaughtered 333
3. The instrument used to slaughter 337
4. The manner of slaughter 338
3. The *sunnah*s of slaughtering 340

10. *'ĪD* SACRIFICES, *'AQĪQAH* AND CIRCUMCISION 342
1. Animals which are sacrificed for *'Īd al-Aḍḥā* 342
1. Its ruling 342
2. The time of sacrifice 343
3. The person who slaughters 344
2. The types of animal sacrifices 345
1. The type of animal 345
2. Its age 346
3. The types 346
3. The rulings before and after the slaughter 348
As for those rulings before the slaughter 348
As for the rulings after the slaughtering 350
4. The *'Aqīqah* 352
1. Its ruling 352
2. The type of beast 352
3. Its age & 4. The type of animal sacrificed for it 352
5. The number 352
6. Its time 352
7. Its meat and skin 353
8. it is recommended to shave the head of the new born on the seventh day and to name it 353
5. Circumcision 353

1. Its ruling 353
2. There is a difference of opinion regarding whoever is born already circumcised 354
3. If an adult fears that he may die as a result of circumcision 354
4. It is reported from Mālik 354
5. The time for the circumcision 354
6. Men circumcise boys and women girls 355
7. It is recommended to invite people to the circumcision-feast which is called *i'dhār* 355
8. The foreskin which is the part which is removed during the circumcision is *najas* – ritually impure 355

Lightning Source UK Ltd.
Milton Keynes UK
UKHW010024070223
416578UK00001B/4

9 781908 892539